THE SOCIAL LIFE OF STORIES

The Social Life of Stories: Narrative and Knowledge in the Yukon Territory

JULIE CRUIKSHANK

UBC PRESS / VANCOUVER

Acknowledgments for the
use of previously published
material appear on page xx
© 1998 by the University of
Nebraska Press. All rights
Reserved. Manufactured in
the United States of America.
♾ The paper in this book
meets the minimum require-
ments of American National
Standard for Information
Sciences—Permanence of
Paper for Printed Library
Materials, ANSI Z39.48-1984.

Published in Canada by
UBC Press, 2029 West Mall,
University of British Columbia,
Vancouver, BC V6T 1Z2
(604) 822-5959
Fax: (604) 822-6083
http://www.ubcpress.ubc.ca
Canadian Cataloguing in
Publication Data. Cruikshank, Julie
The social life of stories :
Includes bibliographical
references and index.
ISBN 0-7748-0648-6 (cloth:
alk. paper); ISBN 0-7748-0649-4
(pbk.: alk. paper). 1. Indians of
North America – Yukon
Territory – Folklore.
2. Oral tradition – Yukon
Territory – History and
criticism. 3. Storytelling –
Yukon Territory. 4. Folklore –
Yukon Territory.
I. Title. E78.Y8C778 1998
398.2'097191
C97-910812-8

To my parents, Kay and Bill, and
to my childhood baby-sitter Alice,
who taught me early the
importance of good stories

Contents

List of Illustrations ix

Preface xi

Acknowledgments xix

Note on Transcription xxiii

1 "My Roots Grow in Jackpine
   Roots": Culture, History, and
   Narrative Practice in the Yukon 1

2 "Pete's Song": Establishing
   Meanings through Story and Song 25

3 Yukon Arcadia: Oral Tradition,
   Indigenous Knowledge,
   and the Fragmentation of Meaning 45

4 Confronting Cultural Erasure:
   Images of Society in
   Klondike Gold Rush Narratives 71

5 Imperfect Translations: Rethinking
   Objects of Ethnographic Collection 98

6 Claiming Legitimacy: Prophecy
   Narratives from Northern Aboriginal Women 116

7 Negotiating with Narrative:
   Establishing Cultural Identity at
   the Yukon International Storytelling Festival 138

Epilogue 161

Notes 167

Bibliography 187

Index 207

Illustrations

MAPS

1. Languages spoken in the Yukon Territory   xxvi
2. The Southern Lakes District, Yukon Territory   xxvii

FIGURES

following page 128
1. Angela Sidney
2. Annie Ned
3. Keish's sister Shaaw Tláa
4. Kitty Smith
5. Three of Kitty Smith's carvings,
   Dukt'ootl', Azanzhaya, and Bear Husband
6. Kaats' being taken by Bear Woman
7. The abandoned wife of Kaats'
   walking away with their child
8. Kaats' and his Bear wife
9. Dukt'ootl', carved by Kitty Smith
10. Carving of Dukt'ootl' in the foyer of
    the Alaska State Museum, Juneau
11. Naatsilanéi
12. Medallion on a speaker's staff or
    song stick in MacBride Museum, Whitehorse

Preface

How do scholars see beyond the norms they use to frame the experiences of others unless those norms are interrupted and exposed so that scholars are vulnerable, seeing what they believe as possibly wrong, or at least limited?

Greg Sarris, *Keeping Slug Woman Alive*

Well, I have no money to leave to my grandchildren. My stories are my wealth.

Angela Sidney, Tagish, March 1974

During the past two decades, I have spent considerable time thinking about stories and about how their meanings shift as tellers address different audiences, situations, and historical contexts. From the early 1970s until 1984, I lived in the Yukon Territory and had the good fortune to work closely with elders engaged in the project of recording their life stories. They and their families wanted to see accounts written in their own words describing memories and experiences spanning almost a century. Ongoing discussions about *how* these words should be recorded, transcribed, and circulated were central to the procedures we followed in trying to develop shared ethnographic authority.

Then, in the mid-1980s, I returned to the university as a student after fifteen years' absence, hoping to learn more about how varieties of knowledge passed on in oral narrative are enlarging scholarly understanding in anthropology and history. There I encountered literature from Africa, Europe, North and South America, New Zealand, Australia, Asia, and the South Pacific addressing questions similar to those absorbing us in the Yukon: questions about oral tradition's potential for translating distinctive cultural meanings to diverse audiences. Both these educational processes — in northern communities and in southern libraries — provided me with more questions than answers about the social lives of stories told both in everyday conversation and in scholarly writing. Two aphorisms seem for me to sum up this quandary: Mikhail Bakhtin's observation that "everything means" tempered by Edward Sapir's reminder that "all systems leak." [1]

This book builds on collaborative work undertaken with three Yukon elders between 1974 and the late 1980s. Their orally narrated life stories told during those years appeared originally in six booklets we produced for distribution in Yukon communities and subsequently in our coauthored volume, *Life Lived Like a Story*.[2] Mrs. Kitty Smith was born about 1890 and lived a full and active life until 1989. Mrs. Angela Sidney's life and observations spanned most of the twentieth century, from 1902 until 1991. Mrs. Annie Ned was born during the early 1890s and experienced a century of change until the end of her life in 1995. Recounting their experiences, they illustrated how narratives that have been passed on orally for generations continue to provide a foundation for evaluating contemporary choices and for clarifying decisions made as young women, as mature adults, and during later life. Such narratives depict humans, animals, and other nonhuman beings engaged in an astonishing variety of activities and committed to mutually sustaining relationships that ensure the continuing well-being of the world. One of the many things these women taught me is that their narratives do far more than entertain. If one has optimistic stories about the past, they showed, one can draw on internal resources to survive and make sense of arbitrary forces that might otherwise seem overwhelming.

Their insights converge with scholarly concerns about how narrative provides a framework for experiencing the material world and how local stories intersect with larger social, historical, and political processes. "When it comes to explaining how it is that humans experience their world in ways that they can make sense of," notes Mark Johnson, "there must be a central place for the notion of 'narrative unity.' Not only are we born into complex communal narratives, we also experience, understand and order our lives as stories that we are living out. Whatever human rationality consists in, it is certainly tied up with narrative structure and the question of narrative unity." [3] If much of the academic literature seems to universalize or to work against the notion that people lead storied lives in distinctive ways, the primary lesson I learned from these women is that narratives providing the most helpful guidance are inevitably locally grounded, highly particular, and culturally specific. What is important is not just knowing the story but sharing the context for knowing when and why it is told so that conversations can build on that shared knowledge.

My thesis is this. In northern Canada, storytellers of Yukon First Nations ancestry continue to tell stories that make meaningful connections and provide order and continuity in a rapidly changing world. An enduring value of informal storytelling is its power to subvert official orthodoxies and to challenge conventional ways of thinking. Such systems of knowledge, as both Greg Sarris and Angela Sidney point out above, can be understood as having the power to inform and enlarge other forms of explanation rather than as data for analysis using conventional scholarly paradigms. My larger question, then, concerns *how* local voices can contribute to theoretical paradigms that frame contemporary scholarship. Skeptical of theoretical tidiness, I have been led to questions raised more than a generation ago by scholars working in very different parts of the world — Walter Benjamin, Mikhail Bakhtin, and Harold Innis. Each wrote about the potential of stories to sustain social life and deplored the consequences when oral storytelling becomes marginalized by more powerful knowledge systems.[4] Though each worked exclusively with written records and from literary sources, the issues they raised have continuing importance and invite contemporary ethnographic investigation of how insistent local storytelling subverts administrative ambition, an issue I pursue in subsequent chapters.

This book also provides an opportunity to explore a paradox that has alternately troubled and exhilarated me during the years that Mrs. Sidney, Mrs. Smith, Mrs. Ned, and I worked together. On one hand, it is evident that written, textual transcriptions of spoken language have the potential to freeze or to arrest speech. In the words of Nora and Richard Dauenhauer, whose fine transcriptions and translations of orally performed Tlingit narrative provide a model for others working with Native American texts, "The writing down of oral literature, no matter how well-intentioned or how well carried out, petrifies it. It is like a molecule by molecule replacement of an organic plant by stone. A petrified log may look like wood, but it is actually stone."[5] On the other hand, during my years living in the Yukon and now regularly visiting there, I continue to marvel at the social lives transcribed texts gain in the communities where they originate and continue to be told. I am especially intrigued by the ways Yukon elder storytellers point to writing as just one more way to tell their stories and to make them part of social practice. Written texts become points of reference narrators can allude to when they want to make socially significant statements to family members, to other members of their community, or to the larger world about the *potential* of stories to make us reevaluate situations we think we understand.

The elders I worked with during the 1970s also insisted that we record and write their narratives in English. There are many reasons for this choice. The Yukon Territory's multilingualism incorporates eight distinct indigenous languages from two very different language families, Athapaskan and Tlingit. For reasons discussed in chapter 1, most people born after the construction of the Alaska Highway in 1943 speak English as a first language. In the mid-1970s, when we began this work, there were no Native language programs in place, nor had orthographies been developed for indigenous languages in the region. All this has changed since the Yukon Native Language Centre came into being in the 1980s.[6] But during the 1970s, the women I worked with had a clear objective. They saw themselves as recording narratives directly for grandchildren who spoke English as a first language, and for whom English had in many ways *become* their indigenous language.

For years, though, I have been concerned that the work that engaged us could be considered an example of one problem the Dauenhauers have discussed — the distortions that occur when literary narratives originally learned in indigenous languages are told and recorded in English. Over time, I have concluded that as long as bilingual narrators can be their own translators and retain a decisive role in the editing process, even stories narrated and recorded in English can continue to have intense and complex social lives in their communities.[7] This book demonstrates some of the ways narrators use versions of narratives, recorded in English, as reference points for animating social meanings that might otherwise be erased.

Chapter 1 discusses authorizing narratives and their consequences. I outline ethnographic particulars about the Yukon, its peoples, and its history, contrasting the narratives presented in written records from the late nineteenth century with those animating contemporary social discourses at the end of the twentieth. Universalizing classification systems that accompanied colonial expansion have inevitably threatened to dislodge or trivialize local systems of meaning, yet Yukon elders have never been deterred from telling narratives that address precise local concerns. The interplay of externally imposed categories with local concepts, though, has consequences for the ways indigenous Yukoners now speak about belonging in the Yukon, and these intersect with regional and global issues of growing concern in the circumpolar north.[8] This chapter suggests that academic narratives — about cultural categories, about narrative forms, about historical periodization — can be enlarged if we take seriously the stories people tell about themselves.

A powerful demonstration of this is the story of Ḵaax̱'achgóok, framing chapter 2. Mrs. Sidney shows how a single story, carefully told, can be employed to convey different meanings to different audiences. She demonstrates first what a story *says* and then what it can *do* when engaged as a strategy of communication. Her use of narrative suggests that oral tradition is better understood as a social activity than as a reified text, that meanings do not inhere in a story but are created in the everyday situations in which they are told. Among other things, she demonstrates that when potential for conflict emerges among people with different perspectives, successful resolution often involves demonstrating how a story can reframe a divisive issue by providing a broader context for evaluating such issues.

Chapter 3 examines some of the problems that occur when complex narratives are wrenched out of context as though their meanings are straightforwardly self-evident. In circumpolar northern regions, for example, oral tradition has recently begun to play at least a rhetorical role in "postcolonial" policy debates. Adding local perspectives to Arctic and subarctic policy discussions is long overdue; however, the technocratic and environmental vortices into which such knowledge is swept may submerge narratives while claiming to learn from them. Management models based on "TEK" (an acronym for "traditional ecological knowledge") draw on oral tradition selectively, as do environmentalist models that more closely approximate a religious paradigm. If management models seem to drain tradition by codifying it on databases, environmental models more commonly adjust the imagery of "original ecology" to fit contemporary environmental concerns. As this chapter demonstrates, indigenous people, caught in the middle, are sometimes compelled to use both kinds of language to claim a legitimate voice in late twentieth-century colonial encounters and may be forced to speak in uncharacteristic ways.

If oral traditions become formulated as indigenous science in one context, in another they are invoked as indigenous history. Chapter 4 examines one case of how oral narrative and written documents contribute to historical reconstruction. My discussion of Klondike gold rush stories centers less on what they disclose about "what really happened" than on what they reveal about social processes. Written and oral accounts from this period reflect contrasting models of social organization on the frontier — bound up especially in ideas about *individual* and *society* — that tell us much about the emerging social order of the day. Comparisons clarify processes set in motion in 1898 by the Canadian government's ambition to authorize its presence (to American miners as much as to "hostile Indians") by documenting, duplicating, dispersing, and legitimizing official accounts of events in writing. These stories connect cascading layers of narrative — of the experiences of indigenous people, of a hastily constructed administrative apparatus, and of how bureaucratic practice begins to erase local knowledge.

Another area where oral tradition confronts official narratives is in museums. Museums tell stories too, and historically their arrangements have been at the heart of classificatory practice. Chapter 5 examines intersecting narratives — some reflecting an artist's life story and others the stories of museums where such works may eventually find a destination. Kitty Smith's carvings portraying narratives she told to illustrate critical turning points in her life also tell stories about museums. Her carvings, discovered in a Whitehorse museum near the end of her life, raise questions about the relation between words and things, between story and object, and between material representations of stories as "texts" and their arrival in museum collections as "artifacts."

Chapter 6 centers on prophecy narratives and moves us to contemporary theoretical debates about competing interpretative frameworks. Conventional academic arguments about prophecy are part of a well-known literature. In North American ethnohistory, one central question has been whether prophetic movements were indigenous or a response to European contact. The sociological literature, shaped by Max Weber, addresses the success or failure of specific prophets, judged in terms of their ability to transform the social and political order. This chapter shifts the emphasis in the study of prophetic movements to a discursive framework, analyzing how contemporary narratives told about prophets by Yukon elders serve as authoritative explanations for disruptive events. Viewed as indigenous ethnohistory competing for legitimacy as an explanatory framework, these stories constitute forms of historical narration that simultaneously question and enlarge scholarly understanding.

Finally, chapter 7 looks at kinds of storytelling that may occur in contemporary public festivals. Performers at the Yukon International Storytelling Festival would probably disagree with much current writing in cultural studies that scrutinizes festivals for evidence of "inauthenticity" or inequality. Local performers insist on telling stories in innovative ways and on their own terms, using this stereotype-filled setting to experiment with cultural translation strategies for diverse audiences. In so doing, they speak directly to some of the larger issues raised throughout the book — Bakhtin's optimism about the transformative power of oral storytelling to destabilize official orthodoxies; Innis's exploration of how oral tradition challenges imperial conceptions of time and space; Benjamin's emphasis on the ability of narrative to interweave information, moral content, and philosophical guidance. Storytellers give optimistic performances enmeshed in the complex political circumstances surrounding the implementation of the Yukon First Nations Land Claims Settlement Act, passed in 1995.

For me, writing this book has been a way to reflect on how experiences, friendships, and study in the Yukon connect with similar experiences in universities, how lessons from one setting may transfer to the other, and in Greg Sarris's words, how criticism can move closer to what it studies.[9] I especially hope this book does justice to those who have taught me — Angela Sidney, Kitty Smith, Annie Ned, Catharine McClellan, and Robin Ridington, as well as to friends and colleagues in the Yukon and in university seminars who struggle with similar issues.

Acknowledgments

This volume owes most to Angela Sidney, Kitty Smith, and Annie Ned, who patiently taught me to hear the many stories a single narrative can convey. But it also owes much to other women and men from Yukon First Nations communities with whom I have discussed stories and whose comments continue to guide my work.

The book builds on research begun twenty years ago and funded initially by the National Museum of Canada, the Council for Yukon Indians, and the Yukon Native Language Centre. More recent research between 1992 and 1995 was made possible by a grant from the Social Sciences and Humanities Research Council of Canada. A sabbatical leave from the University of British Columbia gave me the opportunity to write the manuscript, and a UBC Izaak Walton Killam Faculty Research Fellowship enabled me to spend that year at Cambridge University. I thank both the Scott Polar Research Institute and the Department of Social Anthropology at Cambridge for making me so welcome, for access to their splendid libraries, and for including me in seminars during my time there.

I am especially indebted to colleagues who have commented critically on parts of this manuscript or have discussed it with me in some way. Catharine McClellan has always been ready to read and comment on working papers, and my debt to her is enormous and ongoing. Robin Ridington and Phyllis Morrow each read the entire manuscript closely and made thoughtful and constructive comments, for which I thank them. The book reflects themes in the work of all three, and its subtitle echoes Ridington's *Trail to Heaven: Knowledge and Narrative in a Northern Native Community* as well as ideas that have emerged from years of conversation with him, both as his student and as a colleague. For helpful conversations and critical commentary on parts of the manuscript while I was in Cambridge, I especially thank David Anderson, Tanya Argounova, Barbara Bodenhorn, Paul

Connerton, Mary Core, Erich Kasten (in Berlin), Mark Nuttall, Frances Pine, Marilyn Strathern, and Piers Vitebsky. I am also indebted to the Pembroke College reading group Barbara Bodenhorn organized that year for our lively weekly discussions on the theme of narrative in culture.

I am grateful to colleagues in the Department of Anthropology at the University of British Columbia, and I especially thank Catherine Fenn, Elizabeth Furniss, Linda Mattson, Bruce G. Miller, Leslie Robertson, Nancy Wachowich, Kevin Washbrook, and Wendy Wickwire for ongoing suggestions and commentary on specific parts of the manuscript. Any errors of omission or commission are mine alone.

Of the many colleagues and friends in the Yukon who have spoken to me about their work or have made suggestions over the years, I particularly acknowledge and thank Vera Asp, Paul Birckel, Bessie and Roddy Blackjack, Ida and Henry Calmagane, Alice Carlick, Ron Chambers, Ann Cullen, George and Rachel Dawson, Helene Dobrowolsky, Mary Easterson, Allan Edzerza, Bill Ferguson, Sarah Gaunt, Carol Geddes, Judy Gingell, Austin Hammond, Percy Henry, Sharon Jacobs, Marilyn Jensen, Mary Jane Jim, Stella and Paddy Jim, Ingrid Johnson, Joanne Johnson, Linda Johnson, Margaret Johnson, Kathy Kushniruk, Louise Profeit LeBlanc, Jeff Leer, Beatrice Lowe, Annie MacDonald, Doris Mclean, Joanne Meehan, Eleanor Millard, Patrick Moore, David Neufeld, Elizabeth Nyman, John Ritter, Jim Robb, Edna Leask, Jessie Scarff, Clara Schinkel, Keith Wolf Smarch, Kitty Grant, Ann Smith, Dianne Strand, Gertie Tom, Brian Walker, Dora Wedge, Mark Wedge, and Margaret Workman.

Some parts of this book are revisions of papers that have appeared previously. Chapter 2 is a slightly revised version of a paper that appeared in *When Our Words Return: Writing, Hearing and Remembering Oral Traditions of Alaska and the Yukon*, edited by Phyllis Morrow and William Schneider and published by Utah State University Press (1995); it appears with permission of Utah State University Press. An earlier version of chapter 6 appeared in the *American Indian Quarterly* 18, no. 2 (1994), published by the University of Nebraska Press. Chapter 5, revised here, appeared in *Museum Anthropology* 19, no. 1 (spring–summer 1995), and chapter 7 appeared in *American Anthropologist* 99, no. 1 (2 March 1997), copyright American Anthropological Association 1997. Both are reproduced by permission of the American Anthropological Association and are not for further reproduction.

As Mrs. Sidney, Mrs. Smith, Mrs. Ned, and I agreed, royalties from our earlier book, *Life Lived Live a Story,* are awarded annually to a Yukon student of First Nations ancestry graduating with an interest in oral tradition and planning to undertake postsecondary education. This annual Oral History Award has been administered by the Council of Yukon First Nations and was awarded to Georgette McLoed (Dawson City) in 1993, Lisa Jacobs (Whitehorse) in 1994, Marla Kaye (Old Crow) in 1995, and Teresa Waugh (Whitehorse) in 1996. Any royalties from this book will add to that scholarship fund.

Finally, my thanks to Alice Bennett for her careful editing. As always, I am forever grateful to Garry, Lawrence, and Julian for continuing enthusiasm, encouragement, good humor, and companionship, and to Mary Burns, Dara Culhane, and Anne McCandless for friendship, long discussions, and recuperative walks.

Note on Transcription

The narrators whose stories are discussed in this book are all multilingual, and many speak languages from three distinct families: Athapaskan, Tlingit, and English. In this book clan names, personal names, and place-names in Tagish, Southern Tutchone, and Tlingit are retained in the text. I am indebted to linguists John Ritter, Jeff Leer, Gertie Tom, and Margaret Workman both for years of linguistic instruction and for assistance with transcriptions.

A spelling system for Tlingit has been developed at the Alaska Native Language Center, and standardized writing systems for Yukon Athapaskan languages and for Inland Tlingit are now being developed by the Yukon Native Language Centre. Sounds differ in Tlingit and Athapaskan languages, so the alphabets for these languages also differ. Because I am citing published Tlingit writings recorded by scholars who use divergent spelling systems for Coastal Tlingit and Inland Tlingit, I follow spellings used in those sources and refer the reader to published texts in which individual linguists discuss their spelling choices.

Athapaskan languages and Tlingit are tonal languages, and one major difference in the spelling systems concerns the ways tones are marked. In Tlingit and in one Athapaskan language, Tagish, linguists have chosen to mark high tones and to leave low tones unmarked. However, for complex reasons they have chosen the opposite strategy for a neighboring Athapaskan language, Southern Tutchone, marking low tones and leaving high tones unmarked. Because this system is becoming conventional, I have retained it even though it sometimes looks awkward when a narrator uses words from both languages. Southern Tutchone has another layer of complexity because there are additional distinct rising and falling tones; relatively few Southern Tutchone words appear here, however, so I have left rising and falling tones unmarked.

ALPHABETIZATION

Words in the index are arranged following Southern Tutchone, Tagish, and Tlingit alphabets, which include consonants not found in English. When words from several languages are combined, the alphabetization may seem unfamiliar. The following consonants are ordered thus: ch, ch', d, g, g̲, k, k̲, k', k̲', l, ł, s, s', t, tl, ts, t', tl', ts', x, x̲, x', x̲'.

TLINGIT AND TAGISH ALPHABETS

Tlingit Vowels

Short	Long
a	aa
e	ei
i	ee
u	oo

Tlingit Consonants

Plain stops	d		dl	dz	j	g	g̲
Aspirated stops	t		tl	ts	ch	k	k̲
Glottalized stops	t'		tl'	ts'	ch'	k'	k̲'
Plain fricatives			l	s	sh	x	x̲
Glottalized fricatives			l'	s'		x'	x̲'
Other sounds	m	n	ł		y	w	h

In Tlingit, a glottal stop in the middle of a word is represented by a dot.

Tone

High tone is marked (v́) on short vowels
High tone is marked (v́v) on long vowels
Low tone is not marked

Adapted from "Tlingit Literacy Workshop," 23–25 January 1984, 6–7, Yukon Native Languages Project (now Yukon Native Language Centre), Box 2799, Whitehorse YT, Y1A 5K4, Canada. The Inland Tlingit alphabet has recently been revised, but I follow spellings agreed to at the time these transcriptions were made.

SOUTHERN TUTCHONE ALPHABET

Southern Tutchone Vowels

High vowels   i   ü   u
Mid vowels   e   ä   äw(o)
Low vowels   a
Diphthongs   ay   aw
Nasalized vowels are written with a nasal hook directly underneath the letters: į   ę   ą   ų   ü̧   ä̧   ąw   ä̧w   ąy

Southern Tutchone Consonants

Plain		d	dl	ddh	dz	j	g	gw
Aspirated		t	tl	tth	ts	ch	k	kw
Glottalized		t'	tl'	tth'	ts'	ch'	k'	k'w
Voiceless fricatives			ł	th	s	sh	kh	khw h
Voiced fricatives			l	dh	z	zh	gh	ghw
Nasals	m	n						
Nasal + stop	mb	nd			nj			
Other sounds				r	y	(w)	'	

Tone

Low tone is marked (v̀) on vowels
High tone is never marked; rising/falling remain unmarked below

Adapted from "Southern Tutchone Literacy Workshop," 9–11 May 1984, 6, and "Southern Tutchone Literacy Workshop," 22–24 May 1984, 5, both publications of the Yukon Native Language Centre.

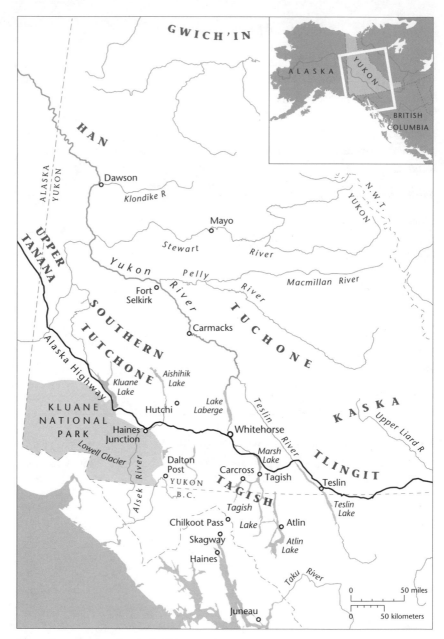

Map 1. Languages spoken in the Yukon Territory

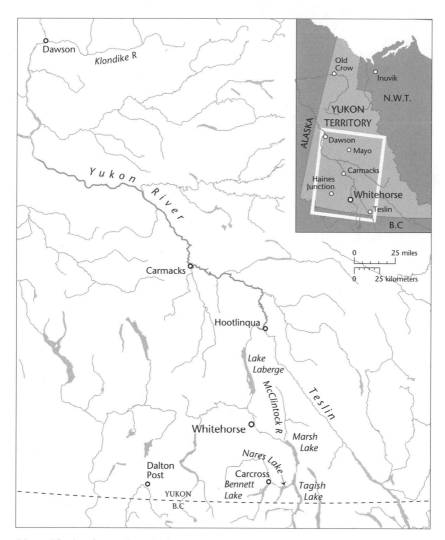

Map 2. The Southern Lakes District, Yukon Territory

THE SOCIAL LIFE OF STORIES

1

"My Roots Grow in Jackpine Roots": Culture, History, and Narrative Practice in the Yukon

I belong to Yukon. I'm born here. I branch here. My grandpa's country, here. My grandma's. That's why I stay here. Nobody kicks me out. No sir! My roots grow in jackpine roots.

Kitty Smith, Whitehorse, March 1974

What the map cuts up, the story cuts across.

Michel de Certeau, *The Practice of Everyday Life*

In *The Practice of Everyday Life,* Michel de Certeau discusses narrative's primary function as one of authorizing, founding, and setting in place ways of experiencing the world.[1] Anthropology's foundational narrative is holistic, and it underscores connection. If economics looks to the mystery of market forces for its primary explanations, psychology to underlying biological and mental processes, and sociology to concrete consequences of social relations, anthropology argues that such features are interrelated and that none can be discussed in isolation. Committed both to comparative studies and to ethnographic methods that involve talking with real people about how they experience their world, organize their behavior, and live their lives, anthropologists argue that in any given society every institution from kinship and religion to economics and art can be shown to be closely connected to every other.

One concept anthropologists use to frame these connections is culture, defined as a uniquely human creation central to everyday lives and practices of all human communities and characterized by our capacity to endow the world with symbolic meanings. Inevitably, this approach draws us to stories people tell about themselves. Stories, like good scholarly monographs, explore connections underlying surface diversity. If anthropology's project has centered on *detecting* subsurface relationships, this book shows how narratives are used to *establish* such connections — between past and future, between people and place, among people whose opinions diverge.

As concepts, though, in recent years both culture and story have begun to look more complicated. Classic ethnographic studies explicating the workings of culture have typically come from societies that seemed relatively small in scale and far away. Ideas about history, about political processes, about global forces sometimes seemed to be missing from early ethnographies, leaving an impression that small-scale societies could be represented as isolated, self-contained units, colliding and glancing off one another but clearly bounded in a timeless stratum designated "traditional." Such portrayals have changed to incorporate hierarchical differences within and between communities created by unequal access to locally or globally valued resources.[2] But if anthropologists no longer think of communities as bounded or homogeneous, we continue to look for the variety of ways continuity, locality, and a sense of belonging are culturally constituted.

Narratives, like culture, may once have seemed capable of invoking seamless closure, but this is no longer so. Few scholars working closely with narrative treat the concept as transparent, even if the idea that stories speak for themselves remains alive in the world. Meaning does not inhere in events but involves weaving those events into stories that are meaningful at the time. Events, after all, are stories known directly only to those who experience them and interpret them to others, who in turn make their own interpretations of what they hear. Personal narratives based on shared metaphors and responses to common problems in one generation may be reworked quite differently by the next. A concept of narrative — like culture — that is more complicated and differentiated provides ways of thinking about how human communities continue to hold together, and about how divisions that at one time seem deep recede and are reworked in the process of building alliances at another time.

Increasingly, anthropologists are historicizing the narratives they tell about culture, looking at how documents, texts, and accounts passed on orally are rendered significant as representations of what has taken place. Anthropologists are consulting written records with more care, just as historians now pay more attention to cultural categories, cosmologies, and symbols. Oriented to the present through fieldwork, anthropologists continue to focus on the contested ways people invoke the past to talk about the present and the present to talk about the past. Including history makes the concept of culture seem less tidy but more interesting.

At the end of the twentieth century, both anthropology and history face challenges about the relevance of their concepts and categories to varieties of cultural experience. Selection of categories is never neutral, and recent scholarly narratives are more conscious of struggles underlying systems of classification and periodization that may subsequently be presented as self-evident, especially those categories designating ownership or membership. In the Yukon Territory, as in many parts of the world, one area where narratives about history and culture collide is in discussions about the nature of *belonging*. Recent literature from Eastern Europe suggests that categories of belonging are precisely where fractures occur most readily during periods of social upheaval.[3] Ideas about belonging provide particular insight into how local meanings are asserted in response to externally imposed classification systems.

This chapter provides some background information about the Yukon, its peoples, and their history and raises instances of how local meanings intersect in consequential ways with externally imposed categories. Here I attempt to construct an account of Yukon culture and history that pays close attention both to written accounts describing political and economic forces that shape contemporary understandings of the Territory's history and to orally transmitted memories of how those forces were experienced in Yukon First Nations communities. I also draw on conversations with indigenous Yukoners who have spent much of their adult lives evaluating the impact of both written and orally transmitted narratives on their land claims negotiations. At the end of the twentieth century both kinds of narrative — oral and written — continue to affect how people speak about history and culture. They may take different forms, but they still intersect, now as in the past.

My thesis, restated, is that Yukon storytellers of First Nations ancestry frequently demonstrate ability to build connections where rifts might otherwise appear. They use narratives to dismantle boundaries rather than erect them. In so doing, they raise significant epistemological issues both about past Western classificatory practice and about contemporary theoretical constructions. If postmodern analyses attribute fragmentation of meaning to late twentieth-century uncertainties, Yukon storytellers have long experienced such fragmentation as springing from the structure of colonial practices that took root more than a century ago. Subsequent chapters demonstrate ways that narrative storytelling can construct meaningful bridges in disruptive situations. When potential for division emerges, successful resolution often involves demonstrating how a story can reframe issues by providing a larger context.

PERIODIZING HISTORY, CATEGORIZING THE WORLD: NINETEENTH-CENTURY NARRATIVES AND THEIR CONSEQUENCES

The writing of history has always involved collecting, analyzing, and retelling stories about the past, yet the very act of collection means that some stories are enshrined in books while others remain marginalized. Sources for remembered history from the late nineteenth-century Yukon include some archived in written records and others passed on orally. They differ partly because the tellers had different goals and objectives, interpreted events differently, and emphasized different experiences. Events are always made into a story by suppressing some aspects and highlighting others, so it should not be surprising that both written and oral histories are based on a selective reading of the past, especially when they are retold to make meaningful connections in the present.

Written records from the Yukon do not go back so very many years — a few fur trade journals from the 1850s, travelers' reports from the 1880s and 1890s, a flood of letters and diaries from visitors who recorded their own stories during the 1896–98 Klondike gold rush. The historical narratives constructed from these records reflect visions of people who considered themselves explorers writing their impressions of a land they presumed to be discovering. Aboriginal oral histories from the same period, transmitted in narratives, songs, place-names, and genealogies reflect an understanding of place by people who saw this land as the center of the world rather than its margin. Like letters and journals, oral histories are not always passed on as complete narratives, but they are much more than documents to be recorded and stored away. Stories about the past continue to be discussed and debated in small communities where oral tradition is a lively ongoing process, a way of understanding present as well as past.

Between 1840 and 1890, a series of newcomers visited northwestern North America. The accounts left behind by fur traders, missionaries, scientists, and others suggest that though each had specific reasons for coming north, they all expected to acquire things of value. The entire project of nineteenth-century exploration can be understood as an exercise in collection and classification. Traders were interested in collecting furs, missionaries in collecting souls, scientists in collecting and classifying facts, prospectors in collecting gold nuggets, and government-sponsored expeditions in acquiring territories.

These are the narratives usually certified as Yukon history. Though orchestrated from a distance, they describe activities that enmeshed indigenous peoples from the upper Yukon River in international markets and relationships long before they had face-to-face encounters with the first strangers. Whatever their motives, many early visitors recorded their observations and impressions in journals, letters, and reports that are valuable to historians but that usually tell us more about Victorian values than about the indigenous peoples described. Yet these very observations often became authorizing statements, the foundation on which policy decisions were made by colonial institutions — the Hudson's Bay Company, the church, and the government. In this way, written documents based on cultural understandings from Europe and from distant North American locations often had serious economic, political, and social consequences for the lives of Yukon peoples.

Fur Traders and Missionaries: The Arrival of Strangers

From 1840 to 1890, Hudson's Bay Company traders and Church of England missionaries were the main international representatives in direct contact with aboriginal people in northwestern Canada. Imperial Britain was emerging from the Industrial Revolution with a strong conviction of its place at the social, economic, and political center of the world. On the surface its representatives — traders and missionaries — had very different objectives and methods, but in practice they often cooperated. Historians often periodize the fur trade as a distinct chapter in Canadian history, as an event or a series of events with a clear beginning and ending. Aboriginal trappers, on the other hand, regard trapping as an enterprise that began long before Europeans arrived and that continues to have social and economic importance in many communities, most recently as a consequence of the activities of animal rights movements that have crippled trapping economies across the North.

Outlines of earlier trade between people living on the Yukon River and their neighbors remain hazy because the earliest items of exchange were perishable. Separated by mountain chains from the Tlingit on the Pacific coast and from the Inuit on the Arctic coast, interior Athapaskans traded skins and furs from the Yukon Plateau for marine products from both seas.[4]

Tlingit traders made annual trips to the interior to trade, bringing dried fish, eulachon oil, shell ornaments, and cedar bark baskets to exchange for tanned furs, moose and caribou hides, finished fur garments and moccasins, and Native copper. Farther north, Gwich'in middlemen brought oil, bone, and tusks from the Arctic coast to exchange for inland furs. Older people still talk about the social contacts such trade provided — partnerships established and marriages cementing them. There are stories about how interior peoples initially met coastal traders, about trade routes they followed, and about dangers Tlinget traders faced crossing glaciers.[5] Clan traditions tell of the arrival of four Tlingit sisters who married into interior communities to formalize trading partnerships, and of the relaxation of ethnic boundaries between coastal and interior peoples over the years.

The European-based fur trade and the arrival of Russian and British traders on the north Pacific coast only intensified existing indigenous trade networks, causing trappers to shift emphasis from the domestic use of furs to their value as objects of exchange. Furs were the marketable resource that initially drew outsiders to the North, the first industry to link aboriginal communities with European economies. With the addition of trade goods, trapping for trade gradually became a central occupation for people living on the Yukon Plateau. Historians and economists have conventionally written about the fur trade as a market-oriented business, examining problems involved in collecting and transporting furs from northern communities to urban centers, tracing linkages between fur production in Canada and fur markets in Europe. Their emphasis has been on how the fur trade articulates with large-scale industrial economies. Anthropologists have been more likely to concentrate on aboriginal producers, looking at procedures followed before the furs reach the trader, examining the kinds of labor involved in both producing and processing furs and the kinds of exchanges that occur as those furs are transformed into commodities. They have analyzed the consequences of such trade for subsistence economies, community leadership patterns, and relations within aboriginal families. Both sets of narratives document a *relationship* that is often explored more fully in oral traditions of people who experienced the intrusion of Victorian values into the Subarctic than in the documentary sources left behind.

Commercial trade dominating the Yukon River after the 1840s was driven from distant centers. Russian and British traders were originally drawn to the Pacific Northwest by sea otter furs, but the European fur markets had no limits: there were never enough furs to satisfy demand in Moscow, London, or Paris. By the mid-1800s, sea otters were all but exterminated, and trading companies turned their attention inland, again relying largely on existing indigenous trade networks. Efforts by the Hudson's Bay Company to establish inland posts during the 1840s stopped at Fort Selkirk when the trader Robert Campbell was driven out in 1852 by coastal Tlingit traders who viewed his arrival in "their" trading territory as an intrusion. Despite his failure, Campbell's efforts have earned him disproportionate weight in oral accounts about first encounters with whites, rendered more recently as accounts of cannibalism by traders at one of his posts.[6]

Ideas of fashion peculiar to a particular historical period in Europe drove the nineteenth-century fur industry. Beaver hats, stoles, muffs, and coats made of Yukon furs were valuable commodities because of their scarcity, cost, and durability. But Europeans were not the only ones interested in fashion. Yukon women experimented with designs made possible by new varieties of beads. Indigenous artistic traditions were elaborated as women began working with different colors and textures, integrating new designs — especially floral patterns — into established traditions. Ideas of beauty, fashion, and art, then, may have influenced the fur trade from several angles, both in the European fashion industry and in indigenous artistic traditions in northern Canada.[7]

If early traders saw advantages in working *with* indigenous knowledge systems, missionaries were committed to a vision that they had a moral obligation to "civilize" and Christianize the world by introducing everyone to the spiritual and cultural values of Victorian Britain. Ironically, the greatest conflicts in the quest for souls came from within the missionary community. Two major agencies were in active competition west of the Great Lakes during the late nineteenth century — the Church Missionary Society (CMS), associated with the Anglican Church, and the Roman Catholic Oblates of Mary Immaculate (OMI). Initially, at least, Anglican missionaries were more successful in the Yukon because of alliances developed with the Hudson's Bay Company during the critical period of nineteenth-century expansion.

Mission programs reflected the evolutionary narrative widespread in Britain at the time, that hunters' moral and material progress would be hastened if they could be enjoined to abandon hunting in order to farm. This idea conveniently served interests of British colonial expansion by justifying repression of other ways of life in the service of expanding cities like London. Church policy took as one of its objectives the transformation of hunters to farmers and, despite the dubious wisdom of pursuing agriculture in a subarctic environment, incorporated garden plots and hayfields into the residential school programs like the one Bishop William Carpenter Bompas and his wife, Selina, established at Carcross shortly after the turn of the century.

As with the fur trade, retrospectively we ask different questions about missionary work. Recent scholarly activity addresses the systematic expansion of missionary pursuits from Europe into North America and the uniformity of the program, despite internal conflicts and competition among the participants. Oral traditions from the Yukon focus instead on the variety of relationships that developed between aboriginal people and individual missionaries who came from different cultural and class backgrounds and brought different styles of operation to their project. Robert McDonald, born to an Ojibwa mother and a Scottish trader on the Red River, was one of the few Anglican missionaries in the Yukon who did not come from England; he is remembered in stories discussed in chapter 6.

Nineteenth-century Christian theology was concerned with fixed meanings — with the idea that there was a single truth. Consequently, missionaries were uninterested in spiritual traditions that guided people living in the Yukon, except when they identified practices they wished to change. A foundational local narrative, largely marginalized in European accounts because it was opaque to newcomers, concerned interaction between humans and animals, more generally conceptualized as relationships between human and nonhuman persons. Everyone understood that humans and animals were born into a world animated by power. At the beginning of time, these beings shared such attributes as language and thought, and animals had the ability to adopt human disguise. In the social contract they shared, such relationships were understood as mutually sustaining. Fur traders who saw animals as commodities and missionaries who categorized humans as distinct from animals and holding dominion over them were ill equipped and disinclined to pay close attention to such epistemology, which nevertheless continued to lend explanatory coherence to local understandings of the world. Whereas missionaries were committed to a single truth, Yukon peoples had no difficulty integrating the new narratives into their own belief systems, as elaborated in chapter 6.

Varieties of History: Extending Empire

By the 1870s other pressures — again from outside the Yukon — were signaling a shift in trading liaisons. With rumors of mineral wealth on the

Yukon River attracting prospectors, independent traders, scientists, map-makers, and journalists continued to arrive. Determined to describe and classify the world they were entering, they left valuable documents that give us an interesting, but inevitably partial, snapshot of what nineteenth-century visitors saw.[8] Two fairly obvious shortcomings — one temporal, one spatial — confront us when we consult these sources. First, the Yukon was experiencing the effects of European intrusion long before most visitors arrived, so most records document the consequences of European intrusion rather than features of precontact life. By the 1890s the Tlingit and Athapaskan fur trade had tapered off. Coastal Tlingit people were already working in canneries, while Athapaskan men and women were selling their labor to prospectors and travelers and taking advantage of the alternative trading opportunities provided by recently arrived independent traders. Second, most early reports from the southern Yukon provide observations from a narrow river corridor. When elders from the southern Yukon talk about early population centers, they refer to places like Hutshi and Aishihik, which rarely appear in written records because they were some distance from the river routes most travelers used.

Older people also tell stories they heard about the earliest travelers. Residents on the upper Yukon River had their own classifications for the strangers, calling them K'och'èn, or "cloud people," because of their colorless skin. A common narrative theme involves a journey made by one man or woman to another dimension of time and space where everything, including people and animals, is white — a winter world where the characteristics of ordinary reality are reversed so that the traveler must be reeducated to understand what he or she is seeing.[9] Some people reasoned that the K'och'èn were visitors from this world. They watched carefully from a distance as the white "cloud people" passed by in their boats. Travelers following the Yukon River regularly reported the absence of local people in such comments as "once again, we saw no Indians today." Oral histories, though, provide ample evidence that indigenous people observed the strangers.

By the 1880s prospectors were arriving on the upper Yukon River, bringing expectations and experiences from the goldfields of California and British Columbia. When questions of territorial ownership arose, they were interpreted solely with reference to competing claims by Canada and the United States, with no suggestion that aboriginal people might have legal claims to the land. Then as now, narratives of nationhood were impassioned and governments were accumulating territories, with the United

States acquiring Alaska from Russia in 1867 and acceding to a boundary line with Canada along the 141st meridian. By the end of the century, though, American prospectors entering the upper Yukon River basin were reluctant to be ruled by Canadian law.

The Klondike gold rush continues to fascinate Western audiences. The allure of gold has deep narrative roots, but its discovery in 1896 coincided with a world depression and gave hope to thousands of unemployed men who could assemble provisions for one winter and set off, encouraged by dreams of fortunes to be found in the creek beds and gravel bars of one small tributary of the Yukon River, the Klondike. All that seemed necessary was a willingness to take the risks involved in traveling to the extreme northwest corner of North America.

Retrospectively, the gold rush seems less glamourous. Many prospectors endured enormous hardships, and few who survived the difficult journey found claims left to stake once they reached the Klondike River. The most enduring effect of the gold rush was establishment of an infrastructure for administering the newly established Yukon Territory from Ottawa, the nation's capital. Institutions dating from this time continue to have far-reaching implications.

The Klondike has generated an enormous literature, but in thousands of pages we find few references to the indigenous peoples who observed and were affected by the changes. Between 1896 and 1900, tens of thousands of men and far smaller numbers of women converged on this one small area. The vast majority came by the same route, climbing the Chilkoot Pass, building rafts, and then traveling down the Yukon River to Dawson City. We are left to imagine the impact of this torrent of visitors on aboriginal peoples living along the route and near Dawson City because so few travelers even mentioned Native peoples in their journals. Chapter 4 examines counternarratives from this period and their long-term implications.

Most whites left the country soon after the beginning of the century. In 1900 the total population of the Yukon Territory had climbed to over twenty-seven thousand, of whom three thousand were classified by the census as "Indian." By 1912 the total population had shrunk to six thousand, and by 1921 to just over four thousand, where it remained relatively stable for the next twenty years.[10] Fur prices remained high well into the 1930s. By then a family's annual cycle included one or more trips to a trading post, and some families built log cabins near posts. There was some seasonal wage work on riverboats, at wood camps, as hunting guides, and on the White Pass railway. More children were attending residential schools. Nevertheless, long-standing social organization continued to provide coherence.

Before the Second World War, there were no major roads in the Yukon and few mechanized vehicles. A few wagon trails remained from mining in the early 1900s and a winter road paralleled the Yukon River from White-horse to Dawson City. Generally, people traveled by foot, dog team, or boat and were separated from other camps by several days' travel. Then one spring day in 1942, three regiments of American soldiers arrived in White-horse with orders to build the Yukon section of the Alaska Highway. A northern road system had been discussed for some years, but the threat of a military invasion from Japan accelerated the task dramatically. Between April 1942 and December 1943, more than thirty-four thousand men were employed constructing a road linking British Columbia, the Yukon, and Alaska. Once again the indigenous population was overwhelmed by large numbers of outsiders with radically different lifestyles. The "second rush," as older people call it, marked another transition with consequences substantially more disruptive than those of the gold rush.

Remembered accounts of Alaska highway construction show that no single narrative captures the experience of aboriginal people living through it. Memories of wartime experience are much debated and have helped people to formulate their contemporary land claims position. Elders speaking formally during the 1976 Alaska Highway Pipeline Inquiry and more personally during the commemoration of the fiftieth anniversary of Alaska Highway construction in 1992 reflected on changes associated with the coming of the road. Short-term consequences included the inevitable impact of another brief population explosion as some thirty thousand soldiers and construction workers arrived practically overnight — including the excitement of new technology, new people, and new ideas, but also the devastation caused by epidemics and dramatic increases in the availability of alcohol.

Long-term changes occurred in two broad areas: in relationships between aboriginal people and land, and in long-standing social institutions associated with family and kinship. Because of overhunting by soldiers during the construction period, large areas of the southwest Yukon were set aside as a sanctuary, effectively barring aboriginal people from their traditional hunting and trapping territories. State-imposed restrictions on hunting and trapping inevitably altered local modes of production. The highway corridor also permitted comprehensive government administration for the first time, and a host of new agencies began to operate in communities, providing social assistance but often usurping roles formerly carried out by extended families — economic support, health care, education, and enforcement of rules. In the short term many of these services seemed beneficial, but the cumulative effect of living in government-administered settlements with no economic base also contributed to difficulties for many families.

BELONGING IN THE YUKON:
LANGUAGE, LAND, AND FAMILY IN THE LATE TWENTIETH CENTURY

Yukon First Nations are linguistically, culturally, and historically diverse. They speak many languages. Their territories stretch from the Arctic Ocean to the Pacific. They have differing histories of contact with other indigenous peoples and with Europeans.[11] In the late twentieth century, when indigenous people speak publicly on their own terms about identity and belonging, they do so in ways that are meaningful at present. Their concepts are rooted in categories different from those of the social sciences, and their formulation of historical periods differs from that devised by historians. But when such concepts intermingle with those used in anthropology, linguistics, history, or economics and become authorized (for example, in negotiations surrounding land claims and self-government), they have consequences. Concepts and categories have the potential to pull people together — to unite them — but they can just as easily be divisive, especially when they become legitimized by "expert" knowledge.

Language, land, and family are central to contemporary public discussions of culture and expressions of belonging in Yukon communities. All three concepts refer to institutions profoundly affected by more than a century of involvement in international economic, political, and social networks. Within any social community, members differ in their experiences of what such fundamental concepts mean — older and younger people, land-based trappers and urban residents, women and men. But when externally authorized categories begin to create cleavages based on conflicting claims to language, to land, or to family knowledge, skillful storytellers frequently contribute by demonstrating — in effect performing — how stories can reconnect people temporarily divided. In subsequent chapters I suggest that this process has long historical roots in the Yukon and that now, as in the past, people use narrative knowledge to establish connections among people potentially at odds. Here I continue to provide background a contemporary narrator would expect from his or her audience.

Language: Forging Connections

Languages spoken in the Yukon Territory are classified by linguists as belonging to two families, Athapaskan and Tlingit. The Athapaskan group encompasses at least thirty distinct languages in northwestern North America as well as several spoken far to the south, including Navajo and Apache. Athapaskan languages still spoken in the Yukon include Gwich'in, Han, Upper Tanana, Tutchone, Southern Tutchone, Tagish, and Kaska.[12] Tlingit is spoken in southeastern Alaska, and following the movement of coastal traders to the high country interior during the nineteenth century, Tlingit became a dominant language in part of the southern Yukon (see map 1).

One striking feature of language use in this region, especially among the elderly, is the fluid multilingualism that seems to have characterized daily life. If the purpose of language is to communicate, no commitment to this goal can be clearer than in northwestern North America, where it seems to have been routine in this century for people to speak not just several languages, but languages from different families. Older women I worked with during the 1970s and 1980s spoke one or sometimes two Athapaskan languages as well as Tlingit and added English to their repertoire as adults. Linguists constructing orthographies for contemporary Yukon languages point to place-names as providing especially vivid linguistic evidence of past multilingualism. Translation of some names is straightforward, but others remain submerged because of complex loan traditions stemming from bilingual times where now only a borrowed name may survive; for example, an original Athapaskan name borrowed and now euphonized in Tlingit. Were it possible to know all the original Athapaskan names, linguists say, we could learn more about the history of each language and the processes of linguistic shift that occurred during the last century.[13]

Contemporary ethnographic maps of the Yukon use linguistic categories to depict territorial boundaries, suggesting firmer divisions than may ever have existed. The boundaries are usually sketched to coincide with river drainages but provide no idea of early population shifts or how many earlier languages may have disappeared. Linguists and anthropologists routinely emphasize the schematic intent and social permeability of such divisions, but once they become accepted techniques for mapping, there is a tendency to reify them — to give them disproportionate categorical weight and to point to them as boundary markers. The convention is simultaneously convenient and problematic.

Origins of names used to designate Yukon languages are obscure. When the first European visitors arrived a century ago, they asked people they encountered what they called themselves and their neighbors, and then sometimes uncritically transcribed what they heard. Some of those names, like Gwich'in or Tlingit, have roots in original languages. Others like Tutchone are opaque, possibly originating in the word dechän or "stick," a term then used on the coast to characterize interior forest dwellers. Elderly speakers of Athapaskan languages use quite different terms to refer to themselves, sometimes dän or den, meaning "people," [14] or possibly Kajìt (Crow) or Ägunda (Wolf), referring to moiety names. If they speak Tlingit they might identify themselves further with reference to clan — Deisheetaan, Yanyeidí, Dak̲l'aweidí, or one of several other prominent Tlingit-named clans. Because there are so many ways to refer to oneself, Yukon First Nations now conventionally use language names as one way to distinguish regional differences. The expansion of the Yukon Native Language Centre's programs in the 1980s and the addition of a Bureau of Aboriginal Languages Services in the 1990s have contributed enormously to discussions of the continuing significance of languages once deemed to be vanishing.

In addition to authorizing territorial divisions, language is sometimes invoked to draw attention to generational boundaries. One distinction, made with increasing frequency, is between those who are said to "have their language" and those who do not. For a variety of reasons — especially compulsory schooling—most people born after the construction of the Alaska Highway in 1943 learned English as a first language. Only in the late 1970s was the idea of Native language instruction in classrooms first given serious attention. Younger students fresh from the stimulation of those programs, addressing elders who often suffered stigma or even punishment for speaking their languages when they were young, sometimes complain that elders do not sufficiently encourage or reward their efforts. Those same older people can only marvel at the inconsistency of educational policies that suppress indigenous languages in one generation and legislate them in another.

But if fractures appear — between linguistic groups or generations — there are countless examples of asserting distinctions to make connections. At a graduation banquet for First Nations high school students in 1993, for example, an elected chief from one community was invited to address the students and asked an elder to translate for him. "I am a young chief," he said, "and do not have my language, and so I am asking my elder to interpret for me." Even though the eighteen-year-old students were unlikely to understand the translation, the public acknowledgment of Tutchone, in this case, gave more ceremonial weight to the event than would have been possible in a speech delivered in English.

A forceful discussion of language also occurred at a three-day elders' festival held in the southern Yukon during the summer of 1994, where the focus remained resolutely on communication. During the weekend workshop, elders from across the Yukon spoke in many languages about many issues. English was the common language of discussion, and because the meeting was being held on Tlingit territory, translation was also provided between Tlingit and English. We met on the edge of Teslin Lake, at a comfortable site where meetings, meals, and entertainment were all hosted by the Teslin First Nation, away from the distractions of town. The meeting included people of all ages, and the expectation was that elders would do most of the talking, giving younger people opportunities to listen.

One of many topics on the agenda concerned how elders' words should be transcribed, an issue long of interest to linguists and students of oral history but more likely to be debated in university classrooms than in subarctic lakeside campsites. The question put to the assembly was this. Recently, proceedings from an elders' conference had been prepared and published using verbatim transcripts of speeches in English. One reader had formally objected that "elders sound unintelligent" when recorded in nonstandard English. This group had been asked to make a decision about whether verbatim transcripts of their meeting should be prepared or whether they should be worked into standard English.

The positions voiced by elders at this meeting were eloquent and impassioned and consistently emphasized communication, audience, and connection. One by one, elders spoke about their view that their words should be transcribed directly as they were spoken. If the academic concern, first raised by Franz Boas a century ago, relates to the inevitable loss in style and form that occurs when narratives learned in an indigenous language are recorded and transcribed in English, the concerns of these elders were different. They spoke about how such words extend connections — to younger people, to cultural outsiders, and across linguistic boundaries within the Yukon. They were less troubled about whether recording oral narrative may inappropriately disembody, decontextualize, and crystallize it than about how the printed page allows readers to "hear" the words of those who are no longer living — in other words, how print enhances possibilities for communication. They unanimously agreed that their words should be transcribed in English as spoken, expressing a commitment to linguistic constructions that are recognizably their own.

In the words of one elder, Percy Henry: "How could we have someone else changing our words — put words in my mouth and change the meaning? It starts from the elder . . . from the grass roots. I've never seen a house built from the top down yet." Another elder added, "Our elders are our lawyers. To take the work they have done and destroy it by changing it is wrong. Then they won't be able to read it. What we have done [in preparing the booklets] you have to respect it and be proud of it. Elders can read. The book should not be changed. We must leave it as it is in order to understand."

Although everyone would agree that ideally multilingual texts should be recorded, transcribed, and printed, they recognize the impracticality of doing this for all public meetings and for a largely English readership. What emerged at this meeting was a strong commitment to extend communication in whatever forms possible, writing being only one way among many. There was also optimism — possibly a result of a history of self-confident multilingualism — that English is just one more Native language, in fact the dominant Native language at the end of the century.

Land and Connection to Place

Articulating past and present connections to place has taken on fresh importance during an era of protracted land claims negotiations. Again, older people describe the relation between humans and land differently than do the younger men and women directly engaged in these negotiations. If elders speak of language as reflecting multilingualism and communication, they speak of land in terms of travel and mobility, frequently constructing life stories as travel narratives. Their understanding of landownership rarely includes formal boundaries and is expressed in terms of knowledge acquired during a lifetime. "My roots grow in jackpine roots!" Kitty Smith reported she told a former commissioner of the Yukon Territory when explaining to him her rights: "I'm born here. I branch here. The government got all this country, how big it is. He don't pay five cents — still he got it all! Nobody kicks me out. No sir!"[15]

Community land claims negotiators, on the other hand, face the difficult task of reconciling the state's narratives about land as bounded units to be owned and operated for profit with their own spatial understanding that stories crosscut maps. Women in their forties who have been involved in the negotiations have given this much thought. In our conversations they have expressed the same point in different ways. In one woman's words, "You know, I think it's all the same thing. People are starting to think about their identity, about who they are. And you know how it is when you start thinking about who you *are*—right away, you think of *place*." Another expressed her concern about the rigidity of the negotiations process: "How can you *own* a piece of land? It's like saying you can *own* a cloud!" Still another expressed her frustration with the categories imposed by land claims agreements on hunting practices in ironic terms: "So, if 'subsistence' means 'food,' and 'nonsubsistence' means 'culture,' how do you get a swan bone for a ceremony?"

My own appreciation of the relation between mobility and connection to land deepened as I recorded stories of lives where a single year could often be mapped as a travel narrative. Speaking about her childhood, for instance, Angela Sidney began,

The earliest time I'm talking about is 1910—I can't remember when I was much younger. I remember we were staying across Ten Mile on that island—they used to call that island "Tagish John Island," and later they started to call it "Old Scotty Island"—it's right straight across Ten Mile. I remember that time—that's year 1910. I remember my father was fishing and we were staying on that island.

She continued to detail the family's activities and her childhood memories during that year. Another time, she began,

This is 1912 I'm talking about, when we went up to Black Lake—T'ooch' Áayi. We traveled around the shore, hunting for moose. From what I remember, we stayed under that gray mountain—Taaghahi—until Christmas, and then we moved to Millhaven. And from Millhaven, we went up to Black Lake. Then, almost at the end of March, we started coming back—back to Carcross or Tagish. That summer we didn't go to Marsh Lake.

And so her narrative continued, incorporating some 230 place-names we mapped together in Tagish, Tlingit, and English languages.[16] Like other elderly women, she described how mobility inevitably decreased as people were consolidated into villages following the wartime construction of the Alaska Highway. Possibly the hardest aspect for these women was confinement to villages where children could attend day schools, but where women could no longer accompany spouses who continued to hunt. Repeatedly, women talked about time with reference to places named in Athapaskan languages and sometimes not seen for years yet still providing anchors for memory. Frequently, too, naming the places reminded women of songs that reenact and commemorate events.[17]

Stories link human history to place. John Joe, almost one hundred years old when we began recording place-names in 1976, explained his view that there is a causal link between understanding the names, knowing the stories associated with names, and living in the world as an adequate human being. He expressed distress that younger people were less knowledgeable about and less interested in these stories than in the past:

Old people used to tell stories to young people. This happened [at] Shatäghay, that one [at] Chezhà, that one at Shatò'she'ee. The stories — you can't tell them now. "You believe that?" they say. Old people, they tell you a story, you've got to listen. When you don't listen, you're going to be crazy. You're going to be crazy, and you're not going to live long.

Near Carcross, Angela Sidney would point to and name the four mountains where Animal Mother or Game Mother hung her trampoline at the beginning of time when she created the first animals.[18] On Tagish Lake, we followed the route taken by Fox when he first gave names to the points of land extending into the lake:

"My brother-in-law," he said. . . .
"From here, you go.
You get down the lake from here.
You go to that K'aa' Deitl'óoní — that means 'where arrows
     are tied up in a bundle.'"
That's Tagish language: Tlingit is Chooneit Wusi.axu Yé.
Now they call it "Frying Pan Island" because it's sometimes
     joined to the shore.
It's across from Ten Mile, Tsuxx'aayí.
"Put bait in the water. From here on, you go. . . ."

They call that mountain behind that place K'aa' Deitl'óoní Dzéłe';
Chooneit Shaayí, Tlingit way.

He's the one, Fox, gave Indian names to all those points on
     Tagish Lake.
They still use them, Indian way.[19]

The surging glaciers in what is now Kluane National Park came alive in very different ways when Kitty Smith told about the copper-clawed owls living in glacier dens or how a shaman caused the Lowell Glacier, Nàłùdi, to surge, blocking the Alsek River valley:

"Ah, that old man!
The top of his head is just like the place where gopher
    plays —
A bare stump."
That kid laughed at him. . . .

Well, that old man is from Yukon, you know.

Summertime, that old [Yukon] man went to Nàlùdi.
He's medicine man, you know, big doctor.
That ice was coming right down from the mountain.
At the end of the ice, a creek came down.
Right there, he sat down.

He said to himself,
"What am I going to do?"
His doctor talks to him.
"You think I'm going to bring that glacier to this mountain?
It's going to be flooded, that side."

His doctor told him,
"You try it. It's going to come."
That old man lay down, right there.
His doctor's working now on that glacier.

It comes down, comes down. . . .
Glacier . . . glacier . . . comes down . . . comes down
Until it's all level with this mountain.

That's the first time it [Lowell Glacier] crossed.
That Indian doctor did that.

After he did that, it crossed another time.
My grandma told me it was like that one time, in her time.
All flooded again, that 1016, Haines Junction, that way.
Talk about gophers die! she said.
Before, that glacier didn't do that.
But after he did that, first time, from there it
    started.[20]

The orientation of different drainage systems in the Yukon took on new dimensions when Annie Ned explained how they were established by Crow at the beginning of time: one to the Arctic Ocean, one to the Bering Sea, one to the Pacific Northwest Coast.[21] A drive along the Alaska Highway is transformed by hearing the names, the songs, the origins of landscape features.

In Annie Ned's words,

You know old people, long time, they call this country
    where they [the places] are.
That's from this man, he tells it.
Next one, he tells it.
That's the way we got it.
Just like you read.

Just like we go to school for that old man.
We bring some wood, bring some water to old people to tell
    us this story.
We don't pick it up for nothing.
Old time words are just like school!

Meanings are embodied in the very performance of naming places. When I asked Kitty Smith whether she would pronounce a list of place-names I read back to her, compiled from her stories, so that I could check spellings with a linguist, she ignored my question and retold the stories, apparently delighted that I was finally learning the names she had taught me.

But mapping names, like mapping the boundaries of territories used by individual trappers, has implications. As background to land claims negotiations, many communities set out to document the extent to which territories near their communities had been used in the past and continue to be used by particular families. Named places can thus be transformed from sites of significance to authorized boundary markers demarcating neighboring groups. Imperceptibly, named places that were formerly an assertion of multilingualism and mobility, of exchange and travel, can come to divide and separate people who were formerly connected. At negotiations surrounding heritage agreements in one community during summer 1991, for instance, debate was generated by the federal negotiators' mandate to offer protection to specific, documented archaeological and historical sites. This clashed with the understanding of many community members that what was at issue was not so much the sites themselves as the relationships *between* sites and the need to protect them by restricting detrimental access to trails between territories.[22]

During final stages of land selection in 1994, some people were publicly expressing concerns about the social consequences of these newly bounded territories. Some parents, for instance, wondered whether their children might be less welcome off settlement lands once boundaries acquire official status. Others were concerned that artificial boundaries may restrict mobility, especially for the elderly: beneficiaries to the settlement must enroll in only one First Nation, but most elders can legitimately claim membership in several communities, making their choice arbitrary. Could this subsequently bring restrictions, some ask, preventing an elder from fishing at a river her grandmother, her mother, and she had used all her life? The decision of the federal government to allocate what is called "land quantum" to each First Nation based on market value means that some communities will receive title to more land than others. Communities on the Alaska Highway, where land is assessed at relatively high values, have smaller allotments than more distant communities, generating potential rifts in situations where allocations may be interpreted as inequitable.

Although the settlement of outstanding land claims in the Yukon has involved enormous commitment and work by many communities and individuals, achievements of one kind come at costs of another kind. Some of the thoughtful ways these issues are addressed in narrative are discussed in chapter 7 in the context of the Yukon International Storytelling Festival. Narratives told at this festival continue to address issues on which there is yet no closure, but they demonstrate that persistent storytelling complicates externally mandated boundaries and categories.

Family and Belonging

Extended family connections remain foundational in Yukon communities. Throughout the world and during most periods of human history, people have relied on culturally variable constructions of family to frame rules of behavior and social obligations. John Borneman suggests that to treat kinship ahistorically, as though it were an evolutionary stage of social organization relegated to the past, is to render it apolitical at the very point where kinship asserts its importance most centrally — in modern nationalism. Kinship indeed provides the axis of non-Western political systems, but it is also "the topos on which 'nationness' is mapped." [23]

Because our experiences of family occur so early in life, there is a human tendency to naturalize our acquired ideas about family. In the Yukon, so-cial relationships are profoundly structured by matrilineal moieties, Crow (Kajìt) and Wolf (Ägunda). Membership as Crow or as Wolf is determined by birth and is passed on from a woman to her children. Because rules of exogamy were strictly enforced in the past — disobedience was consid-ered incestuous and was punishable by banishment or death — one's father was always a member of the opposite moiety, and every domestic unit in-cluded both Crow and Wolf. Historically, alliances were repeatedly forged between moieties by marriages, partnerships, and trade, linking people from widely dispersed areas in networks of familiar responsibilities. In southern Yukon Tlingit communities, moieties further incorporate clans whose members can usually name a common ancestor in the distant past, if not necessarily the precise genealogical links.

Such a system has broad advantages. It immediately situates everyone, since kinship affiliations can be determined immediately by answers to simple questions like "Who is your mother?" or where names are clan-owned property, "What is your Indian name?" Until recently, preferred patterns of postmarital matrilocal residence ensured that elderly people were provided for by sons-in-law. A woman would be likely to continue working with her mother, aunts, and sisters after marriage, and together they might raise their children. Her husband, joining her family at least for an initial year or two, would hunt with her brother, and as opposite moiety brothers-in-law, they might become permanent trading partners even after the couple became more independent. A man would come to know two hunting territories well — the one where he was raised and also his wife's. A woman would retain detailed knowledge of berry grounds and the loca-tions of vegetable roots and plants, critical during periods of scarcity.

Moiety and clan arrangements have continued to guide behavior at criti-cal times of life — birth, puberty, and death — as well as on numerous less formal occasions. At death, for instance, opposite moiety relatives can be counted on to take care of mortuary arrangements, and after an appropri-ate interval, the bereaved clan may repay them with a potlatch.[24] Con-temporary potlatches support an effective redistribution system whereby one moiety performs services for another and later receives repayment. Be-cause every household unit includes members of both moieties, goods pot-latched by one side may well remain within the same domestic unit.

Another way of understanding relationships is as reciprocity between providers and dependents. In the past, every group needed to maintain a balance between people who were able to provide necessities of life and those who depended on them. Each person began life as a dependent child, became a provider in adulthood, and resumed dependent status again in old age. An elderly woman, for example, might spend one winter with one group of children and grandchildren and another winter with other family members. An able-bodied man or woman might join a group temporarily. Both lateral and generational relationships, then, were characterized by reciprocity.[25]

With increasing intrusion of the state into family affairs, both sets of relationships have become problematic. Contemporary efforts to formalize tradition with reference to "traditional justice systems," for example, offer belated attempts to accommodate moiety, clan, and generational relationships in decision making by the very legal institutions that attempted to erase them a century ago, an issue explored in chapter 4. Current efforts to revitalize older principles of social control require codification of relationships that would not have occurred in the past. Furthermore, men and women now elders in their late sixties and seventies, who are enjoined to work toward building such institutions, experienced during their teenage years the forceful disruptions dismantling kin-based relationships after construction of the Alaska Highway in the 1940s. The epidemics associated with highway construction, consolidation in highway communities, the introduction of the Family Allowance Act (1944–45) used to enforce residential school attendance, and the Revised Act to Provide Old Age Assistance (1952) (which strained relationships between those who had cash and those who did not) were central to their formative years.[26] In a contemporary context, relations between generational groups are sometimes strained by what one younger person has described as a "culture of disapproval" emanating from some elders. His interpretation is that, given the social disruptions this generation of elders experienced, they are sometimes less patient with young people than elders may have been in the past. Mrs. Sidney's narrative and Mrs. Smith's carvings discussed in chapters 3 and 5 suggest that clan and generational differences are not necessarily new and that storytelling practices may long have addressed such contradictions when they arose.

CONTEMPORARY EXTENSIONS OF ORAL TRADITION

When Yukon First Nations began doing research for land claims in the late 1960s, one of their initial objectives was to document their shared experiences as aboriginal people throughout the Yukon in order to present their claims collectively as a united organization. With the settlement of that claim, they are struggling to develop ways of working together while still recognizing long-standing regional and cultural differences. They argue that the terminological shift from "Yukon Indians" to "First Nations" significantly foregrounds multiplicity of perspectives rather than homogeneity.

In the late 1990s, increasing attention is being paid to indigenous perspectives on the past — in the South Pacific, Africa, and North and South America. Yukon oral traditions are also reaching wider audiences. At the annual Yukon International Storytelling Festival, discussed in chapter 7, elders speak to large crowds of attentive listeners. Northern Native Broadcasting Yukon has produced videotaped documentaries on historical and contemporary issues that are televised across northern Canada. The Yukon Historical and Museums Association sponsors annual conferences, like the one described at the beginning of chapter 2, where elders, academics, and other visitors exchange ideas on topics of common interest. The Heritage Branch of the Yukon Territorial Government funds First Nations to conduct their own oral history projects. The Yukon Native Language Centre continues to document languages, place-names, narratives, and history and to ensure that these become incorporated into the regular school program. The Council for Yukon First Nations has worked with the Department of Education to develop a community-based curriculum for use in Yukon classrooms. The Bureau of Aboriginal Languages Services supports a broad range of translation services in communities.

The endurance of oral tradition in the Yukon speaks to the persistence and adaptability of narrative as a framework for bridging social fractures that threaten to fragment human relationships. Storytelling also raises questions about the relation between knowledge remembered and embodied in narrative and its translation to broader audiences. Remaining chapters investigate these processes in greater depth, both as they occurred in the past and as they continue in the present.

2

"Pete's Song": Establishing Meanings through Story and Song

In collaboration with Angela Sidney

Ethnographies always begin as conversations between anthropologists and our hosts, who are also in conversation with each other. If we are fortunate some of these conversations take unexpected turns, develop into genuine dialogues, and continue over many years. Dialogues open the possibility that we may learn something about the process of communication, about how words are used to construct meaningful accounts of life experience. In this way they differ fundamentally from structured interviews, where one of the participants claims the right to both pose the questions and interpret the responses.

It was my good fortune to have an ongoing dialogue with Angela Sidney, an elder from the Yukon Territory, for more than seventeen years. Our conversations began at our first meeting in 1974 and continued until the end of her life in 1991. Even though she can no longer participate actively in our dialogues, they continue whenever her words surface unexpectedly while I am puzzling about some problem, just as she undoubtedly hoped they would (fig. 1).

Angela Sidney described herself as a Deisheetaan (Crow) woman of both Tagish and Tlingit ancestry. Born in 1902 near the present village of Carcross in the southern Yukon to Ła.oos Tláa (Maria) and Ḵaajinéek' (Tagish John), she was given the Tlingit name Stóow and a second Tagish name Ch'óonehte' Má. Her lifelong interest in passing on the knowledge she had acquired about the relation between her mother's Tlingit and her father's Tagish ancestry brought us together. We began our conversation with a simple contract: I would record her life history for family members, and in return she would become my teacher — a role that intrigued her because it tested her pedagogical skills in new ways.[1] In addition to a brief life history prepared for family members in 1975, she was able to publish several booklets of narrative, family history, and place-names that are widely circulated in her community.[2]

One of the chief intellectual pleasures of this witty, warm, thoughtful woman was trying to convey, across cultural boundaries, the subtle lessons about human behavior she had learned during her lifetime. She was born shortly after the Klondike gold rush, so her experiences encompassed almost a century of startling institutional changes — the brief but turbulent influx of prospectors at the turn of the century, the establishment of ecclesiastical residential schools, the involvement of indigenous trappers in an international fur market, the construction of the Alaska Highway, the development of an unstable mining economy, and the expansion of government infrastructure. But she was also intensely interested in changes that had occurred during the previous century. Her parents and grandparents had taken part in the flourishing trade between coastal Tlingit and interior Tagish peoples during the late nineteenth century when Tlingit customs, clan names, and language were introduced inland. Her understanding of all these changes came from her lifelong attention to oral tradition. In our dialogues, she defined her task as teaching me how oral tradition continues to explain not just the past but also contemporary issues.

In this chapter I attempt to convey something of how she used oral history to teach, confounding any simple definition of what oral history is or does. The central thesis guiding her work was that while oral tradition can indeed broaden our understanding of the past, it tells us even more about the present. Her concern about the importance of communication through storytelling underscores the value of performance theory to studies of oral tradition. Her great skill came not just from remembering and knowing the stories, but from knowing how to use them appropriately in different situations to produce the effect she knew good stories can create.

When Angela Sidney and I began working together, my own understanding of the term "oral history" was fairly superficial. I was delighted by our collaboration because it seemed to me an ethically sound way of doing research — with a clear set of issues for me to investigate and a substantive product for Mrs. Sidney and her family. I assumed that I would be documenting details of social history as it had affected indigenous people in northwestern Canada, a perspective lamentably absent from most of the written records. My earliest questions were framed with reference to the Klondike gold rush, the construction of the Alaska Highway, and their effect on the lives of people who had always lived in the region.

Mrs. Sidney responded patiently but firmly, in each case suggesting that I begin by recording a particular story — perhaps one about a boy who stayed with Salmon People, or a girl who married a star, or one about the woman stolen by Grizzly. Eventually we recorded dozens of narratives in which a protagonist traveled under the water, beyond the horizon, or to the skies to learn about other dimensions of reality. Despite my initial sense that we were moving further and further from our shared objective of preparing an orally narrated life history, I gradually came to realize that she was consciously providing me with a kind of cultural scaffolding, the broad framework I needed to learn before I could begin to ask intelligent questions.

One of the stories she told me was about a coastal Tlingit man named Ḵaax̱'achgóok. Briefly, Ḵaax̱'achgóok was one of the famous Tlingit ancestors of the Kiks.ádi clan. One autumn he went hunting sea mammals with his nephews, only to receive a sign that hunting was now dangerous for him and he should return home. Reluctantly, he destroyed his spears and returned to his winter village, but eventually it became unbearable to him that his wives should have to beg for food and that they should be treated with disrespect while he remained at home. Setting out to sea once again with the same nephews, he was blown off course and became lost. Eventually they washed ashore on a small island. Ḵaax̱'achgóok spent the following months devising ways to feed himself and his nephews and perfecting a method to mark the sun's points of rising and setting against the horizon. When he was sure that it had reached its most northerly point and stopped moving, he set sail for home, using the sun's rising and setting as steering points for navigation. Despite his successful return, he faced the difficult business of acknowledging how much life had changed during his absence.

The narrative of Ḵaax̱'achgóok's journey is a powerful one, and no single interpretation can begin to convey all the meanings that emerge in varying tellings by different narrators from different historical periods. John Swanton recorded a version told by a Tlingit storyteller in coastal Alaska shortly after the turn of the century.[3] More recently, Nora and Richard Dauenhauer worked with Tlingit narrator Mr. A. P. Johnson to record and translate bilingual versions in Tlingit and English.[4] Catharine McClellan recorded two versions with Angela Sidney, one in 1949 and another in 1951, each containing details not included in Mrs. Sidney's later version of the story, presented here.[5] Robin Ridington points out that attention to solstices as marked by sunrise and sunset occurs in stories told in other Athapaskan communities, and that the Dunne-za have a similar story and describe solstices as a point when "the sun stops."[6]

It is important to hear Mrs. Sidney's more recent version of the story of Kaax'achgóok in her own words. Here I focus on her retellings of his adventures in different contexts because she was so explicit about the way a single rich narrative can be used to convey a range of messages. She first told me this version of the Kaax'achgóok story in 1974. Once she was sure I had mastered the narrative and understood the content, she never told the full story again in my presence. Instead, she made regular mention of it in our conversations in the same way that she referred to other stories she was teaching me. She used it as a point of reference both to discuss her personal development and to interpret and connect a range of events that might otherwise seem unrelated. Angela Sidney understood, as only the most talented storytellers can, the importance of performance — how performance involves not simply a narrator but also an audience, and how narrator and audience both change with time and circumstances, giving any one story the potential range of meanings that all good stories have. Once she was sure I understood the context of knowing the story, our conversations were able to build on that shared knowledge.

After presenting the story in Mrs. Sidney's own words, then, I will discuss her original telling of the narrative to me in 1974; her account, several years later, of how and why she first told the story publicly in 1945; her subsequent explanation of why she had the right to tell the narrative; and her much more recent use of that narrative to commemorate a specific event in 1988. Her various tellings vividly reveal the way a skillful storyteller is able to use what appears to be the same story to convey a range of meanings. Each performance is historically situated as the teller, the audience, and the intended meanings shift to meet the occasion.

First, then, the story, as Mrs. Sidney originally told it to me in 1974.

I was ten years old when I heard this story first.
My auntie, Mrs. Austin, told me the story first time.
Later I heard my father tell it to the boys.
This is the song I gave to Pete.
I'm going to tell how we claim it.

This is a true story.
It happened on salt water, maybe near Sitka.
It goes with that song I sing — I'll tell you about it.

This man, Ḵaax̱'achgóok, was a great hunter for seal.
He was going hunting at fall.
He has eight nephews on his side, his sisters' sons.
Ḵaax̱'achgóok is Crow and so are those boys.
They all went out together in a boat.
Early in the morning, they left.
Fog was down low on the ocean.
He's captain: he sat in the back, guiding that boat.

He heard a baby cry that time, "Wah, wah."

"Stop. Listen. Stop that, baby, now!
Don't you know this is Ḵaax̱'achgóok's hunting ground?"
He listened quite a long time.
Here it was baby seal crying.
That's bad luck.
That voice even called his name, "Ḵaax̱'achgóok."

So he told his nephews that's bad luck:
"Let's go back."

They came back that same evening.
He brought up his boat, paddles, spears, and he tells those
    boys to chop it all up.
"I'll never hunt again."
He knows it's something. It's bad luck to hunt now.

After that, he just stayed home, I guess.
Anyway, he didn't hunt anymore that one year —
Stayed home all year until fall.
Maybe he goes out a little bit, but he never hunts.

Finally, someone else killed sea lion.
They invited both those two wives of Ḵaax̱'achgóok.
When those wives of Ḵaax̱'achgóok came back, he asked the
    youngest one,
"Did they give you any fat? Any fat left over they give you
    to bring home?"

"No, just meat," she answered.

Then he asked his older wife,
"Did they give you any fat to bring home? Any left over?"

"No, no fat, just all meat."

"How come they're so stingy to not give you women any fat!"
He thinks maybe his luck will change.

Next morning he asks his older wife,
"Go ask your brother if I can borrow his boat.
I want to go out just a little ways.
Want to borrow boat, spear, hunting outfit.
I'm lonesome — tired of staying home."

She goes to her brother.
"I want you to lend my husband your boat, spear, your
    hunting outfit.
He wants to go out just a little ways.
Not far."

"Okay," he says.
"The boys will bring it over later this evening."
He's got eight boys too.
That's Ḵaax̱'achgóok's wife's people, Wolf people — they
    call them Killer Whale on coast —
That evening they packed over a brand-new boat — dugout.
Spears, oars, everything in there already.

Ḵaax̱'achgóok tells those wives,
"You girls better cook up meat in salt water for us."
Next morning, those boys get water ready in sealskin.
Cook things.

Then, when they are ready, Ḵaax̱'achgóok goes out again.
Not far, north wind starts to blow.
You know north wind blows in falltime?
Ḵaax̱'achgóok thinks,
"Gee, we should go back while it's not too rough.
Let's go back," he tells his nephews.
They turn around.
Right away, that wind came up — they row and row.
Soon waves are as big as this house.

Ḵaax̱'achgóok is captain: what he does, the rest of the boys do.
He throws his paddle in the boat.
Those boys do that too.
Ḵaax̱'achgóok pulled up a blanket and went to sleep.
Those boys, too, they sleep.
They went the whole night and the next day like that.

Toward the second morning, Ḵaax̱'achgóok woke up.
He feels the boat not moving, but he hears waves sucking back.
He pulled the blanket down and looked.
By gosh, they drifted onto an island —
Nice sandy beach.

"Wake up you boys. What's this I hear?"
It sounds like when the wave goes out, goes back.

Next oldest boy looks up too.
"Yes, we're on land," he said.
"Well, might as well go on shore."

Those boys run around.
They see a leaf like an umbrella —
It's a stem with a hole that is full of rainwater.
"Frog leaf," they call it.

"Eh, save that [fresh] water."
Each has his own sealskin water bag.
He looks around.
"Take your time.
Go back and see if there's a good place to make a fire."
They found a good place, sheltered from the north wind.

"Let's go there."
Big trees around there.
They make brush camp out of bark.
They carry that bark with them in boat.
Just that quick they had camp put up.
Look for wood — lots of driftwood.
"You boys are not to run all over. We'll check all around first."

On the south side of the island, there's a rocky point.
All kinds of sea lions, seals, all kinds of animals.
When they're on rocks, the tide is out.
He thinks that's the best time to club them.
That's what they did.
Each boy made a club.
They killed off as much as they needed —
Sea otter, sea lion, seal.
Not too much — just what they can handle.
He told them to look after that meat good.

Some people say he was there over a year —
Some say 'til next spring.
He dreamed he was at home all the time.
"I gave up hope, then I dreamed I was home."

That's the song I sing for you.
I'm going to tell you about it and tell you why I can sing it
And why we call it "Pete Sidney Song."
I'll tell you that when I finish this story.

That man, Ḵaax'achgóok, he always goes to north wind
     side every day.
He goes out on the point — never tells anyone.
He marks when the sun comes out in the morning —
Marks it with a stick.
In the evening, he goes out again,
Marks a stick where the sun goes down.
He never tells anyone why he does this.
He just does it all the time.
Finally, that stick is in the same place for two days.
He knows this marks the return of spring.
Then the sun starts to come back in June, the longest day.

In the meantime, he said to the boys,
"Make twisted snowshoe string out of sealskin.
Dry it; stretch it.
Make two big piles.
One for the head of the boat, one for the back of the boat."
Finally, when the sun starts back in June,

He sees it behind the mountain called Tloox, near Sitka.
In June, that sun is in the same place for one, two days.

He tells those boys just before the end they're going to start back.
Tells those boys to cook meat, put it in seal stomach.
Once they're out on the ocean, there's no way to make fire
So they've got to cook first.
They prepare ahead.
Sealskin rope is for anchor.
When the sun goes back again on the summer side, they start.

"Put everything in the boat."
He knows there's a long calm time in late June when the sun starts back.

No wind —
They start anyway.
They think how they're going to make it.
Those boys think, "Our uncle made a mistake.
We were okay on the island, but now we are really lost."

Row, row, row.

Finally, sun came out right in front of the boat.
Evening, goes out at the back.
Ḵaaẋ'achgóok anchors the boat and he tells those boys to sleep.

I used to know how many days that trip took — it's a long
    time, though.
I was ten when I heard this story first —
My auntie Mrs. Austin told me the story first time.
Later, I heard my father tell it to the boys.

Sundown.
They anchor the boat when it goes down on the steering side.
Next morning, the sun came out same way at the head of the boat.
He knows what is going on —
They're right on course.
They keep doing that I don't know how long.

Finally, one time, just after the sun goes down,
He sees something like a seagull.
When the sun comes up, it disappears.
Evening sundown, he sees it again.
Four days, he sees it.

The second day he sees it, he asks,
"What's that ahead of our boat? Seagull?"
They think so.
Where could seagull come from in the middle of the ocean?

They camp again.
It gets bigger.
Finally it looks like a mountain.
They don't stop to rest anymore!
Four paddle all day — four paddle all night.
Their uncle is their boss: he sleeps all day, I guess. Don't know.
Finally, they see it.

Early in the morning, Ḵaax̱'achgóok's oldest wife comes
    down to cry for her husband.
That youngest wife they already gave to another husband.
Finally, all of a sudden, she sees boat coming.
She quits crying — she notices how her husband used to paddle,
Same as the man in the boat.

She runs back to the house.
"It looks like Ḵaax̱'achgóok when he paddles!
Get up! Everybody up!"

"How do you expect that?
It's a whole year now.
You think they live yet?"

Then he comes around the point —
People all pack around that boat.
They took him for dead — already made potlatch for him.
So he gave otter skin to everyone who potlatched for him.
Sea otter skin cost one thousand dollars, those days.

Then he sang songs he made up on that trip.
He made one up when he gave up the oars.

"I gave up my life out on the deep for the shark."

That song he gave to G̲aanax̲.ádi people.

Then he made up a song for the sun who saved him:

"The sun came up and saved people."

He made that song during winter
And he sang it when he made a potlatch.

Then that song he sang,

"I gave up hope and then I dreamed I was home."

That's the one I sing.
Deisheetaan people, we own that song,
Because long before, our people captured K̲aax̲'achgóok's
    brother.
When they started to make peace, he sang that song and gave
    it to us for our potlatch.
Then we freed his brother. That's how come we own it.
That's why we claim that song.

LAYERED TELLINGS
Narrative as Text

Angela Sidney's story of K̲aax̲'achgóok can indeed be written down and read as a text, one of many she told me in the course of preparing her life history. When she first told me the story in 1974, her primary objective was to have it tape-recorded and transcribed in her own words. We read over the written text carefully and made the minor changes she suggested. At her request, it appeared in a booklet of narratives by three Yukon elders, *My Stories Are My Wealth,* printed for use in Yukon schools.[7] Once an orally narrated text is printed, though, it is open to a range of interpretations by readers as well as by listeners.

There is no shortage of ways to approach the K̲aax̲'achgóok story if we regard it simply as a self-contained narrative. For example, because of the thematic attention to the sun in Mrs. Sidney's version, it has sometimes been highlighted in Yukon classrooms at the end of June, presented as an example of indigenous perspectives on the summer solstice, a significant day north of the sixtieth parallel. Mrs. Sidney was pleased by this acknowledgment and even agreed to tell the story and to be interviewed by a local radio station on 21 June one year near the end of the 1970s.

Given the structural parallels with *The Odyssey*, the story has also been interpreted as an example of powerful epic narrative. The hero's journey, constructed around disappearance, extensive suffering, and eventual return, dramatizes a theme common to much world literature. Like all good literature, the story addresses fundamental human problems. The psychological dimensions of returning home after prolonged absence were certainly on Mrs. Sidney's mind in other versions she tells, discussed later in the chapter. The story of Ķaax̱'achgóok undeniably constitutes a work of literature: bilingual texts of another version of this narrative, in both Tlingit language and in English, have been presented in exquisite detail by Richard and Nora Dauenhauer in *Haa Shuká/Our Ancestors,* their first volume in a series titled Classics of Tlingit Oral Literature.[8]

Alternatively, we might ask whether this narrative incorporates events from historical time. Ķaax̱'achgóok was a famous ancestor of a named clan, the Kiks.ádi Crow clan, and it is conceivable that his journey might be traced to a known historical figure. The possibility of incorporating orally narrated accounts into ethnohistorical analysis seems to give oral history rather elastic promise, particularly when so much northern scholarship rests exclusively on written records. Yet a literal interpretation of the events in the story is too narrow.

Such diverse possibilities suggest good reasons for paying attention to the story of Ķaax̱'achgóok as text, with a range of conventional avenues for hearing its content — as a reflection of mythology, history, ethnology, language use, and psychology. Too frequently, though, textual analyses begin and end with these questions. As Paul Ricoeur reminds us, there is a difference between what a narrative *says* and what it *talks about.*[9] Had Angela Sidney not referred to it again herself, I might simply have interpreted it just as one among other fine examples of oral narrative from northwestern North America.

Narrative as Gift

Some years later, in 1981, Angela Sidney and I were firmly engaged in the process of recording her life story. By then I understood that the dozens of narratives we had recorded and transcribed really did provide a framework she could refer back to when she talked about her own experiences. Repeatedly, she explained choices she had made or advice she had given with reference to narratives learned from parents, aunts, and uncles — narratives exploring the subtle relation between human and superhuman domains. Her narrative allusions and interpretations always *added* a dimension to whatever event we were discussing.

She talked about Ḵaax̱'achgóok again on 6 July 1985, this time in a very different context. Her son Pete, then in his seventies, was visiting one afternoon, and though he had obviously heard the story many times before, she took the opportunity to explain, with him present, why it had such significance for his life. Pete was one of many men from Yukon First Nations who served overseas during World War II, and this day she talked about how difficult his absence had been for her. "Five years he's gone — just like that Ḵaax̱'achgóok story I told you." [10]

During his absence, she said, she and her husband bought their first radio, "so we could listen to where they're moving the troops so we would know where he is." When the war ended, her son sent her an airmail letter from Europe announcing his imminent return: "DEAR MOM, I'M BOOKED FOR CANADA. TOMORROW I'M LEAVING." With a map, she and her husband calculated how long it would take to cross the Atlantic by ship to New York. When he arrived in New York, he sent a telegram. "LANDED SAFELY IN U.S." From there they estimated that it would take four days for him to cross the continent to Vancouver by train. She allowed another four days to travel up the west coast of the country by ferry, and an additional day to ride inland on the narrow-gauge White Pass and Yukon Railway to his home in Carcross, Yukon. "From the time he got on the boat from Vancouver, we're counting the days again. Well — *I'm* counting the days — I don't know if the rest do!"

As the excitement mounted, her husband asked her how they should celebrate the occasion of his return. She described the feast she planned to give and the people she intended to invite. "'And then,' I told him, 'I'm going to sing that Ḵaax̱'achgóok song!' And my Old Man said, 'Gee, I didn't know you were so smart to think like that! That's a *good* idea.'" When Pete arrived home, then, his gift — the greatest gift she could give him — was the song sung by Ḵaax̱'achgóok when he returned home. "That's why we call that 'Pete's song.' 'I gave up hope, and then I dreamed I was home.'" [11]

But the story does not end there, because her right to sing the song was immediately challenged by men of her father's clan who were senior to her.

Her narrative about how her clan acquired rights to use that song, and hence her own decision to make a gift of it to her son, forms an integral part of the next version of her story.

Narrative as Settlement

Tagish people in the southeastern Yukon adopted Tlingit-named clans sometime during the nineteenth century. As on the coast, rights to use songs and stories remain firmly grounded in clan membership, which is traced through the maternal line. Angela Sidney, like her mother, was born into the Deisheetaan Tlingit clan, and her son Pete also belongs to her clan. Her father's cousin Koołseen (whose English name was Patsy Henderson) was the senior living member of her father's Daḵl'aweidí clan, and he challenged her right to sing the song at this celebration. As a relatively young woman in her early forties at the time, this put her in a vulnerable position. She recalled, "[He] told my mother, 'It's not you fellows' song, that song. You can't use that song!' He asked Johnny Anderson about it, and Johnny Anderson said, 'No, it's not a Deisheetaan song.'"

Mrs. Sidney explained how she demonstrated to him that the song had been given to Deisheetaan by the Kiks.ádi clan, and that she really was using it in an appropriate way. Ḵaax̱'achgóok, she explains, belonged to the Kiks.ádi clan (which, like Deisheetaan, is grouped with Crow or Raven clans). Sometime in the past, a dispute arose between the Deisheetaan and Kiks.ádi clans. A Kiks.ádi man — "Ḵaax̱'achgóok's [clan] brother" — was taken by Deisheetaan clansmen as a slave in payment for an offense committed against them. As hostilities escalated, the two clans met and negotiated a conventional settlement: an exchange was worked out so that the Kiks.ádi man was returned to his kinsmen, and they in turn gave the Deisheetaan clan the Ḵaax̱'achgóok song. Because songs are among the most important property owned by clans, the dispute was considered settled.

To confirm that as a Deisheetaan woman she was acting appropriately, Angela said she did further research. She traveled down to the coast, to Skagway, Alaska, to meet with Tlingit elders there. She told two senior elders, Maggie Kodenaha and Bert Dennis, what had occurred and asked them to judge whether she had acted appropriately.

I told her [Maggie Kodenaha] all about how I sang that song when Peter came back and when I made that dinner for him. I called everybody from across the river to his welcome dinner, and I sang it before we started out that dinner and I said that Ḵaax̱'achgóok song was our song. And Uncle Patsy didn't believe it. So I went to Skagway too, and I asked Maggie Kodenaha and she told me all about it. She told me about the war we made and that's how come he gave us that song. Ḵaax̱'achgóok made lots of songs. He made songs for the sun and he made songs for when he shoved his paddle in their boat, and *that* song he gave to G̱aanax̱.ádi. And that sun song, I don't know who he gave it to. He just kept it for himself, I guess.

He [Ḵaax̱'achgóok and his clan members] gave that Ḵaax̱'achgóok song to *us* in place of his brother. That's why we use it. That's why *I* use it. That's why I gave it to Pete when he came back from the army, because he just went through what happened to Ḵaax̱'achgóok. He drifted away in the ocean, but he finally came back. I asked all about that, too . . . [before I used the song].[12]

Narrative as Commemoration

Angela Sidney was forty-three years old when she first performed the Ḵaax̱'achgóok story and song in 1945. More recently, at the age of eighty-six, she decided to use this story again, this time in a very different public setting. By now she was acknowledged as a senior elder storyteller in the Yukon Territory. She was in great demand as a storyteller in schools and had performed at the Toronto Storytelling Festival in 1984. She was widely credited as the inspiration for the annual Yukon International Storytelling Festival described in chapter 7. She had been awarded the Order of Canada by the governor-general of Canada in 1986 for her linguistic and ethnographic work. At this stage in her life, no one was going to challenge her right to tell whatever story she chose.

When the new Yukon College complex officially opened in Whitehorse in 1988, she was invited to take a formal role in the ceremonies, and she was asked to give the college a Tagish name. Although I was now living outside the Yukon Territory and was unable to attend the opening celebrations, Angela Sidney and I met several weeks later, and she described her performance. To commemorate the event, she told me, she had sung the Ḵaax̱'achgóok song because it conveyed her feelings about what Yukon College could mean to young people in the Territory.

Her audience was a very mixed one this time, including hundreds of non-Natives as well as members of First Nations from throughout the Yukon. It is not at all clear that the meaning of her story was self-evident to her listeners, but she was single-minded in her commitment to present them with a story they could think with, if they chose to do so. Because she could not be sure her audience would understand her reasons for telling it, we discussed the idea of distributing the text of her story with some additional commentary so others could recognize why she had chosen it. And so we did.

The reason I sang this song, is because that Yukon College is going to be like the Sun for the students. Instead of going to Vancouver or Victoria, they're going to be able to stay here and go to school here. We're not going to lose our kids anymore. It's going to be just like the Sun for them, just like for that Kaax'achgóok.[13]

ESTABLISHING MEANINGS THROUGH STORY AND SONG

With the growing discussion about local knowledge, indigenous perspectives on history, and comanagement of natural resources in northern Canada and Alaska, there is sometimes a tendency to treat orally narrated accounts as collectible texts that can in turn be reduced to sources from which "data" may be extracted. Researchers pose questions about landscape, flora and fauna, history, ethnography, language, psychology, and social behavior. In their search for answers, they may look to orally narrated accounts — sometimes going directly to living elders, other times searching archival collections for accounts recorded in the past.

The implication is that oral sources are somehow stable, like written sources, and that once spoken and recorded, they are simply there, waiting for interpretation. Yet anyone who has been engaged in ethnographic fieldwork knows that the content of oral sources depends largely on what goes into the questions, the dialogue, the personal relationship through which it is communicated. Oral testimony is never the same twice, even when the same words are used, because the relationship — the dialogue — is always shifting.[14] Oral traditions are not natural products. They have social histories, and they acquire meaning in the situations in which they are used, in interactions between narrators and listeners. Meanings shift depending on how fully cultural understandings are shared by teller and listener.[15]

The persistent idea that oral testimony can be treated as data is not so different from Franz Boas's conviction a century ago that the actual telling of narratives remained relatively uninfluenced by the observer and that the "native point of view" could be gleaned from recorded texts of myth and folklore. Two problematic conventions have emerged from this assumption. First, as Dell Hymes points out, the words of a single speaker have often been glossed over in the name of an entire community, as though the speaker were merely some kind of information conduit. Second, ethnographers have normally gone on to assume full authority for these ethnographic products.[16]

If we think of oral tradition as a social activity rather than as some reified product, we come to view it as part of the equipment for living rather than a set of meanings embedded within texts and waiting to be discovered. One of the most trenchant observations of contemporary anthropology is that meaning is *not* fixed, that it must be studied in practice — in the small interactions of everyday life. Such practice is more likely to emerge in dialogue than in a formal interview. In her retellings of this one story, Mrs. Sidney shows how she is able to communicate meanings that are both culturally situated and highly personal. She readily acknowledges that her interpretation could be contested by other community members. She claims only that she has made every effort to present it as she understands it from her own research.

Angela Sidney's use of the story of Ḵaax̱'achgóok demonstrates the way she uses narratives as a kind of cultural scaffolding on which to construct the story of her own life. It is one of many complex narratives she asked me to record after she had expressed interest in the project of documenting her life experience. As our work progressed, she repeatedly referred back to specific stories, interrupting her narrative with comments like, "You remember that story about . . . ? Well, I told you that one already. That's the one I'm talking about now." And then she would show how that story could illuminate some event that had occurred during her own life. Her construction of her life story relied heavily on this full range of narratives as points of reference.[17] Such stories, then, can be both culturally specific and highly personal.

Angela Sidney's various tellings of the Ḵaax̱'achgóok story remind us that when we approach oral tradition there is more involved than textual analysis. Her point, in her various retellings, is to show how oral narrative is part of a communicative process. First, she demonstrates, you have to learn what the story *says*. Then you learn what the story can *do* when it is engaged as a strategy of communication. Unless we pay attention to why a particular story is selected and told, we understand very little of its meanings. Her point in retelling stories about Ḵaax̱'achgóok is precisely to show that a good story, well used, can not merely explain but also add meanings to a special occasion.

Her tellings raise questions about the stability of story, narrator, and audience over time. After establishing Ḵaax̱'achgóok's story as one full of possibilities for interpretation, she made it central to three *other* narratives several years later. One of her stories referred to an event that had occurred more than a century before; another was tied to an important event in her own life, one that had happened forty years earlier; a third commemorated an event with significance for the future. In her tellings, there is no simple analogue between the narrative and a reified oral history.

But if stories are historically situated, so are narrators. Mrs. Sidney was very much aware of how her own evolving role as performer changed on different occasions. In 1945 she was a relatively junior woman speaking in front of elders who challenged her right to tell the story. The point of her next version, referring back to the late 1800s, was to establish her emerging ethnographic authority as she conducted research in conversation with her elders. In 1974, as a woman in her early seventies, she saw herself as a teacher, both to me and to the "schoolkids" who might read her narrative. At her fourth telling, in 1988, she was positioned as an acclaimed senior storyteller in the Yukon, unlikely to be challenged by anyone, but also less likely to be understood by her heterogeneous audience. The net effect of her bringing the four versions together in recording her life history was to demonstrate *how* she established the authority to tell and to attribute meanings to one story during the course of her lifetime.[18]

Listeners change too, and Angela Sidney always had a careful eye for her audience. Because she took seriously the goal of demonstrating her communicative competence, she took responsibility for ensuring, at each telling, that her audience understood what she was saying.[19] The 1974 telling was for novices — for me and for the "schoolkids" who needed to learn the story outline. This was very different from the 1985 version, told in the presence of her son to invoke an event from 1945, his arrival home from military service in France. Her son was an interactive audience: he knew the story well, but he also had his own version of the events. He kept trying to interject details about his own journey. On that occasion, though, Mrs. Sidney saw this as *her* story, and she intervened firmly whenever he stopped to breathe. No one was going to interrupt her telling this time! Giving him the gift of the Ḵaax̱'achgóok story had been a pivotal event in her emerging role in her community. Her husband's delight with her intelligence ("Gee, I didn't know you were so smart to think like that! That's a *good* idea.") was countered by her paternal uncle's disapproval ("It's not you fellows' song, that song. You can't use that song!").

Her account of how she gave this song the name "Pete's song," then illustrates both the consensus by which cultures celebrate their sense of collectivity and the oppositional process by which difference and boundary are maintained. That a culture is shared does not mean that all individual interpretations will be the same, but it does guarantee that conflicting interpretations are significant.[20] Publicly challenged, Angela Sidney conducted her own ethnographic research with Tlingit elders who confirmed her legitimate, inherited clan right to tell the story, to sing the song, and to give such a gift. Part of her reason for insisting on retelling the story in 1985 was to show her son (and me) that an audience of elders who themselves took the roles of cultural experts about questions of Tlingit oral copyright had publicly endorsed her choice in 1945. Her various audiences — those elders, her son, myself — could appreciate and understand the role of narrative and song as statements about clan identity.

In 1988 her audience changed again, this time to a very diverse gathering attending formal ceremonies commemorating the opening of the local college. Although Angela was pleased with her own choice of K̲aax̲'achgóok story to represent the symbolic importance of the college for the community, she was quite sure that many members of this audience, hearing the story for the first time and lacking a context for recognizing it, would fail to understand her meaning. She understood that effective performance of oral tradition requires more than performers and performances — it also demands an expressive community sharing similar expectations.[21] She puzzled later about how to make her point in a different way — in other words, how to demonstrate her communicative competence to this very mixed audience. Eventually she concluded that it would be appropriate to extend our dialogue, reproducing in printed form the narrative she had originally recorded with me and adding a short explanation. We arranged for its publication in the *Northern Review,* a journal published at Yukon College.

In conclusion, Angela Sidney's story draws on a traditional dimension of culture to give meaning to a range of contemporary events. During the years we have worked together recording the events of her life, she has repeatedly demonstrated that she thinks and processes information with reference to the narratives she learned as a young woman. She has shown that she organizes, stores, and transmits her insights and knowledge of the world through narratives and songs describing the human condition. Her narrative is as much about social transformation of the society she lives in as it is about individual creativity. Her point is that oral tradition may tell us about the past, but its meanings are not exhausted with reference to the past. Good stories from the past continue to provide legitimate insights about contemporary events. What appears to be the "same" story, even in the repertoire of one individual, has multiple meanings depending on location, circumstance, audience, and stage of life of narrator and listener.

Angela Sidney spent much of her life demonstrating how this process works, and today younger women and men in her community continue to draw insights from the methods she used to teach. The words she used to end one of our dialogues on a winter afternoon say it most clearly: "Well," she concluded, "I've tried to live my life right, just like a story."

3

Yukon Arcadia: Oral Tradition, Indigenous Knowledge, and the Fragmentation of Meaning

In 1982 the Yukon Historical and Museums Association convened a modest conference on early human history in the Yukon Territory. Archaeologists, some with decades of experience working in northern Canada and Alaska, were invited to participate along with elders from Yukon First Nations. The laudable aim of this meeting, unconventional at the time, was to encourage scientists from across Canada to meet local elders in a setting where they could exchange knowledge about environmental factors affecting regional history. To ensure informality, the conference was hosted in the small community of Haines Junction, headquarters for the Champagne-Aishihik First Nation, rather than in Whitehorse, the Territory's capital and a more conventional conference venue.

More than a hundred people — adults and children — crowded into the community hall on a brisk Saturday morning in autumn, many driving considerable distances. Local elders filled the front row while organizers prepared coffee and assembled slide carousels. Throughout the day, archaeologists successively presented papers about their past and current research projects and responded to questions from engaged audiences. After sitting patiently listening until late afternoon, Mrs. Annie Ned, a Southern Tutchone elder close to ninety years of age at the time, rose to her feet asking, "Where do these people come from, outside? You tell different stories from us people. You people talk from paper — Me, I want to talk from Grandpa." Thus claiming her authority, she began telling her own stories about subjects of the day's discussions — early caribou migration routes; trade between coast and interior; her aunts' and parents' experiences of the Klondike gold rush; her own memories from early in the century. When I had first heard Mrs. Ned's narratives several years earlier, I had slim basis for understanding what she was saying. When we began working together during the 1970s, my initial objective was to learn how indigenous women had experienced the tumultuous changes brought to the Yukon during the twentieth century. It rapidly became clear that Mrs. Ned and her contemporaries were approaching our project with a very different model of life history. I had expected our discussions to trace the effects on their lives of the Klondike gold rush, missionary-run residential schools, construction of the Alaska Highway, and other disruptive events. I was also intrigued by how these women talked about subjects studied seasonally by visiting scientists — from the human consequences when glacier-dammed lakes emptied catastrophically into the Alsek River valley to changing migration routes of the Porcupine caribou herd — and whether narrative traditions about such events could provide scientists with information not available from other sources (fig. 2).

Eventually I came to view both projects as flawed by my attempts to impose a conventional academic framework that might evaluate such accounts as historical or scientific data. These women kept redirecting our work away from secular history and toward stories about how the world began and was transformed to be suitable for human beings. The more I persisted with my original agenda, the more insistent each was about the direction our work should take. "Not now," Mrs. Ned and others would reply to my questions. "Write down this story about that man who stayed with caribou." Or "Listen to this story about the boy who stayed with fish." Each woman explained that such stories were important to record as part of her personal history. If I expected to learn anything, they implied, I needed to become familiar with pivotal narratives "everybody knows" about relationships among beings who share responsibility for maintaining the social order. Although my initial concern was that they were narrowing our focus by insisting on the primacy of traditional stories, it became clear as we continued working together that they were actually enlarging our project. My additional discomfort about recording in English timeless narratives learned in Athapaskan (Dän) languages, given inevitable losses incurred in translation, was met with their confidence in their own translation abilities and their insistence that English is just one more Native language spoken in the Yukon. Gradually I learned how narratives about complex relationships between animals and humans, between young women and stars, between young men and animal helpers could frame not just larger cosmological issues but also the social practices of women engaged with a rapidly globalizing world. Stories connect people in such a world, and they unify interrupted memories that are part of any complex life. Rooted in ancient traditions, they can be used in strikingly modern ways.

The narratives seemed to act as translation devices for explicating both prosaic and dramatic events of everyday life. Mrs. Ned was born near the old settlement of Hutshi sometime during the 1890s, before births were formally registered. The forces tearing through the lives of people in this region during the twentieth century sometimes meant loss of a partner, death of a child, encroachment on territories and family life by traders, missionaries, government agencies, and resource extraction ventures. Such crises had to be endured, particularly by women others depended on — aging parents, daughters, sons, and partners. Narratives provided the foundation for local ethnohistory, helping people incorporate unfamiliar events into larger stories by connecting them with previous experiences. Such knowledge was neither passively stored nor encapsulated in individual narratives; rather, its telling involved active engagement with the world, and its performance in a particular situation made a specific point. Hence stories were often about the *telling* of stories and about the circumstances in which they were formerly told.

And so, on that afternoon in 1982, I was intrigued to hear how Mrs. Ned would address her audience in the Haines Junction community hall. She spoke at length, relating some stories I had heard before and others new to me, including one about her acquaintance with Skookum Jim, the codiscoverer of the gold that triggered the Klondike gold rush in 1896. "I almost married Skookum Jim," she commented wryly, startling listeners who knew him only as an emblematic historical figure.[1]

At the time, Mrs. Ned's intervention was both singular and memorable for her audience. In the 1990s, when elders are more routinely invited to make presentations to northern conferences, such an interjection would not be unusual. There has been a dramatic shift in popular discourse during the intervening years, and the idea that indigenous peoples should represent themselves rather than be represented by others (such as archaeologists or anthropologists) now meets widespread, commonsense approval. In Arctic and subarctic Canada, one consequence of this shift has been that references to local knowledge or indigenous knowledge are increasingly incorporated in public discussion, suggesting that additional voices are being included in public debates. But are they? And if so, how? And if more voices are included, whose are still left out?

A decade after Mrs. Ned intervened at the Haines Junction conference, I reviewed a draft bibliography titled "Indigenous Knowledge in Northern Canada," consisting of 550 carefully annotated entries.[2] My own work with Mrs. Ned and with other Yukon elders was listed among books and articles on such topics as aboriginal rights, animal behavior, archaeology, ethnobotony, land use, language, oral tradition, material culture, resource management, spirituality, subsistence, traditional clothing, and many more. I located many of the sources and read further. I found academic papers and research reports, conference proceedings and speeches, management plans from all levels of government and from nongovernment organizations like the Association of Canadian Universities for Northern Studies and the Canadian Arctic Resources Committee. The bibliography included reports by indigenous organizations usually overlooked in academic citations; the Labrador Inuit Association, the Avataq Cultural Institute, the Dene Cultural Institute, the Inuit Cultural Institute, the Council for Yukon Indians, and the Inuit Circumpolar Conference.[3] The ASTIS CD-ROM database yielded two hundred additional references and a sense that indigenous knowledge is indeed a burgeoning field of study.[4]

Moving to international literature dramatically increased the pool, with materials on indigenous knowledge from Africa, Asia, and Latin America. Reports, conferences, publications, and newsletters on this topic have recently been funded by UNESCO; the International Union for the Conservation of Nature (IUCN); the United Nations Man-in-the-Biosphere program; the World Wildlife Fund (WWF); the World Conservation Strategy; the World Commission on Environment and Development (the Bruntland Commission); the World Bank; and the Arctic Environmental Protection Strategy (AEPS), signed by the eight countries with Arctic territories.[5] Recommendations arising from the 1992 United Nations Conference on the Environment (the Earth Summit) in Rio de Janeiro "clearly establish traditional knowledge and traditional practice among the pillars of sustainable development."[6] The sheer scope of the literature raises questions about whether a growing tendency to present indigenous knowledge as somehow free-standing — to give it what one student of African agriculture has called "spurious epistemic independence" may be propelling us away from questions about what can be learned from local knowledge and toward assigning reified meanings to abstract concepts.[7]

Critics have cautioned that there is a danger that local knowledge will be absorbed uncritically into ideological critique, foreclosing opportunities to explore alternatives. Arne Kalland, for instance, questions using a term like "indigenous" to describe something as precise as local knowledge. Though convenient, it describes a relationship between particular peoples and a surrounding nation-state rather than knowledge shared by members of a community. Such an adjective carries symbolic weight yet is broad enough to include a variety of groups with proliferating self-designations.[8] Cultural knowledge is learned and passed on locally and does not inhere in reified political categories. Yet once the term "indigenous knowledge" becomes ideologically embedded, it gets welded to other ideas that inevitably sweep up local views in its vortex. What may be overlooked is local knowledge — learned, shared, and passed on locally—and this may be a more helpful characterization.[9]

In *Language and Symbolic Power,* Pierre Bourdieu questions how we come to frame everyday practices as autonomous, homogeneous, internally bounded objects of knowledge amenable to prescribed kinds of analysis. Drawing his examples from the field of linguistics, he argues that conventional scholarly approaches too often assume an object domain without reflecting on the social, historical, and political conditions whereby some languages and dialects are suppressed while others gain both authority and associated rights to analyze or translate those very linguistic forms that have been marginalized.[10] This paradigm defies the collective weight of twentieth-century scholarship by treating knowledge as though it were somehow neutral. If we are going to investigate the proliferation of ideas about a topic as complex as indigenous knowledge, he might say, we need to concern ourselves with the social conditions under which such knowledge becomes defined, produced, reproduced, and distributed (or repressed and eliminated) in struggles for legitimacy.

Given the aristocratic history of indigenous knowledge studies, Bourdieu's concerns are especially relevant here. Repeatedly framed as a foil for concepts of Western rationality, typologies used to characterize such knowledge vary wildly across time and space under names like "primitive superstition," "savage nobility," "empirical practical knowledge," and "ancestral wisdom," terms that inevitably reflect more about the history of Western ideology than about ways of apprehending the world. Such classifications have never been neutral and have gone hand in hand with extension of empire, suppressing beliefs defined on a continuum from the demonic and dangerous to the irrelevant "survivals" suitable for antiquarian collection. Inevitably, such studies were justified as serving the best interests of peoples whose ideas were eradicated in the service of evolutionary models of progress. Late twentieth-century recasting of ideas formerly dismissed as superstition and now reincarnated as knowledge produces strange juxtapositions. In northern North America, for example, ideas once dismissed as "animistic" are now transformed to iconic status as "indigenous science," though in a form that satisfies a North Atlantic preference for classificatory studies projected as traditional ecological knowledge, or TEK.[11] Thus recast, indigenous knowledge continues to be presented as an object for science rather than as a system of knowledge that could inform science.[12]

But knowledge is recast differently in different contexts. In Germany, for example, indigenous knowledge has been romanticized by the environmental movement as original ecology at the same time that it provides an animistic foil for the contemporary European human rights movement. At the Checkpoint Charlie Museum marking the former boundary between East and West Berlin, a small, tired-looking replica of a totem pole labeled "Totem pole, 18th [*sic*] century — from the estate of Zan [*sic*] Grey, 1875–1939" stands near the entrance to an exhibit depicting the history of human rights in twentieth-century Europe.[13] The label reads:

For Indians there existed no code of human rights, as we know it. Their behaviors were decisively determined by tradition, by fear of their tribal chieftains as well as a respect for a cosmic-magical order. Individual chieftains are remarkable in that they are closely connected with certain animals, from which they derive their power. By means of the totem pole standing at the entrance of their dwelling they convey this power and their will to maintain and exercise justice.

Local knowledge, it seems, can be used to symbolize whatever is convenient.

The rest of this chapter looks critically at themes emerging in circumpolar literature about environmental issues of serious concern in northern regions. The idiom of ecological crisis in which much of this work is embedded reflects an escalating certainty that the world is changing faster than our understanding of it. Daily reports of environmental disasters cause particular distress in the Arctic and Subarctic, where people who until recently saw themselves as distanced from industrial pollution now discover that atmospheric currents concentrate contaminants at the poles, endangering ecosystems and creating potentially devastating consequences for subsistence hunting.

The burgeoning literature on indigenous knowledge, then, is not neutral and has consequences for the people whose concepts it addresses and incorporates. Three strands especially deserve discussion. First is a growing literature on themes of resource management and sustainable development. Second, much environmentalist writing looks to First Peoples for alternative ways of thinking about environment. Third, indigenous organizations negotiating with different levels of state government are producing their own materials on environmental issues. Although these narratives all address notions of a common good and increasingly share a lexicon, they originate in different domains. The processes by which local concepts become incorporated into Western narratives often seems strangely distant from Mrs. Ned's advice about listening to "different stories."

INDIGENOUS KNOWLEDGE AND RESOURCE MANAGEMENT

If particular concepts lend substance to shifting policy regimes, comparing rhetoric of northern development from the mid-twentieth century with that of comanagement as we approach the millennium raises questions about how much the language we use clarifies administrative guidelines and how much it obscures them. During the early 1970s the Yukon member of Parliament, Erik Nielsen, confidently asserted on more than one occasion his dream that Whitehorse, the Territory's capital, could become the "Pittsburgh of the North." Such views were common then but became publicly questionable during the Mackenzie Valley Pipeline Inquiry when Justice Thomas Berger, appointed to chair the hearings, solicited views from small communities throughout the Mackenzie Valley. He concluded that prevailing modes of resource extraction by nonlocal interests should be reframed as a choice between a "northern frontier" and a "northern homeland" and recommended against the construction of a gas pipeline through northern Canada until the federal government undertook its legal obligation to settle land claims.[14]

On the surface, proliferation of government-sponsored workshops in the 1990s on sustainable development, indigenous knowledge, and comanagement might be interpreted as a small but significant policy shift. The impetus for such exercises is clear enough: they are grounded both in widespread reevaluation of large-scale economic development schemes and in the highly politicized context of indigenous claims to land and autonomy. One paradox, though, is the expectation that indigenous northerners should contribute their observations and interpretations of environmental phenomena only now, in the wake of the Chernobyl explosion, the *Exxon Valdez* oil spill, and recognition that polar latitudes are among the most polluted on the planet. Even more ironic is the expectation that they should make these contributions at national and international levels, as members of conference panels and regulatory boards, rather than at a local level where such knowledge could make an actual difference.[15] Such a formulation seems to suggest that indigenous traditions should provide answers to problems created by modern states in terms convenient for modern states.

Both administrators managing environmental programs and elders living with the consequences of environmental deterioration probably agree that things no longer work as they should, though their expressions of causality are likely to differ. Elders can point to local evidence of growing imbalances in the relationship between humans, animals, and the lands and waters they inhabit. Government officials more often look to international solutions, concluding that humans have made serious errors and must revise global management strategies. With pressure growing to include indigenous representatives in regimes like the Arctic Environmental Protection Strategy, more managers embrace the rhetoric of indigenous knowledge. Though they may profit from attachment to causes perceived as morally sound, they increasingly use the language of science to speak of the need to collect, classify, translate, and use such information.

Northern hunters have long maintained land-based economies and are undeniably in a position to make unique and fine-grained empirical observations. In many instances their knowledge exceeds that of North Atlantic scientists. But that knowledge is encoded both in distinctive paradigms and in seminal institutional arrangements for converting those observations into everyday practice, and these may get stripped away in translation because they do not travel easily across cultural boundaries.

The acronym-filled rhetoric of traditional ecological knowledge, or TEK, provides a rich arena for assessing both what happens to local knowledge swept into debates now framed as global and the consequences of universalizing formulations when they are played back at a community level. An issue of the Canadian Arctic Resources Committee newsletter devoted to this topic begins with an editorial urging that "an effective system . . . be developed to collect and classify native knowledge, particularly with respect to northern resources, environment and culture." [16] A newsletter published by UNESCO called *TEK Talk* states its purpose as "to further the recognition and understanding of TEK, to promote the application of TEK in the decision making process, and to promote networking among those interested in TEK." [17] The Commission on Ecology of the International Union for Conservation of Nature (IUCN) has established a Working Group on Traditional Ecological Knowledge, one of whose objectives is "to develop and promote ways of harnessing, recording, analyzing and applying traditional ecological knowledge for the conservation of nature and natural resources." [18] And the list goes on, much of it embedded in the so-called gray literature of commissioned reports.

A proliferation of titles like "Capturing Traditional Environmental Knowledge," "Harvesting Traditional Knowledge," "Integration of Indigenous Knowledge," and "Preservation, Transmission and Utilization of Indigenous Knowledge in the Industrial Epoch" suggests how conventional the language is becoming.[19] One pilot project in the Bering Sea is centered on "beluga whale TEK,"[20] while another project on Hudson Bay enters information on databases packaged as "traditional ecological knowledge and management systems" or TEKMS.[21] In northern Scandinavia discussions of the importance of "taxonomic research . . . codification . . . and flexible report systems"[22] raise questions about what this actually means. A description of one of these projects in the *World Wildlife Fund Bulletin* is unhelpful:

Following the research in the communities, draft reports will be prepared of the *documented information*. The *mapped information* will then be entered into a Geographical Information System (GIS). From this, it will be possible to prepare maps on different themes (migration, feeding, calving, and so on) and to present *visual displays* of traditional knowledge in addition to the written record. This winter, each of the communities will be addressed and asked to *review the draft reports and maps*. This will give the elders and hunters an opportunity to go over the information and to see if there [are] any gaps and to *correct any mistakes*. (My emphasis)[23]

The overwhelming impression given by such descriptions is that indigenous knowledge is essentially uncomplicated, that acquiring it is primarily a technocratic classification exercise, and that managers are the ones best equipped to identify the appropriate parameters and categories. Thus formulated, TEK can sometimes seem little more than the application of a rule constructed by the analyst who both sets the terms of the debate and ultimately authorizes what constitutes indigenous knowledge.[24] What seems to be missing in this objectivist paradigm is any sense of how such issues are discussed in local communities.

In 1982 one caribou biologist who heard Mrs. Ned speak at the Haines Junction meetings later accompanied me to visit her at her cabin thirty miles north of Whitehorse on the Takhini River. Mrs. Ned had referred to the enormous herds of caribou she remembered seeing at Kluane Lake and Aishihik Lake during her childhood. There is archaeological evidence that such herds once traveled much farther south than they do now, though none have been seen in this area in recent memory.[25] Two subspecies of caribou formerly ranged the southern Yukon — the large herds of Stone caribou (*Rangifer arcticus stonei*) and the Osborn caribou (*Rangifer arcticus osborni*), which travel in smaller groups. Scientists are still unsure of the reasons for their appearance and disappearance. This biologist was interested in learning what Mrs. Ned could tell him and had specific and careful questions he hoped to ask her.

Of the elders I worked closely with, Mrs. Ned was the most curious about what scientists and archaeologists were really up to. She was pleased to see him and provided thoughtful answers to his questions. When caribou came in winter, she told him, the sound of their hooves could be heard for miles as they clattered across the lakes. On one occasion, large numbers broke through when their weight was more than the ice could support, and she described how difficult it was for hunters to retrieve the meat and for women to tan hides soaked and frozen in this way. She went on to tell him about one of the last times caribou came in this direction. A man with shamanic powers disappeared when he was taken by caribou. His kinsmen struggled to entice him back to the human world. They could see what appeared to be a single caribou on the lake, but once they heard it sing this shaman's song, they understood that he had been transformed and knew what their obligations were:

Already moose were getting short when caribou came.
Lots of caribou around here when I got my kids,
Used to be [1910–15].

When lake froze in winter,
When caribou came,
It was just like horses, same.
You could hear their feet making noise,
Making noise [imitates hooves on ice].
Lots of caribou covered up these hills.

I want to talk about this story:
Old people tell this story.

One time, caribou took people.
That man had a little bit of doctor, I guess;
Well, caribou took him.

Everybody felt bad: he was gone.
His wife was left alone.

Right in the middle of the lake, they heard caribou singing
    his song.
People don't know what to do —
They tried to get him.

One man said, "Well, let's go. We're going to try."
Yeah!

They've got bow and arrow, that's all — they have no gun yet.
It was a long time ago, I guess.
They heard that man's song.
I think it was wintertime.
Wintertime.

That caribou just lay down in the middle of that ice.
All the time he stayed in the middle.
For a long time, they watched him.
Whenever they tried to come to that caribou, all the time he
  watched them.
He looked from person to person,
And all the time he didn't sleep.

One man told them he was going to do it.
Then he sneaked in. [She shows how he wrestled with the
  caribou and held it down.]

The caribou spoke:
"You smell," he told people.

Well, that man knew how to talk to caribou.
"What about your kids?" they asked him.
"Your kids are crying for you," his own brother told him.
"What's wrong with you?"

In a powerful voice, Mrs. Ned sang for us the song they heard.

Gradually and with great difficulty, through a series of elaborate rituals,
people were able to bring the man back to the human world even though
the transition was immensely difficult for him and he was never again able
to hunt caribou:

He couldn't help it.
So they brought him. They brought him home.
They took him home!
I guess his wife is glad: he's got kids too!
His wife came, and his kids.
He held his kids' hands, but for his wife, nothing.
He doesn't know her yet.

Well, they took him back.
They told him.
Then they watched him
They made a camp for it [away from the human camp].
Somebody watched him there.
He wanted to go!
He doesn't eat their food — he only eats willows.
You know what that means!
But they kept him the other side of the fire.

Then he came back to person.
But he can't hunt caribou anymore.

This was way before my time, but I saw lots of caribou.
They came back, caribou.
All this mountain was covered by caribou.
Used to be we had caribou not too long ago when my kids were
    growing up.

One time lots of caribou fell through the ice, one lake:
I called my husband back to get the meat.
My mother-in-law came to get the skins.
She got enough that time: she had her son with her.
But they are hard to clean when they fall in that way.
That's the last time caribou came this way.
That's the last time we saw caribou come.

But they didn't come back? How come?
That man came back to person.
Then he knew where moose are, where caribou are.
He tells them, but he can't hunt them.

That's the last time caribou came this way.
Since then, nothing.

Mrs. Ned went on to talk about how this story was bound up with her second
husband's powers and the story's significance for his life. If Mrs. Ned's
narrative were to be included in an enterprise like the one described above
in the *World Wildlife Fund Bulletin*, it is difficult to say how (follow-

ing the author's terminology) it would be "reviewed" or "visually displayed" and what "gaps" would be filled. Mrs. Ned and her contemporaries would be unlikely to "verify" such a story, though they might suggest that listening to it closely could generate different strategies for different listeners, depending on their individual life trajectories. In all likelihood, it would drop out of the database because it confuses rather than confirms familiar categories.

By the 1990s Yukon elders were accustomed to holding their own conferences and workshops. Now managers more commonly request invitations to make presentations at *elders'* conferences. From the perspective of at least some Native northerners, renewed attention to sustainable development can appear increasingly interventionist and intrusive, and consequently these presentations are rarely smooth expository addresses. A recent federal government policy framed as "devolution" has resulted in reassignment of some managers from Ottawa to northern communities. Locally, this sometimes looks rather like entrenchment of state systems at a regional level and has the effect of making people in small communities even more subject to regulation. Managers in turn are put in the difficult position of mediating between communities and the bureaucracy, having to make compromises between competing interests while carrying out government directives.

At an elder's festival in the southern Yukon held in the summer of 1994, a fisheries biologist made a presentation about the contentious catch-and-release program requiring anyone who catches a fish below a specified size to release it back into the water. This program has proved deeply problematic for local elders, who speak forcefully about how such a practice violates ethical principles because it involves "playing with fish" that have willingly offered themselves. The biologist, while expressing sympathy with this position, nevertheless explained as clearly as he could the relation between fish size and future fish stocks, arguing that rational resource use and long-term management would ultimately enhance the aboriginal fishery. An elder, shifting the field for discussion, responded by reviewing the story, familiar to the other elders there, of the "boy who stayed with fish." A youngster, showing hubris by making thoughtless remarks about fish, trips and falls into a river. He is swept into a world where all his normal understandings are reversed. In this world, fish occupy the human domain, and all the cultural behavior he has come to take for granted is shown to be foolish and wrongheaded. Gradually he becomes initiated and properly socialized into his new world, and when, the following year, he is able to return to the human world through shamanic intervention, he brings back an understanding of the fundamental relationships enmeshing humans and salmon in shared responsibilities for the health of salmon stocks.[26] Again, it is unclear how this knowledge, broadly understood in the southern Yukon, could be translated into the language of TEK.

As Phyllis Morrow and Chase Hensel have reported from Alaska, terms like "comanagement," "sustainable development," and "ecological crisis" are highly negotiable and have no analogues in Native American languages. To suggest that they are somehow bridging concepts may constitute taking control of the dialogue in ways that both mask deep cultural disagreements and restrict the range of ways of talking about these issues. Institutionalizing such language, they suggest, simultaneously narrows available strategies of discourse and sets precedents that redefine Native cultures through Western categories.[27]

Bruce Kapferer examines a parallel process that he calls "bureaucratic erasure" at work in contemporary Australia. He situates his argument both in Weber's analysis of bureaucracy and in Foucault's discussion of how taxonomic systems emerged and developed in the sixteenth and seventeenth centuries. At the heart of Western bureaucratic practice, Kapferer suggests, is the systematic fracturing and fragmentation of human experience. The resulting taxonomic schemes tend to take their structure from surface features and are inclined to stagnate, resulting in "the virtual draining of content from the categories, and the disappearance of life, sometimes the object of their concern, from their analytical orders."[28] Categorical practices that distance people from lived experience have real consequences. Kapferer argues that these processes are intensified in new cultural orders established as a result of growing bureaucratic, scientific, technical, and military management, in conditions sounding rather like those accelerating in the Arctic.

INDIGENOUS KNOWLEDGE AND ENVIRONMENTAL MOVEMENTS

In broadly based environmentalist literature, we encounter a relationship with indigenous imagery both more encompassing and historically more complicated than that discussed above, but also subject to more trenchant critique. If technocratic models seem to drain tradition by reducing it to codifiable data, environmentalist literature more commonly incorporates the imagery but reshapes it to fit contemporary concerns. Emerson, Thoreau, Karl May, and others independently drew inspiration from what each imagined to be American Indian beliefs, and their legacy has continued in the transformation of Black Elk, Chief Seattle, and others into environmentalist icons whose words have been reshaped to a present-day idiom.[29] Critiques of this paradigm make it clear how such imagery, while representing itself as a rejection of modern alienation from nature, actually reformulates modernism's most enduring narratives — environmental determinism and evolutionary progression — by positing Native Americans *as part of* nature and arrogating the mantle of moral truth for environmentalism, pervasively reformulated as "us." In a collection of essays analyzing how environmentalist appropriations of Asian imagery have entered into Western ideological constructions, Ole Bruun and Arne Kalland argue that globalizing environmental narratives are the latest version of a modernism whereby we universalize our concerns and project them onto others. While in no way minimizing the seriousness of environmental crises, their critique is directed at the tactical appropriation of Asian and Native American concepts in these debates. Local knowledge *is* important in these discussions, they insist — far too important to be transformed into Western myth.[30]

Two questionable axioms underlie juxtapositions of Arcadian past with contemporary environmental mayhem. One, well represented in North Atlantic writings, is the axiom that Native Americans lived in harmony with nature before the arrival of Europeans. This position, though it contains elements of truth for particular times and places, ignores substantial evidence to the contrary.[31] It becomes reframed in much environmental literature as a backward projection of contemporary views and then goes on to accumulate new baggage. Thus reformulated, Native Americans held long-term perspectives and engaged in highly rational behavior that sounds suspiciously like intuitive foresight of modern management strategies. The image has them relying on clear-cut evidence for the relation between harvest size and population size, adjusting their activities accordingly, and sharing with contemporary moderns a model based on notions of scarcity.[32] Such creative reconstruction ignores the extensive work by scholars documenting worldviews that animals are infinitely renewable rather than inevitably scarce, that they give themselves to hunters, with whom they share a complex world and to whom they are bound by ties of kinship and reciprocity.[33] It further ignores research demonstrating that indigenous hunters often had to rely on opportunistic strategies — to take what they could when they could in order to survive.[34] It completely overlooks the wide range of Native American subsistence strategies, including crucial variables like population size and resource availability. Small foraging populations inevitably alter their environments less than societies with higher population densities relying on farming, and Native Americans employed a variety of strategies for making a living and were never passive occupants of the land. But thus naturalized, the original ecologist, to use Ann Fienup-Riordan's term, is transformed into a noble savage with modern Western sensibilities.

A second axiom postulates that if people in a particular society express respectful attitudes toward the environment, they will inevitably behave circumspectly toward it.[35] Such arguments are grounded in a discourse about the ideological embeddedness of Western science, and they presuppose a fundamental link between a society's philosophical perspectives and the behavior of its members. Frequently cited examples include Judeo-Christian mastery of nature embedded in models of progress, or Cartesian fracturing of subject and object that relegates physical and social sciences to separate domains. Societies that do not so clearly set concepts of nature and culture in opposition, runs this argument, will demonstrate more reverential forms of behavior toward the natural world. But this view too errs on the side of romanticism and an overly simple understanding of the relation between ideology, norms, and behavior. Sociologists have shown that norms do not determine behavior in any society, though they may retrospectively allow us to legitimize our actions. To confuse the two is to oversimplify more complex processes. It also follows too closely the commonsense notion that expressions about nature are empirical statements about ecosystems, when a Durkheimian interpretation might view them as statements about social organization. In a framework where animals and humans are understood to share common states of being that include family relationships, intelligence, and common responsibility for maintenance of a shared world, the rights and obligations obtaining to relationships among people also extend to the natural world. Interaction with the physical world, then, *is* a social relationship, and consequently it is rarely straightforward.

The pitfall of both axioms — one linking hunters with harmony, the other conflating norms with behavior — is that each so easily becomes a weapon when indigenous people fail to pass arbitrary tests of authenticity. George Wenzel documents how the animal rights movement first appropriated and incorporated Inuit traditions into antiharvesting campaigns and ultimately turned those same arguments against Inuit people, whom they came to define as enemies because they now use modern technology for hunting. In the anthropology thus invented by the animal rights movement, Inuit culture has been redefined and idealized on Western terms. Hence "the word 'tradition' becomes a semantic telescope that is used the wrong way round. What is distant is good and what is contemporary is bad because it has been tainted by modernity." [36] The offended response of some urban environmentalists toward any infraction of that idealized matrix is exemplified in a disturbing comment from an activist in the International Wildlife Coalition who was involved in the antisealing campaign that devastated Inuit economies during the 1980s: "I own the Native culture. I bought it with my taxes. I own about two-thirds of it . . . that's how it survives. There would be no Indian culture today if it wasn't for the fact that southern Canadians pay for it" (Stephen Best, cited in Wenzel, 158).

Despite surface differences, models based on TEK and those based on environmentalism share contradictions. TEK, modeled loosely on ecological science models, heads in bureaucratic directions. Original ecology models, more conventionally phrased in religious terms, posit indigenous peoples as stewards of profound ecological knowledge. Both models force indigenous people to speak in uncharacteristic ways; both ultimately redefine aboriginal cultures in Western terms by projecting North Atlantic concerns as global. But if, as Marx suggested, some ideas "migrate" better than others, the distinction between these models may reflect Engels's thesis that rising classes embrace ever more materialistic perspectives (like a scientizing TEK), whereas declining classes resort to increasingly fantastic beliefs (like New Age environmentalism) in an effort to deny to themselves that their power is diminishing. [37]

A situation in subarctic Siberia provides a revealing comparison with North America. In Yakutsk, Piers Vitebsky observed how a religious model rather than a management model animates public discussion yet is equally subject to fragmentation. During the 1930s, shamans were among the most persecuted Soviet citizens. They were tortured, imprisoned, and killed, and their suppression seemed largely complete. Two generations later in the 1990s, shamanism has reemerged (though without the shamans) as a kind of Asian essentialism, incorporated into Sakha nationalism as part of a cultural society in Yakutsk known as Kut-Sur, translated roughly as "Soul-Reason." [38] Vitebsky discusses how in this case the global idiom of environment, presented as inalienable wisdom, is used to legitimate claims of one ethnic group to resources (in the Sakha case, diamonds) at the expense of other ethnic groups in the region. Sakha urban professionals and schoolchildren alike are reeducated about cardinal points and distinct layers of their cosmology in classrooms by instructors using flip charts and other Western pedagogical techniques. Thus fragmented and packaged as facts, rather than lived as Bourdieu's *habitus*, shamanic ideas are stripped of their narrative power to link past, present, and future.[39] Parallel processes are documented in Colombia, where instructors hold workshops and use tape recorders to teach shamanism reformulated as indigenous science.[40]

Conceivably, utter suppression of religion in Siberia during the Soviet era may make that region especially receptive to concepts of knowledge formulated in religious terms, just as long-term marginalization of local environmental knowledge in the North American Arctic may be provoking hospitable responses to a scientizing project in that region. Despite superficial differences, both paradigms share a tendency to shatter the holism of local knowledge by simply eliminating the parts that do not, in Marx's terms, migrate easily. Once appropriated, ideas can be relocated and welded to a dissident ideological agenda, a process that has been discussed elsewhere as the erasure of memory.[41]

Indigenous Knowledge in Neocolonial Encounters

Conflicting ideologies about sustainable development, environmental crises, and indigenous rights intersect differently in the Amazon, Asia, the South Pacific, and northern Canada. Conceptions of knowledge become strained at this awkward conjunction of ideology with the lives of real people, especially in late twentieth-century colonial encounters. If conflicts in some parts of the world center on enormous corporate profits flowing into pharmaceutical coffers from medicinal plants whose uses have long been known by indigenous peoples,[42] in northern Canada attention is directed to land, to self-government, and more recently to economic benefits deriving from northern research projects.

The terms of current debates often appear set. Indigenous leaders find themselves sharing a public stage with other interest groups and compelled to address issues in language authorized by the apposite setting. In liberal democracies, claims to specialized cultural knowledge carry some weight when they have public support, but to garner such support this knowledge must be presented as simultaneously rooted in long-standing tradition, relevant to the modern world, and transparently accessible to broad audiences. By the mid-1990s, too, there is an emerging populist backlash to indigenous knowledge, fed by economic retrenchment. One example comes in the synopsis of a recent report titled "Market Solutions for Native Poverty," prepared for the conservative C. D. Howe Institute, based in Vancouver. Its editor argues that "traditional knowledge is dramatically at odds with the requirements for success in industrial society" and urges the federal government to phase out transfer payments to aboriginal communities and redistribute resources to those willing to make the transition to urban society and economy.[43] Another article charges that government requirements for including traditional knowledge in environmental impact assessment hearings leading up to approval of a proposed diamond mine in the Northwest Territories amount to "the imposition of religion on Canadian citizens."[44]

Three strategies used by indigenous people in northern Canada illustrate difficulties arising when they engage in formal, public exposition of their cultural traditions. Each strategy incorporates paradoxes intensified by universalizing discourses of science, spirituality, economics, law, or politics. One example, from a recent land claims case, highlights the seeming improbability of performing indigenous knowledge on its own terms in a contemporary court of law. A second concerns the measured success achieved by Canadian Inuit translating their knowledge as TEK. A third outlines contradictions discerned by a perceptive speaker invited to participate on a First Nations panel addressing an environmental conference.

Oral Tradition in the Courts

In the case of *Delgamuukw v. B.C.*, brought before the Supreme Court of British Columbia in the late 1980s, hereditary chiefs of the Gitksan and Wet'suwet'en First Nations presented their claims to ownership and jurisdiction of lands in northwestern British Columbia. In so doing, they took the enormous risk of trying to state their relationship to the land on their own terms, from their own perspective, using long-standing oral traditions as a medium to present arguments to the court.

Acknowledging that they were addressing a court of law with institutionalized procedures for resolving conflicts, they formulated the narrative thrust of their legal argument to match that court's requirements. A critical issue for the judge centered on the concept of social organization, and he required the plaintiffs to demonstrate to the court both that they had lived in organized societies before European contact and that they continued to do so. He also required them to produce evidence linking past social organization with contemporary social institutions.[45] Gitksan and Wet'suwet'en leaders gave formal evidence about the antiquity of their house and clan system and contended that linkages between past and present could be demonstrated through traditions passed on orally. Addressing the court in its own language, they identified oral tradition as their *declaration of title*.

Knowledge of land, they continued, cannot be divorced from knowledge of social organization. They referred to two distinct kinds of tradition — the Gitksan adaawk (defined as sacred narratives about ancestors, house and clan histories,[46] and territories) and Wet'suwet'en kungax (songs about trails between territories central to Wet'suwet'en houses). Their statement of claim asserted that *expressions of ownership* are made through adaawk, kungax, songs, and ceremonial regalia; that *confirmation of ownership* through totem poles gives those expressions a material base; and that *assertion of ownership* to specific territories was now being made in this court through specific claims. Marshaling their own legal traditions in addition to those of the court, their hereditary chiefs appeared in ceremonial regalia and publicly enacted narratives, songs, and dances that had formerly been performed only within a community context, presenting these as statements linking history, performance of adaawk and kungax, and land.

They urged the judge to recognize the symbolic importance of oral tradition, stating that the case before the Supreme Court should not depend on the literal accuracy of these histories to establish connections between social organization and land tenure. Oral tradition is more than literal history and should not be reduced to mere historical data, they argued, although it does provide evidence for scholars studying the past. For a variety of reasons discussed elsewhere, Justice McEachern rejected their assertions about broad concepts embodied in oral tradition, finding that they did not conform to juridical definitions of truth: "I am unable to accept adaawk, kungax and oral traditions as reliable bases for detailed history but they could confirm findings based on other admissible evidence."[47] Despite the appellants' admonition not to evaluate the oral traditions against positivistic definitions of "truth," the judge rejected their value as evidence for precisely this reason.

The final judgment, printed, published, and distributed in a bound volume titled *Reasons for Judgment,* provides a powerful example of the unequal weight accorded to different narratives. The inescapable lesson seems to be that removing oral tradition from a context where it has self-evident power and performing it in a context where it is opened to evaluation by the state poses enormous problems for understanding its historical value.

Arctic TEK

Canadian Inuit have been successfully using models centered on traditional ecological knowledge, though not without costs. The devastation wrought to Arctic economies in recent years by European antisealing campaigns has made them extremely wary of the environmentalist movement, and many communities prefer to address the critical environmental issues by building closer associations with social and physical scientists. They have achieved extraordinary successes in an international forum. The Inuit Circum-polar Conference (ICC), composed of Canadian Inuit, Alaskan Inupiat and Yupiit, Greenlanders (and joined recently by Inuit from Arctic Siberia), was established in 1977 and has held official observer status at the United Nations since 1984. The list of ICC's accomplishments is impressive. Members have obtained positions on such international committees as the World Conservation Strategy, the International Working Group for Indigenous Affairs (IWGIA), the Arctic Monitoring and Assessment Program (AMAP), and the Conservation of Arctic Flora and Fauna (CAFF) and have established an Indigenous Peoples' Secretariat within the eight-country Arctic Environmental Protection Strategy (AEPS).[48] They were prominent at the 1992 United Nations Conference on the Environment in Rio de Janeiro and played a role in the 1993 International Year for the World's Indigenous Peoples.

Forging broad alliances can risk disengaging leaders from local issues, but Inuit appear to have successfully linked concerns about global change with local, territorially based knowledge, at least in some communities. Inuit leaders have become aware of the potential benefits from involvement in scientific research, arguably one of the few renewable economic resources in the Arctic, and of the need to secure such benefits for local communities. The Hudson Bay Program had by 1993 received $1.5 million to document resources shared by twenty-five Inuit and Cree communities surrounding Hudson Bay;[49] the "Beluga TEK" project in Alaska has now extended connections to Siberian Inuit;[50] the long-term Nunavik project funded by the Makivik Corporation has provided a training ground for local expertise.[51] All these projects have helped to define local ideas about how research should be conducted and how knowledge should be transmitted, largely because of their emphasis on local control.

As Vitebsky points out, though, privileged positions negotiated by some groups, like the Inuit, may come at the price of an advanced commoditizing of their indigenous knowledge.[52] Despite current successes, the language of TEK moves away from familiar expression of worldview and increasingly enmeshes them in bureaucratic management strategies. The Hudson Bay Program, for example, with its "Traditional Ecological Knowledge Management Systems" (TEKMS) was described by its director as providing "a data base for predictive modelling, for forecasting and for selecting harvest areas" and as helping Inuit and Cree "bring forward their knowledge in such a way that it can be integrated into the cumulative effects assessment."[53] If Inuit now gain undeniable advantages by linking their knowledge to the authority of quantifiable and empirical science, claims based on reification of TEK may eventually strand them on a slippery slope between politicizing of that knowledge and its rationalizing by government. Sissons has documented how incorporation of Maori knowledge into New Zealand social service programs creates new problems for Maori communities as knowledge becomes codified, formalized, amd rationalized in the context of state power.[54] Accepting the language of TEK may bring immediate benefits for those who use it successfully, but this is a globalizing exercise. Fragmentation, objectification, and standardization of knowledge by encroaching bureaucracy carries unanticipated costs.

The applicability of TEK models is even more difficult for more heterogeneous groups. Associating indigenous knowledge with local territories can become complicated when territories are defined as bounded units, as in current land claims negotiations. During the mid-1970s many northern communities set out to map their use and occupancy of lands, surprising outsiders by the extensive territories known intimately by individual trappers. Two decades later, those same maps are sometimes reinterpreted as representing firm boundaries separating neighbors. Given inevitable differentiation among communities unequally endowed with visible cultural history, claims to territorial knowledge can be used to generate hierarchy and inequality and to set communities in competition with one another for shrinking resources.

Environmental Agendas and Indigenous Knowledge

A more circumscribed example comes from my discussions with participants in environmental conferences. Environmental meetings provide a platform where indigenous people may find sympathetic and influential audiences. As with TEK, one option speakers have is to use a rhetoric familiar to their audiences even when this forces them to speak in untypical ways. A more challenging option is to try to complicate their listeners' perceptions, but results can be disappointing where audience members bring clear expectations about what they want to hear. A woman of First Nations ancestry invited to be a panel member at one of the many environment conferences held in the North during the early 1990s reported insightfully about difficulties facing speakers in such settings.[55]

Two elders and three younger speakers more familiar with such meetings were invited to address approximately one hundred registered participants. An elder began by telling a story from her childhood about how she and her playmates had once behaved casually and inappropriately toward plants, and how this had frightening consequences that none of the children ever forgot. She concluded her lengthy narrative by saying that children now are not spanked frequently enough.

My colleague followed. Uncertain about how completely the audience was able to appreciate this narrative and what they might make of the unexpected reference to spanking, she confronted this issue directly. She began by thanking the elder and alerting the audience to the importance of the narrative they had just heard, explaining that it was rarely shared with strangers and that they were fortunate that an elder was speaking to them so frankly about things usually discussed only among closely connected acquaintances. She explained that this was one of many narratives addressing fundamental issues of respect between humans and other living beings. She pointed out that people in her community do not make a distinction between human affairs and the physical environment, and that the Western idea of environment as a redeemable object to be "saved" was unfamiliar to elders. The reference to spanking, she noted, might best be understood as a concern elders sometimes express about lack of discipline, rather than referring to a representative practice. She went on to talk about how specific stories convey the inseparability of environment from everyday life.

A second speaker adopted a different strategy, one that works effectively in many meetings. He spoke of the concept of respect — respectful behavior toward other human beings and between humans and nonhumans. Accustomed to using this language to speak to large audiences, he may have seemed to some to overgeneralize by using such phrases as "we always respected our elders" and "we always respected our women." When an audience member requested a clearer definition of the term "respect," this panelist responded, again conventionally, that it is impossible to translate some concepts from indigenous languages to English. The previous panelist, trying to formulate a more optimistic response, proposed that while "respect" is indeed an English word used only recently, it might be thought of as referring to attention to subtlety, especially in the relationships among humans, and between humans and other living things.

A third panelist, possibly observing the difficulty of cross-cultural translation in this setting, framed her presentation with reference to the importance of cardinal points and the sacred medicine wheel to indigenous people. Even though the concept of the medicine wheel lacks historical

roots in the Subarctic, this panelist may have judged that it would be recognizable to her audience, and she was the only one of five speakers to elicit
applause. In experiments to reach broad audiences who come with universalistic expectations and expect to understand what they hear, familiar
strategies are inevitably the most effective in the short term, but they too
have costs.

In making public presentations, speakers have limited options. They may
construct their arguments by setting local concepts in opposition to Western concepts — partly in order to make the distinctions clear. This usually
involves drawing a contrast between an indigenous religious self (grounded
in familiar symbols like medicine wheels or respect) and a Western materi-
alist "other." Such boundaries may be rhetorically effective, but asserting
them puts indigenous people in the unenviable situation of having to live
up to unreasonable and unrealistic standards. In such situations tradition
becomes treated as purity, modernity as corruption, and wearing blue jeans
or eating pizza as evidence of inauthenticity.

CONSTITUTING KNOWLEDGE?

Discussions of what constitutes knowledge fit into familiar debates — about
our tendency to fragment understanding of the world into categories like
nature or culture, and about our human inclination to hold the world together through narrative storytelling. Issues of knowledge, power, and
voice, familiar topics in social sciences, are now entering environmental
sciences, generating questions about how far we should embrace models
characterized by linear relations and described in mathematical equations.
Postmodernism's thesis that knowledge in the contemporary world is always and everywhere contested has gone a long way to challenge master
narratives of scientific progress.

But postmodernism is now a model seriously interrogated. Anthony
Giddens responds that though uncertainty is understandable, we have
come to accept the idea of a postmodern world only because change occurs
at such a disorienting pace that we have never grasped the complexities of
modernity, and that if we did we would see its universalizing tendencies
increasing rather than diminishing.[56] Bruno Latour goes further, suggesting that we have not yet even *become* modern.[57] Defining modernity as the
successful (if impossible) separation of nature from culture, he identifies
1989 as a critical year. The fall of the Berlin Wall demonstrated human
incapacity for grand social engineering in the same year that major environ-

mental conferences in Paris, Amsterdam, and London demonstrated our inability to "fix" the environment. Northern aboriginal people may not make firm distinctions between nature and culture, but neither do the rest of us, Latour argues, and the proof lies in our production of hybrids like zygotes, hydroelectric power dams, and holes in the ozone layer that are both natural and cultural objects. Our flawed categorical distinction between "nature" and "culture" is a by-product of our own arbitrary classification systems. Nature, in other words, is not a "natural" object. Our categories no longer fend off confusion. Viewed in this light, attempts to sweep indigenous knowledge into outmoded categories seems seriously defective.

Investigating the variety of ways humans construct knowledge has long been a central concern of anthropology. Anthropology's main contribution has been to formulate this in a holistic sense, emphasizing connections between social worlds and ideas. If some of the more acrimonious debates in the humanities and social sciences fragment along a materialist/idealist axis, anthropology has more often tried to show how material circumstances and ideas are *both* concrete social products, how they interact, and especially how local concepts and formulations can complicate hegemonic, commonsense globalizing agendas, often in surprising ways.

A few months after Mrs. Ned addressed her audience in the southern Yukon, in a very different part of the world British social anthropologists held their 1983 decennial conference formulated around the problem of how to make anthropological constructions of knowledge more relevant — in other words, how to encourage their appropriation. Reassessing that initiative a decade later, Marilyn Strathern summarizes the startling range of settings in which such appropriation is happening — from memoranda on "the culture of the workplace" being issued by corporations like British Petroleum and the bodies governing universities to public discussions of culture in the art world. Recontextualizing knowledge, Strathern points out, is not and never has been a neutral activity, even though it produces some appropriations that are more welcome than others. No one, least of all anthropologists, can act as the gatekeeper controlling how constructs get used, but we can evaluate the proliferating consequences of a translation project that may once have seemed more straightforward. One important aspect of a concept like indigenous knowledge, she notes, is that it has made visible the division between anthropology's claims and the claims of those whose ideas it studies.[58]

Pierre Bourdieu might take a more pessimistic view. Referring to the inevitable damage that occurs when ideas are separated from the settings in which they are produced, he suggests that repatriating exported products is both naive and dangerous, since it provides a simplified instrument of objectification. Knowledge in hunting societies is encoded at critical points in a belief system, sustained over centuries, that conceptualizes animals and humans as sharing a common world and their connections as mutually sustaining. When it becomes incorporated into a Western framework, it is reconstituted to formalize relationships between people and becomes embedded in hierarchy and inequality.

One of the many things I learned from working with Mrs. Ned and her contemporaries is that their extensive knowledge is not amenable to direct questions, nor can it be easily formulated as a set of rules. It must be demonstrated so that others can see how it is used in practice. Such knowledge is a relational concept, more like a verb than a noun, more process than product, and it cannot easily be construed as a written, formally encoded, reified product. Once it is, and once it becomes authorized in this way, it begins to accumulate different meanings, a topic explored in subsequent chapters.

What are the consequences of categorical practices that distance people from lived experience? How does authorizing knowledge change its social function? Is a passion for universalizing peculiar to the West, or is it part of a more global process? How northern local knowledge becomes bound into larger narratives and whether it can maintain its own integrity remains to be seen, as does the form such transformations may take in different geopolitical circumstances.

4

Confronting Cultural Erasure:
Images of Society in
Klondike Gold Rush Narratives

The Canadian economic historian Harold Innis developed a deep and enduring interest in oral tradition. Best known for his economic thesis that mercantile capitalism inevitably produces margins as it exploits them, he attributed Canada's very existence to profits it offered imperial Britain, both as a source of unprocessed staples — furs, gold, cod, and timber — and as a market for commodities manufactured in distant industrial centers.[1] Investigating how empire manages the awkward problem of administering far-flung territories, Innis was drawn to history of communications. He argued that a crucial feature of administration is classification and control of activities in the hinterland and authorization of official observations, categories, and statistics in written texts. Although this undertaking is conventionally rationalized as both producing knowledge and serving the interests of those administered, it invariably occurs at the expense of existing regional traditions. Colonialism is simultaneously economic and intellectual.[2]

He went on to investigate historical mechanisms by which literacy has displaced the authority of the spoken word, tracing the demise of oral tradition in Egypt, Babylonia, Greece, and Rome. He came to view Socrates as the last great exponent of oral tradition and his death at the beginning of the fourth century B.C. as coinciding with a shift from customary law to formalized judicial codes.[3] Until then, Innis maintained, oral tradition had given vitality to the written word and had actively prevented concentration of power because a society that accords orality a central place could not be disciplined to the point of political unity.[4] Innis was especially intrigued by the ways oral tradition worked in conjunction with writing to provide a model for dialogue, which he saw as a model for social action.[5] "My bias is with the oral tradition . . . and with the necessity of capturing something of its spirit," he concluded. "The quantitative pressure of modern knowledge has been responsible for the decay of oral dialectic and conversation."[6]

Innis's views about the creative potential of oral tradition mirrored those of his contemporary Mikhail Bakhtin, also writing during the 1930s and 1940s, though from more constrained circumstances in Stalinist Russia. Neither could have encountered the other's work, but their approaches were similarly eclectic. Bakhtin, like Innis, was drawn to the open-ended possibilities inherent in oral dialogue and the thoroughness with which totalitarian regimes worked to suppress it. He saw what he called the "dialogic," relational possibilities of conversational storytelling as a model intrinsically opposing authoritarian speech. In terms applying equally to the capitalist frontier of subarctic Canada and the communist frontier of subarctic Russia, Bakhtin formulated the problem of history as its tendency to foster apparent randomness — for the order of events seemingly to disintegrate. And he saw active narrative storytelling as a constraining, countervailing force, working to hold things together. His larger point mirrors that made by Innis: narrative challenges hegemonic institutions.[7]

Ironically, Innis carried out his economic studies in northern Canada and his historical investigation of classical oral tradition without ever seeming to connect the two. Despite a prodigious appetite for labor-intensive research that took him across northern Canada and an open admiration for the work of his colleague Edward Sapir on indigenous languages, he never seemed to juxtapose his economic analysis with living oral traditions in his own country, reporting regretfully that "we have no history of [oral tradition] except as . . . revealed darkly through the written or printed word."[8] One of economic staples Innis turned his attention to was gold, that most liquid of commodities, which can be traded for any other. He attributed Canada's westward expansion to Britain's search for gold, found in extraordinary quantities in the extreme Northwest.[9] Had he been aware of some of the interplay between oral traditions and writing occurring in the encounters between the expanding state and indigenous residents of the Klondike goldfields, he might have observed dynamics similar to those that so intrigued him in ancient Greece — the processes set in motion when writing began first to overwhelm narrative traditions, then to actively domesticate or suppress them.

This chapter examines alternative accounts of two events that are now footnotes in recorded histories of the Klondike gold rush. In each case, writing helped to authorize official reports. But the same events also appear in orally narrated life stories I recorded with elderly Tagish and Tutchone women, who incorporated versions of these incidents into the stories of their own lives. One set of narratives concerns the original discovery in 1896 that triggered the rush; the other concerns conflict between Tagish people and prospectors passing through their territory two years later, resulting in the Territory's first murder trial. Elsewhere I have discussed each event separately with reference to the advantages of incorporating perspectives from oral tradition in historical reconstruction,[10] but my questions here differ and are closer to those Pierre Bourdieu raised about the symbolic power of language. Accounts of the past, including oral storytelling, are not just abstract objects of study, texts for analysis; their telling is bound up in social-historical and power relations. What consequences follow when different narrative models intersect on a "frontier" where they are accorded unequal social weight?

When images of the Klondike gold rush appear in the larger world, they usually echo clear-cut narratives of the frontier. What seems to fascinate readers of Robert Service's poems about "a land where the mountains are nameless" or Jack London's drama of individual men in stark confrontation with nature is their clarity, enhanced by elements bound up in North Atlantic folklore about gold. Remembered as a "poor man's gold rush," the gold strikes in 1896 coincided with a world depression and seemed to offer opportunities to thousands of unemployed men.

The paradox, of course, is that the mountains were *not* nameless and were home to people rooted to place by narratives of connection.[11] To indigenous people, North Atlantic myths of individual autonomy set in opposition to a hostile land were probably incomprehensible, so little did the frames of reference overlap. If the problem facing individual prospectors in the late 1890s was how to escape economic constraints and forge autonomous identities, the problem for indigenous families was how to hold communities together and maintain networks of connection in the face of overwhelming pressures brought by the influx of thirty thousand to forty thousand men traveling through their territories. Although we do not have even rudimentary census figures for the upper Yukon River before the twentieth century, comparative figures from the adjacent Northwest Coast show population losses on the order of two-thirds by the 1890s from epidemics of smallpox and measles.[12] Oral accounts indicate that diseases were also decimating interior families during the same period. The gold rush was ultimately part of a larger, less glamorous operation than our folklore acknowledges — the expansion of the new Canadian state into the margins of northwestern North America. As Innis suggests, the most pervasive effect was a new regional infrastructure — forms of legal and political organization, largely established through writing.

Two sets of narratives are summarized here. The first initially appears to be about a unique individual, Skookum Jim, or Keish, whose name is officially linked with the "discovery" of gold on the Klondike River.[13] The second is more apparently a story about communities: the death of a white prospector and the subsequent trial of four Tagish men charged with his murder cast into sharp relief conflicting ideas about law and collective responsibility. I argue here that one critical difference in these narratives is the way they construct the categories "individual" and "society." I suggest that models of connection and autonomy collide in frontier cultural encounters and that the boundaries are *not* coterminous. Nevertheless, when indigenous stories become subsumed within official frontier narratives that make sense of them using taken-for-granted categories, combining them can carry serious consequences. The administrative penchant for documenting, classifying, and authorizing accounts of such events has ensured an extensive written archive that outweighs the more lightly narrated oral versions. Any attempt to evaluate them retrospectively has to take account of their relative placement in *hierarchies* of narrative.

SKOOKUM JIM AND THE DISCOVERY OF GOLD
Written Accounts

A central figure in all accounts about the discovery of gold in the Yukon is a Tagish man named Skookum Jim.[14] When William Ogilvie employed him in 1887 as a packer to transport supplies over the Chilkoot Pass, he marveled at the heavy loads Keish could carry, so the Chinook word Skookum, or "strong," was added to his English name.[15] Ogilvie went on to become the Yukon Territory's first commissioner and later published an official account of the gold rush after interviewing the participants about the staking of Discovery claim. He describes Jim's association with the white prospector George Carmack, who was by then the husband of Jim's sister Kate. In 1896 Jim, Kate, Carmack, and Jim's sister's son Charlie reportedly set out from their home at Carcross near the head of the Yukon River system, to go prospecting downriver on the Yukon. In *Klondike,* Pierre Berton paints a one-dimensional picture of Skookum Jim, describing him stereotypically as a "giant of a man . . . with eagle's nose, straight as a gun barrel . . . the best hunter and trapper on the river." But he goes on to speculate that "Jim longed to be a white man, in other words a prospector. . . . He differed from the others in his tribe in that he displayed the white man's kind of ambition." [16]

Near the Klondike River they met another prospector, Robert Henderson, who told Carmack he knew a good place to look for gold and was willing to share the information with him, but not with his Indian companions. Incensed, Jim, Charlie, and Carmack went on their way, and when they accidentally found gold a few days later very close to the place Henderson had identified, they chose not to go back to tell him. In the rapid staking rush that followed, Henderson missed out and became the tragic figure in the drama, defeated by his own hubris. [17]

Jim, Carmack, Kate, and Charlie went briefly to Seattle with their new-found wealth, and their escapades there were reported with considerable glee by newspapers — possibly apocryphal stories about Kate blazing the path to her hotel room with a hatchet, stories of Kate and Jim and Carmack throwing nuggets from their hotel room window — gold rush stories typical of the genre. [18] Then life began to sour. Carmack married a white woman and sent Kate back to Carcross. Charlie drowned in 1908 after falling off the Carcross bridge. Jim continued to prospect, making lengthy trips along the Teslin, Pelly, Macmillan, Stewart, and Upper Liard Rivers, but he never made another major strike, and his health began to deteriorate. He died in 1916. [19]

Oral Accounts

In recounting stories of their own lives, both Angela Sidney and Kitty Smith gave significant place to stories of people whose experiences were entwined with their own. Their accounts draw on foundational narratives about relationships between human and superhuman beings who share the world and about expectations attached to moiety and to clan membership. The importance of exogamous, matrilineal moieties and Tlingit-named clans was strengthened in the southern Yukon interior during the nineteenth century by trade and intermarriage with coastal Tlingit. Within any family, adult siblings were careful to observe rules of avoidance; however, the eldest brother had a definite commitment to see to the welfare of his sisters who were members of his clan. [20]

Skookum Jim was the cousin of Mrs. Sidney's father: their mothers were sisters, making the two men brothers by the Tagish system of kinship reckoning, and consequently he was her uncle. She knew him from the time she was a child until his death in 1916 and helped nurse him during his final illness. Kitty Smith married Skookum Jim's sister's son; after their marriage, she came to know her husband's aunt, Kate Carmack, and heard the story of the discovery many times from her.

Jim, whose Tlingit name was Keish, was born during the mid-1800s at the height of trade between Tlingit and Athapaskans. His Tagish mother and Tlingit father married in a conventional alliance between coast and interior, and they had eight children who reached adulthood — two sons and six daughters.

Mrs. Sidney's account emphasizes not the exceptional man, but his social context: his acquisition of a frog helper, his encounter with "Wealth Woman," or Tl'anaxéedákw, his exemplary assumption of responsibility for his sisters. Elsewhere, fuller accounts appear in the words of women who narrated their individual life stories,[21] but Mrs. Sidney's account provides an explanation very different from that in gold rush literature. She interprets Keish's behavior from this perspective rather than as reflecting any desire to be a prospector or to discover gold. As a young man, he once saved the life of a frog trapped in a deep hole:

He hears something making a noise.
'Whoo . . .' — just like sand pouring down.
So he stopped and listened.
Here there was a ditch alongside the house where they dig up the sand
    and put it on the moss for roofing.
That's what they used, long time ago.

So he went to the edge and he looked down.
Sure enough there was a big frog — coast frogs are bigger than these
    frogs, you know.
Long way from water, too, they said.
Here it was trying to jump up and trying to get back but it fell down.
Kept doing that, I don't know how long.
Gravel fell down with him — that's what's making the noise.

Anyway, Skookum Jim saw it, so he looked around for a board.
Here he found a board and he shoved it down that hole
And then that frog crawled on that board.

So Uncle Skookum Jim lifted it up.
He lifted it up and carried it and took it down to the creek —
There must be a creek there — this is Dyea.
So anyway, he left it there.
He let it go.

[Later the same frog returned to him on two occasions, first in its animal form when it healed a wound he had sustained:]

And here he feels something tickling him there —
That's why he looked down.
Here it was a frog licking that sore place.
That's what it was that woke him up.

My mother saw it and then she just got a board or something and put the
    frog on that.
It never jumped too, nothing, just stayed like that.

Well, my mother used to have silk thread and beads and stuff too.
She was good then — she wasn't blind then.
They gave that frog silk thread and some beads.
They put swan down feathers all around him too.[22]
Then she took it down to the creek and left it there.
That's payment for Skookum Jim to that frog.
They paid him.

[Still later, she says, the frog appeared to him in the form of a woman who directed him toward his fortune downriver with a gold-tipped walking cane:]

"You saved me one time," she said.
"I was almost starving and I was just about going to die.
And here you saved me one time.
And I'm the one that saved you too when you were sick.
When you were sick, I saved you.
I helped you.
I medicined you.
That's why you got better."
That's what that lady's supposed to tell him because he dreamed that.

And that lady told him when she gave him that walking stick:
"You're going to find the bottom of this walking stick.
You're going to find it this way."
So he looked at it, and gee, everything is shining, looks like gold.
"Look this way," she said, pointing to Atlin, "Look this way."
He looks and sees just like a searchlight coming up.
"That's not for you though; that's for somebody else.[23]
You go down this way and you're going to have your luck,
Your walking stick" [indicating down the Yukon River].
That's what that lady is supposed to tell him.

Tagish people credit this animal helper with a significant role in his eventual discovery of gold.

Keish's encounter with Tl'anaxéedákw was equally significant. She is a complex mythological figure who rewards anyone who hears her, catches her, and follows a prescribed ritual. Both Jim and Charlie heard her but were unable to overtake her, says Mrs. Sidney. Consequently the money that came their way after the discovery did not last:

They were camping there in the lakeside when they heard that baby crying.
Skookum Jim heard it — then Dawson Charlie heard it.
Here they got up to go after it.
Patsy [Henderson] went with them — he went a little way, but he got
    scared, started crying — he was still a kid yet.

"Crazy me," he tells us later.
"That's why I never get rich."

And they tried to chase it around — around the lake.
It kept disappearing.
That's why their money didn't last after they found gold.
They found money all right, but it didn't last.

Catharine McClellan has compared accounts of both the frog helper story and the story of Tl'anaxéedákw, showing how these narratives are part of a larger body of indigenous oral literature that provided a conventional framework for explaining unprecedented events.[24] She suggests that Tagish people were particularly concerned about maintaining intellectual consistency when they explained the dramatic contradictions accompanying the gold rush. Using a customary cognitive model helped make strange events seem more comprehensible.

But while superhuman explanations may have helped Tagish people to explain the discovery, Mrs. Sidney and Mrs. Smith also give considerable weight to Keish's assumption of social responsibility. Keish and his brother both married coastal Tlingit women, but during the 1890s the elder brother died in one of the influenza epidemics sweeping the coast, leaving Jim solely responsible for the safety of his sisters.

Three of Keish's sisters also married coastal men, but in each case illness and death took a toll. The first sister contracted influenza and died shortly after her marriage. Since marriages were essentially contracts between kin groups rather than between individuals, her husband's clan requested that a sister be sent to replace her, and the Tagish family complied, sending Aagé. But before this marriage could take place the groom fell ill and died, and his maternal nephew (who was his sociological equivalent) was selected to replace him as Aagé's new husband. They had a daughter, but just before the birth of their second child, *he* also died in difficult circumstances. The young widow asked to be allowed to return to Tagish, and her husband's family agreed, but only on condition that she leave her eldest child with them to be raised by her cowife. The marriages, the deaths, and the loss of her first child had taken a toll, and for a variety of reasons Aagé asked her mother to look after her other daughter when she left with a prospector, remembered only as "Mr. Wilson." In this way she became the first of Skookum Jim's sisters to go downriver with a white prospector.

A third sister, Kate or Shaaw Tláa, also married a coastal Tlingit man, who then died of influenza. As in her sister's case, Kate's husband's Tlingit clan wanted to keep her and give her an appropriate husband. But her mother, back in Tagish, was so deeply distraught by the loss of her daughters that she insisted Kate return. The startling number of deaths was forcing people to improvise when remarriage of widows was concerned: a fourth sister had recently taken a white prospector and trader named George Carmack as her husband, but she too died of influenza, which was by now working its way into the interior. Kate's mother insisted it was more appropriate for Kate to return to Tagish as the wife of her deceased sister's white husband than to remain on the coast. Partnerships between brothers-in-law were very important, and after Carmack's incorporation into this family, he and Skookum Jim became allies. But shortly afterward, Carmack and Kate followed her sister downriver, where rumors of gold were attracting prospectors. A fifth sister died a tragic death when she and her daughter were caught in an unexpected winter storm on a mountain pass as they returned from a funeral potlatch (see fig. 3).

In a very few years, then, Keish lost one brother and three sisters: of the surviving three sisters, two had gone down the river with white prospectors, leaving only one still in Tagish. Local people insist that Skookum Jim was *not* prospecting with Carmack in 1896, that he was living on the southern lakes preoccupied with learning the whereabouts of his two sisters. In Angela Sidney's words,

In the first place, he wasn't looking for gold. Skookum Jim went downriver to look for his two sisters because he missed them. They were gone two years already — he didn't know if his two sisters were alive or not. That's why he thought he'd go down the river too — to see if he could find his sisters, Aagé and Kate. They were strict about that kind of thing, old people.

She went on to describe how a party was selected to go, who was chosen, who stayed behind, and why. Her own parents went part way, as far as Lake Laberge, but turned back when they considered how difficult it would be for their elderly parents to survive the winter if they were delayed.

Kitty Smith's husband, Billy, was one of the young men who was left behind to look after his mother. Mrs. Smith heard the story many times after her marriage from the perspective of Kate, who was living in Carcross by then. She also heard repeatedly about Jim's anxiety that winter because of his sisters' disappearance. Dawson Charlie finally insisted on going with his maternal uncle to search for the women.

In each account, the actual discovery of gold is almost incidental to the point of the main story — Skookum Jim's journey down the river to find his missing sisters. The pattern of a protagonist who uses special powers to undertake a journey to find his wife or sisters is familiar in narratives from this region.[25] Oral traditions use metaphors of connection to explain Skookum Jim's actions just as written records rely on metaphors of frontier individualism, but the explanatory narratives in each case reflect different understandings of how society works.

Stories of the aftermath focus on the interplay between wealth and tragedy. After gaining the initial wealth, each man became caught up in a lifestyle that cost him his family. Keish's wife left him and returned to her coastal Tlingit family. Her parents were disturbed by their daughter's violation of custom and brought her back to Carcross, but Skookum Jim no longer seemed to care. She took their son, and Jim kept their daughter Daisy. Dawson Charlie's wife left too; alcohol played a part in his accidental death a few years later. Kate returned to Carcross alone, abandoned by George, who took their daughter south with him.

Written accounts, then, portray Skookum Jim in an individualistic frontier genre — as a rather flat and one-dimensional character, "an Indian who
wanted to be a white man," the lone prospector-trapper whose efforts are
ultimately rewarded. Oral accounts from members of his community who
knew him personally describe him as a man impelled by social and cultural
motives — a strong sense of responsibility for his sisters and an ability to
communicate with and be guided by superhuman helpers. In both versions
he exhibits qualities of an "ideal man," but those ideals differ dramatically.
I will set aside for the moment the issue of how such contrasting genres
may reflect and enforce contrasting views of individual achievement while
we consider another incident from the same period.

THE DEATHS AT MARSH LAKE
Written Records

The second event chronicled here is less prominent in published accounts
of the gold rush, usually appearing only as a sentence or footnote in
books praising the success of the Northwest Mounted Police in suppressing
"hostile Indians." [26] I had encountered official versions of Skookum Jim's
achievement well before I heard contrasting stories from elders who knew
him, but it was verbal testimonies about the ricocheting consequences of
the arrests of four young Tagish men in 1898 that initially led me to written
records. Annual reports of the Northwest Mounted Police and newspaper
accounts from the *Klondike Nugget* yielded some information, and court
transcripts at the Public Archives of Canada even more. When I first read
them, however, I did not sufficiently appreciate Innis's point about the
links between empire and communication and the need for early Yukon
officials to scatter independent and sometimes conflicting reports to various administrative destinations. Letters and reports to the secretary of
state, the Department of Justice, Northwest Mounted Police headquarters,
and various comptrollers and commissioners were later assembled and are
now stored in the Public Archives of Canada. Comparing them connects
cascading layers of narrative — stories of a trial, of a hastily constructed
administrative apparatus, of indignant miners, and of indigenous people
whose lives continued to be affected by the events — and illuminates more
general issues surrounding the social life of these stories a century later.
As with narratives about Skookum Jim, differing conceptions of individual and community animate the accounts. Here, though, the stereotypes in written accounts shift from "good Indians" (who, like Skookum

Jim, appear superficially understandable) to "bad Indians" (who make trouble).[27]

According to police and trial records,[28] on 10 May 1898 a wounded prospector, Christian Fox, stumbled into a cabin at Marsh Lake and reported that he and his partner Billy Meehan had been fired on by Indians and that Meehan was dead. Ten days earlier, the two had reasoned that by turning up the McClintock River and portaging their goods across the divide to the Hootelinqua (now Teslin) River, they could take a shortcut to Dawson City. About twelve miles up the McClintock they broke through the spring ice and abandoned this plan, stopping to build a boat for their return trip (see map 2).

On 2 May they met two Tagish men, Frank and Joe, returning from the Hootelinqua to Marsh Lake and short of food. The four camped together that night, and the following morning the Native men moved on, camping less than a mile away and returning the following day with a third man named Dawson. During the week the two camps had frequent and friendly contact, and a week later the Tagish were joined by a party from Marsh Lake — a man named Jim, three women, and two children. Once the boat was finished, Frank asked for a ride downriver for himself and two of the other men and, this agreed, helped the prospectors load up. At the last moment the Tagish men seemed to change their minds, so Fox and Meehan pushed off alone at about 11 : 00 A.M. on 10 May. Twenty minutes later they were fired on from the shore. Meehan was killed instantly, and a bullet entered Fox's shoulder. He recognized Joe holding a gun and saw others fading into the bush. Aware that he was drifting toward them, he paddled with his good arm and reached the opposite shore, headed for the nearby hill (known in the Tagish language as Mbesh T'áy) to avoid detection, and followed its crest to Marsh Lake and the cabin of William McIntosh, who summoned a doctor and sent a message to the Northwest Mounted Police station at Tagish, thirty miles away. A posse of miners hastened upriver to retrieve the boat and found the prospectors' goods piled next to the river.

Corporal Edwin Rudd, assigned to the case, arrived the following day, interviewed Fox, and headed up the McClintock with several assistants. On the evening of 12 May they found Jim's camp and more of the prospectors' belongings. Jim denied killing Meehan, protesting that he had "shot but not killed" the surviving prospector. He was arrested (as was one of the children, "Rabbits," later released) and jailed at Tagish. On 15 May Rudd discovered tracks heading toward Lake Laberge, and he and his men went directly there. During the following week, police kept under surveillance

the Native camps at both Marsh Lake and Lake Laberge, forbidding anyone to help the fugitives. On 23 May the men surrendered and were arrested. Frank, the youngest, offered to lead Rudd to Meehan's body, which
was recovered from the river and brought to Tagish for a postmortem.

The prisoners were detained for two months at the Tagish police post
until a location for their trial could be determined. During their incarcera-
tion, they were variously photographed, sketched, and described by travelers passing by the post on their way to Dawson. A Presbyterian minister
was moved by their interest in stories of Jesus.[29] A French traveler seemed
mildly disappointed by their ordinary appearance, noting "Rien sur leur
visage impassible ne denotée le criminal" as he sketched them eating
soup.[30] Photographs show them standing in chains — two look self-as-
sured, a third looks less certain, and Frank — still a boy — seems bewildered
and frightened.[31] Their names are recorded in written records as Joe, Jim,
Dawson, and Frank Nantuck. An inscription beneath one photo reads,
"Indians at Tagish Post that shot Meehan and Fox on the McClintock,"
and beneath another, "Group of Murderers, Police Camp, Tagish." At the
trial, their ages were estimated as between fifteen and nineteen, though
some reports guessed that Jim might be as old as twenty.

With political boundaries newly established, the question of proper jurisdiction for a trial arose, demonstrating the complexities of administering
distant territories. The Yukon Territory had just acquired separate legal
status from the Northwest Territories on 13 June 1898, one month after
the incident, and there was enthusiasm for a show trial in the Territory's
new capital, Dawson City. Police Superintendent Steele wrote to his supe-
riors requesting that a judge be brought to Tagish, enabling the men to be
tried close to home and saving the wounded witness a difficult journey.[32]
Weeks after the trial was over, he received a response (written 2 August)
assuring him that a newly appointed judge would be arriving soon to hold
the trial in Tagish. In one of many communication lapses related to this
case, Steele replied on 23 August, almost a month after the trial had ended,
that he had already sent the prisoners to Dawson, where he understood
"they are now undergoing their trial."[33]

The prisoners, meanwhile, were transferred to Dawson City in mid-July
and were tried on 28 and 29 July 1898 in the Supreme Court of the Northwest Territories, Provisional Judicial District of the Yukon, with the Hon-
orable Mr. Justice Thomas McGuire presiding. A Dawson City newspaper,
the *Klondike Nugget*, conveys the general atmosphere in which the trial
was to occur, with a 16 June headline blaring "Indians Shoot White Men

to Rob Them of Their Supplies" introducing an article describing this as "one of the most cold-blooded crimes committed since the rush to the gold fields began." Six weeks later on 27 July, the day before the trial began, the same newspaper was confidently predicting conviction in headlines announcing "Deliberately Tried to Kill Their Benefactors for the Outfits" and "The Treacherous Instincts of the Aborigines Will Get Their Necks Stretched with Hemp."

After the trial, on 3 August the judge submitted to the secretary of state an official handwritten narrative clarifying his procedures. It is worth summarizing at the outset, because it includes background information not in court transcripts. He begins by noting that the prisoners were "very imperfectly acquainted with English," speaking "Tlinkat," and expresses his conviction that the interpreters selected by the court, "two gentlemen, McLoed and Lear, who swore they could speak and understand the language of the Indians,"[34] were competent to ensure that "the proceedings [were] very carefully and fully explained . . . to the prisoners charged." The judge went on to explain how, through these interpreters, he spelled out the alternatives available to the prisoners — for instance, the kinds of excuses that might be considered legitimate. The prisoners "were asked if they had any excuse or justification or reason for so doing — any quarrel — but they said they and the whites were 'good friends' but some white man a year or two years ago had killed two Indians. On these statements, I entered a verdict of 'Guilty' in the case of these two Indians 'Joe Nantuck' and 'Dawson Nantuck.' Jim said he did not kill Billy — and a plea of Not Guilty was entered for him."[35]

Joe and Frank were tried separately so that the Crown could use young Frank as a material witness against Jim. Jim's trial was held first, on 28 July, and Frank's was held on 29 July. The court selected a Mr. F. H. Lisle "an advocate of many years' experience"[36] to act on their behalf. Mr. F. C. Wade was the Crown prosecutor. Names of six local miners were drawn from a hat as jurors for each case. No Native witnesses were called.

Although the accused men undoubtedly understood Tlingit because of long-standing trade with Tlingit neighbors, their first language would have been one of the Athapaskan languages spoken at the head of the Yukon River — Tagish or Southern Tutchone — and Tlingit would have been a second language for them, as it most certainly was for the official interpreters, whatever they swore. In court, however, the issue of translation of cultural categories soon came to outweigh any issues of linguistic translation. Critically, this was *not* a miner's lynching trial (though many spectators might have preferred that) but a reasoned, careful demonstration of British judicial sensibility brought to the frontier — a demonstration as much to American miners as to Indians that the law of empire now prevailed. Frank's appearance as a witness, on 28 July, initially faltered on the issue of how he could take the all-important oath, ceremonially affirming the link between literacy (the Bible) and truth. The judge began with a series of questions, all directed to Frank through the interpreters: "Is he a Christian? Has he any knowledge of God? Has he any religion of his own at all . . . any fixed and clear belief in a future state of rewards and punishments?" When this yielded no fruitful results, the judge moved to more complex epistemological ground, asking the interpreter to ascertain whether Frank believed that his own death would be "just the same as for a cow or moose or any other animal," a question to which Frank could finally respond in the affirmative. Judge McGuire continued, "I want the interpreter, if he can reach his intelligence, to see if he has anything corresponding to a form of making an oath" (20), to which Frank replied that of course he understood what it meant to tell the truth, and the examination began.[37]

The judge urged Frank to "state his story" (22), but when Frank began to tell the same story as Joe and Dawson, that he and the prospectors were indeed friends but that white men had previously killed two of their friends, it was recorded but went unheard. Frank stated that after these earlier killings he had made up his mind to kill a white man, and he agreed that he had viewed these prospectors as candidates when he first met them. He and the others accused had all decided to kill them without ever really having to discuss it, he insisted. They shared responsibility equally, and (in the words of Frank through his interpreters) they "all had the same mind" and "were all just the same as one of them . . . all just like one" (23–25). When asked whether his older companions had influenced or compelled him to participate, he repeated that "no one told him to do it — it was just made up by all of them — no one man suggested it." He described how they had decided that Joe and Dawson should aim at the stern while he and Jim would shoot at the man in the bow. The outcome of three bullets entering Meehan and only one hitting Fox caused Frank and Jim to categorize their actions as "not successful" rather than as "not guilty."

As the trial progressed, what seemed to incense spectators was the refusal of the accused either to provide elaborate explanations for their actions or to show remorse. Their silence in the courtroom was taken to mean that the "facts" spoke for themselves. Again, the *Klondike Nugget* editorialized on 3 August:

The questions put to the murderers by the judge through the interpreters showed them to be wholly deficient in the most ordinary morals. Their cunning, also, was of a low order. They could plot to destroy the two men in the boat and steal their goods but appeared to be stolidly indifferent to the results of the admissions they were making, though it was repeatedly impressed on them. Questioned about their knowledge of God or a future state, everyone was surprised to find that they knew nothing about either one. Even the "Great Spirit" and the "Happy Hunting Grounds" of the North American Indians were unknown to them.

The judge, who presented himself as a man of reason, was also a man of categories and spelled out for the jurors, in calm detail, the relation between the cultural logic of the court and their collective duty to society. He explained that their duty was "to find as to the facts," while his was "to apply the law to the facts" (28). He instructed them first about categories of killing. Homicide, for instance, included "culpable homicide" and "nonculpable homicide"; culpable homicide could in turn be divided into "manslaughter" and "murder." Murder, he instructed them, was defined by intentionality: where there was an intention to kill plus evidence of killing, there was murder (29). But the judge pointed out that there are instances of "justifiable killing," which he described in gendered terms as including cases when a man shoots to protect himself, his wife, his family, or his house "from robbery or violence." This defense, he said, could transform the definition of killing from murder to common assault.[38] To contrast this with unjustified killings, he drew a metaphorical Venn diagram of this case for the jurors. The accused were friends with the parties they attacked. There was no sudden quarrel. This was not a case of self-defense. Hence he drew the meticulous conclusion that the accused had "no excuse for what they did if, indeed, they did anything" (34).

Another important categorical distinction firmly divided "guilty" from "not guilty," and he reminded the jury of the scrupulousness of the court in clarifying these categories to the accused (31). When Jim was arrested by armed police at his camp in the bush on the evening of 12 May, he was, in the judge's words, "duly warned by the police out of an excess of caution to be careful about making statements because they might be used against him." In other words, he was told *not* to tell his story. But Jim insisted on explaining his actions and, in the words of the judge, "blurted [his story] out without being asked." The judge then reminded the jury that "what [Jim] is said to have said to the interpreter [in the camp] would not be reliable evidence for you to have acted upon" because the police officer testifying in court could have no way of evaluating the accuracy of the translation that night. *But,* said the judge, when the same officer testified in court about his understanding of what Jim had told the interpreter, and that statement, transcribed in court by a court reporter, was translated back to Jim, who agreed that this accurately represented his words at the time of his arrest, *that* became Jim's official story (16–17). Henceforth the judge referred to this as Jim's "admission" (32), adding that "every precaution was taken to obviate even the appearance of asking him anything except was he guilty or not guilty of the charge." By this convoluted reasoning, then, Jim's "story" became one he told in his camp to an interpreter who translated it to a police officer, who in turn told it in court, where it was transcribed by a court reporter and then reinterpreted by (non-Native) translators to the defendant, who was given a final opportunity to choose which of two categories it fell into.

Finally the judge digressed into the area of categories of humanity and put his mind to the contrast between what he called "civilization" (30) and what he called "lower orders of humanity" (33, 34). Noting that the Statute Book makes no distinction, he concluded that neither should he. Proclaiming that all are the same under the law (a position that necessarily erases alternative conceptions of law), he reminded jurors that "we have a great many Indians here and it is important that you should not lightly or carelessly consign one of them to the gallows, but it is just as important that you should not, through any mistaken idea of tenderheartedness or sympathy omit to do that which is a very unpleasant duty . . . but is, nevertheless a duty" (36). He urged caution and advised the jury not to convict if they had reasonable doubt, but he held out that final category as an option only if they determined that one of the accused was actually absent at the time of the shooting. In Frank's case, he suggested the possibility of clemency.

The judge ended his instructions to the jury by underscoring distinctions between individual and society. If four men collectively agreed to do this, each was individually responsible for carrying out the act, regardless of which bullets actually killed William Meehan (33, 36). The jurors, on the other hand, represented "society," and in the judge's words, "You are now acting as arbiters [for Our Sovereign Lady the Queen] in a matter which affects the safety and peace and lives of human beings" (35).

The jury found Jim guilty. In Frank's case, they recommended clemency because of his age and his willingness to discuss the events. Newspaper accounts continued to symbolize the young men as representatives of "savagery," contrasting them with "order" brought by the judiciary. Not only did the accused not respond in institutionally appropriate ways in the courtroom, they also failed to conform to the stereotype of noble savages, as revealed by their lack of knowledge about the "Happy Hunting Ground." When the prisoners failed to play their expected part, editorial attention shifted to the judge, noting that "not one in the courtroom but was sympathetically affected by the venerable judge's suppressed emotions at sentencing those intellectual children to death." [39]

No witnesses had been called on behalf of the accused, but almost immediately the Anglican bishop, William Bompas, petitioned the Yukon's commissioner and the Department of Justice in Ottawa, in two letters, one cosigned by six missionaries, commenting on the "exceptional intelligence of at least two of the young men" and asking that the sentences be commuted and the prisoners put in the care of the mission. Bompas made three points. First, he argued that customary laws in the region were strict and could escalate if the four men were seen to be unfairly executed. Second, he pointed out that both government and miners had been seizing Indian land without any compensation. Third, he noted that despite rumors of Natives' being harmed and clear cases where they had been fired on by whites, the local people had been largely hospitable and that such a verdict worked against continuing good relations. [40]

From here the rules must have become even more opaque to the prisoners. The sentence was to be carried out on 1 November 1898. At the end of October, word came that Frank's sentence had been commuted to life imprisonment in the British Columbia Penitentiary, but during subsequent appeals no attempt was made to act on this. Appeals were launched on various grounds: first, that 1 November was "All Saints' Day," and the prisoners could not be hanged on a statutory holiday, even one celebrated only in Quebec; second, that the sheriff responsible for carrying out the executions had not been properly sworn in. At the last moment, on the morning of 1 November, the execution was postponed to 2 March 1899. A further appeal was launched in January, charging that the prisoners had been tried in the wrong court. The Yukon Territory was established as a separate jurisdiction by the time of the trial, but no court was yet in place; consequently the case was heard by the Supreme Court of the Northwest

Territories, which by then had no legal jurisdiction over Yukon affairs. Once again the execution was postponed, this time until August.[41]

As these appeals dragged on, the prisoners became demoralized and ill. Both Frank and Joe died in February 1899 of "pulmonary troubles." At the time, the sheriff in charge noted that the other two brothers were "commencing to be sick, in the same way as the other two were, and I think it is very doubtful if either of the remaining condemned Indians are alive to suffer the penalty of the law on the 4th August, 1899."[42] The police officer in charge noted in his annual report that "the suspense of a long reprieve had very much disheartened these Indians." Jim and Dawson Nantuck were executed on 4 August 1899.

The Oral Accounts

This event had enormous repercussions for Native families in the southern Yukon and is recalled painfully and in considerable detail by elders. Again, oral accounts from Yukon elders provide us with an interpretation quite different from that in written records. They elaborate on the response Judge McGuire heard, but dismissed, when he asked the accused men to present him with some excuse for their behavior.

Kitty Smith was a child at the time, living two hundred kilometers west of Tagish, at Dalton post. Her mother, Tatl'èrma, had moved there to live with her husband's family after her marriage. One of the four men accused of killing the prospector was Tatl'èrma's brother, and the young woman was "called home" immediately along with other members of the Crow moiety. Two of Tatl'èrma's uncles, her mother's brothers, came with the news that Tatl'èrma's mother was in deep despair because of her son's arrest and removal to Dawson City and no longer wanted to live. "When her son was hanged, my grandma said, 'I don't know if I can forget it, that Whitehorse River way. I wish they would throw me in the water when I die so I could follow down. My son got lost that way." Tatl'èrma returned with her uncles, arriving back at Marsh Lake at the height of an influenza epidemic. She became ill and died without ever seeing her child again.

Mrs. Smith described what she was able to piece together about the events many years later. Sometime early in 1898, she said, an old lady from Marsh Lake either found or was given a can containing some white powder which she mistakenly assumed was baking powder. The powder may actually have been arsenic, used in the refining of gold.[43]

I don't know what happened. . . . Indians don't know. . . . I guess something was wrong. I don't know. . . . Somebody found that can, some whiteman place. A little baking powder can. An old lady found it — an old lady just like me. People have got flour. A young fellow was staying with his grandfather. They've got flour and, well, they ask for baking powder.

"This looks like the one that cooks bread." Well, nobody can read, you know.

They cooked the bread. It raised the bread, too! Then they gave it to the dog, first time. But the dog died too slow; that was the trouble. Then the boy died and then his grandpa died. They use that stuff to make gold, they say. That's why I guess they did that.

Used to be they didn't kill people for nothing, long time ago. When they get over it, then they're friends together. This way, however many people died, they're going to pay them. Then they're good friends again, see? . . . They kill them to make it even. Then they make a big party. They make a big song.[44]

Angela Sidney heard the story from her mother, who was at Tagish when it happened and knew the actors. Her understanding is that the can was found by the boy who died. He took it home to his opposite-moiety aunt, his uncle Tagish Jim's first wife, Gokhakat. At her urging, he made some bread. He fed it to the dog, then ate some himself and gave some to an older man, his "grandpa." By the time they realized the dog was dying, it was too late to save the men.[45]

By custom, the responsibility for avenging the deaths fell to clan members of the deceased. Mrs. Sidney states this explicitly: "They were all Crow, all one nation — brothers, cousins — like that." There were conventional, customary ways of resolving such a painful incident, and they were understood by everyone. When a victim was a member of one moiety and the attacker a member of another, formal negotiations were necessary to arrange fair compensation for the death. The social group the attacker belonged to was responsible for opening negotiations. Either the death of a social equivalent of the victim or a negotiated repayment in goods would be satisfactory compensation.[46]

Oral accounts suggest that the two prospectors, Meehan and Fox, were seen as representing the "clan" of white people responsible for the incident. The visits the Native men made to the prospectors' camp may have been intended to give the prospectors an opportunity to open negotiations. Mrs. Sidney acknowledges that the two men were chosen randomly as social equivalents of the deceased. She even includes the name of the hill where the Crow men decided to act, Tl'adaake Tene, as part of her story.

There's four of them: John Joe's brother; Whitehorse Billy's brother; that boy whose brother got killed; and one more, the one they call Sagwaaye, I think. Four of them, four boys, they all got hung. They took them down to Dawson.

That was because they shot that whiteman. They were coming down the McClintock River. They were up the river someplace. Here they were coming down again and here these boys were at a place called Tl'adaake Tene, means "on top the hill road." That's what it means, Den k'e [in Tagish language]. They were resting there, and here they saw this boat coming and that boy said: "That's what they do. They go round in the bush all the time. That's their fault my brother died." And he picked up his gun.

The rest of the boys told him, "Don't do it."

Just the same, he started shooting them. And he shot one. And then the other one fell down too and they both float around.

Just before their boat went down the point they see one man get up again. They said, "One man got up again! One man got up again! Anybody got shells?" Shells all gone. Nobody. They say Whitehorse Billy's brother had shells. Just the same he didn't want to give them.

And I just know that part.

But I hear from other people that they drowned. And even that Sagwaaye, he wasn't with them. He was up the road camping someplace. They even took him too. He died for nothing! He was at the camp. They were all Crow, all one nation. Brothers, cousins, like that.[47]

That only one prospector actually died when two people had previously been poisoned may account for the accusation in court that the prospectors' goods were also "stolen." Whatever the interpretation, it is very likely that the four saw themselves as taking absolutely appropriate action to settle the deaths of kinsmen.

But when they returned home and explained what they had done, Mrs. Sidney says, their uncle urged them to flee and go into hiding. They traveled some forty miles across country to Lake Laberge, but there they were advised by an influential chief, Jim Boss,[48] that they had nothing to fear and should return home. Clearly there were conflicting opinions about whether they had reacted correctly or incorrectly in killing the prospector. In Mrs. Smith's words, "Well, they don't know, that time. . . . They don't know police business."

Mrs. Sidney's mother told her daughter years later about going to Tagish post and seeing the men chained: "Here she saw those boys. They all had chains on their feet and a big ball on the end, and she just cried and lifted up her hands toward them. Nobody knew what year it was or how long after they got killed. That's what I heard. That's the way I understand it. That's what my mother told me."

DOCUMENTING JUSTICE

Orally narrated stories have social histories, and their telling bears traces of the situations they emerge from. There are many stories embedded in re-membered accounts of the Klondike gold rush, and during the three-year centenary celebrations spanning 1996–98, some are more likely than others to be discussed, debated, and retold. They persist both because they appeal to the popular imagination and because they are rooted in general social concerns that seemed especially problematic at the time. They explore contradictions in social organization at the same time that they dramatize cultural ideals. More interesting than the question of which versions more accurately account for "what really happened" is what differing versions tell us about the values they commemorate. One critical difference in the narratives is the way they construct categories of individual and society, and especially how boundaries between those categories are established. Another concerns their asymmetry in hierarchies of narrative that foreground some stories and marginalize others.

If stories about Skookum Jim present two contrasting pictures of an emblematic individual, accounts of the Marsh Lake tragedy certainly reveal equally conflicting visions of society and social justice. The disparity reflects a situation where one institutional order has dramatically displaced another in the matter of a few years. The first Northwest Mounted Police inspector, Charles Constantine, reached the area of the upper Yukon River in 1894. Four years later we have the full force of the British judiciary imposing the death sentence on indigenous men for upholding their traditional justice system. And yet "the facts" are essentially unaltered in these contrasting narratives: what changes is the context in which they are interpreted.

Between the discovery of gold by Keish in summer 1896 and the arrest and trial of the Nantuck brothers in summer 1898, more than thirty thousand would-be prospectors and miners converged on one small area of the Klondike River. The newcomers' prototype was Horatio Alger, and the virtues they extolled were individualism and plucky self-reliance. They brought their own myths about both Western and Native societies, and these myths played a significant role in the ways newcomers structured their accounts. Unfamiliar "others" — the indigenous peoples — readily became symbols for contradictory values.[49] "Good Indians" appeared to share some of the values of the newcomers, and Skookum Jim's accidental discovery earned him such dubious compliments as "an exception to his race" and "an Indian who wanted to be a white man." Such interpretation had less to do with qualities Skookum Jim may have exhibited than with the newcomers' desire to confirm the advantages of an emerging social order in which individualism was a value widely shared, if problematic.

But as we have seen, by 1898 Natives were already dealing with unprecedented changes. Individual autonomy was not a troubling issue for Tagish men because the ability to act independently was essential for survival in a hunting society. Their major concern was to maintain integrity of their core social institutions, already under enormous pressure from economic dislocation, illness, and death. Oral accounts from Tagish society show the struggle to achieve consistency between old values and changing circumstances. Oral accounts about Skookum Jim attribute his success not to individualism but to his continuity with long-standing cultural values — his acquisition of an animal helper, his successful encounter with Tl'anaxée-dákw, his efforts to maintain the unity of his Dakl'aweidí clan, and his resolution to carry out his responsibility toward his sisters and nephews.

Accounts of the deaths at Marsh Lake are equally embedded in contrasting ideas about individual and society. For the newcomers, an attack on two prospectors was disconcerting and incomprehensible because it challenged their view of their enterprise. Hence it could only have been perpetrated by "bad Indians." In the writings of these early travelers, indigenous people are always present, but they are portrayed as part of the landscape, as backdrop, not as actors in their own right. Newspaper reports at the time of Meehan's death begin with self-righteous indignation, continue by denigrating the accused, and conclude by wallowing in *tristesse* about the enormousness of the white man's burden. Years later this theme is reformulated as a triumphant moment for northern justice in Longstreth's history of the Northwest Mounted Police: he describes the incident as "a serious racial situation," noting comfortingly that "it was largely due to this forgotten incident that the thousands of prospectors in the Yukon solitudes far from the main river could rummage for their precious colors in peace."[50]

But from the Native perspective, their classification of the newcomers as members of a cohesive group — like a clan — and their attempts to impress on them the rules of the country met with an incomprehensible reaction. The stories passed on orally make the same point as those told about

Skookum Jim. They provide coherent narrative translations of events that have no familiar prototype. Unprecedented events occurred. An anomalous case was strategically interpreted based on past experience. Cultural practice encompassed a new event. There is no suggestion in either oral or written accounts that the accused wanted to deny what they had done, but the explanation they gave to the judge — the one that he recorded in his notes — that "they and the whites were 'good friends' but that some white man a year or two years ago had killed two Indians" was so incomprehensible to the outsiders that it was given no weight.

Again, parallels between the perspectives of Innis and Bakhtin are illuminating. Innis pointed to the state's overweening ambition to assert itself during periods of territorial expansion by monopolizing and systematizing information and by routinely silencing local traditions that do not fit official categories. Bakhtin looked for cases where narrative successfully resists such domestication, marginalization, and erasure. Observing the chilling transformations occurring in 1930s postrevolutionary Russia, Bakhtin concluded that there must be forms of resistance more effective than the violent replacement of one set of leaders by another, and he looked for inspiration to the social practice of everyday spoken language. He was especially drawn to processes set in motion by conversational forms of oral storytelling. The metaphor underlying his model of communication was that of a centrifuge with two countervailing forces — authoritarian speech displacing local ideas to the margins, and irascible orality magnetically straining to hold a center.[51] A century later, orally transmitted stories about Keish foregrounding superhuman beings and social connection continue to provide interpretations of events resisting official depictions. Stories connect, as by centripetal force, those areas of life that seem to be disintegrating.

Stories about the deaths at Marsh Lake are less easily harmonized and provide a clearer example of how narratives bear the imprint of the institutions that produce them. Analyzing medical institutions as sites of narrative production, A. J. Saris targets voicelessness and narrative erasure as critical issues for narrative studies. He points to the naive, if commonsense, notion that orally narrated stories somehow connote "experience near" phenomena as transparent texts. Nothing could be further from the truth, he insists, as he analyses how institutions filter what is relevant, erase what is troublesome, silence or force to the edges what they do not want to hear.[52] Bourdieu uses the term "institution" to connote any durable set of relations that allows individuals with power, status, and resources to enact what their spoken words claim to perform. He cites legal discourse as the classic example of this because of its power to bring into existence the very conditions it utters; in other words, the law begins by constructing a situation in which the evidence is said to be verifiable, and it uses prescriptive language to bring about and affirm the verification.[53]

In asserting imperial ideology, the judge was especially conscientious about being seen to be fair and to be serving interests and values shared by everyone. He carefully employed what Bourdieu calls the strategy of neutrality by using "politically unmarked political language, characterized by a rhetoric of impartiality, marked by the effects of symmetry, balance, the golden mean and sustained by an ethos of propriety and decency"[54] as he set out to establish what he frequently and casually refers to as "the facts." But what becomes critical in this context is not what is being said but the social conditions of narrative production (in a courtroom), reproduction (in official transcripts), distribution (to various government agencies), public legitimation (through newspaper reports), and erasure (of the defendants).

In effect, facts get established by enacting silences. Despite the judge's frequent admonition to the accused to "state your narrative," that is not what he really means. An institution differs from a dialogue in that it sets constraints on what stories can be told and when they are admissible. There are things to be said, and there are ways of saying them. When Frank does state his narrative, his reasons for the deaths are dismissed without comment. When Jim's narrative is translated in the courtroom, he is accused of having "blurted it out" at the wrong time and of thwarting the scrupulousness of police who advised him *not* to state his narrative. By judicial alchemy his narrative is then used to sentence him to death.

A secondary narrative would interest Innis. One of the objectives of this trial was to document the successful performance of law on the frontier, but time and distance played a role in fragmenting the procedure. As noted earlier, Superintendent Steele sent an early request that a judge be brought north to hear the case at Tagish where the witness and arrested men were waiting; weeks after the case had been tried more than three hundred miles downriver in Dawson City and the sentences imposed, he received an answer promising that a judge would soon be arriving in Tagish for the trial.[55] The order commuting Frank's sentence, signed by the minster of justice on 22 September, was sent from Ottawa to Vancouver, British Columbia, and then hand carried north by Mr. Duff Pattullo, who left Vancouver by boat on 2 October, passed by Tagish on 10 October, and proceeded by steamer to Dawson City, where he gave it to Sheriff Harper.[56] Letters written by the bishop of the Yukon to both the minister of justice and the secretary of state on 3 August 1898, requesting alternative sentencing for the young men, received a reply written in Ottawa on 28 October, a mere three days before the execution was originally scheduled to take place, denying the request but responding that extension of clemency to Frank should satisfy their concerns.[57] Mail sent from Dawson City during the first week of November, after the first postponement of the executions, was lost in an accident on the river at Hootelinqua, creating a vacuum in which no one wanted to take responsibility for subsequent decisions: the deputy minister of justice wrote a terse letter on 4 January 1899 demanding that duplicate copies of all lost reports be forwarded to Ottawa.[58] The extensive documentary record also tells a story about the inertia accompanying the movement of paper and the expedient decisions that can be made in a vacuum.

The issue of whether the trial had taken place in the correct jurisdiction and whether such a jurisdiction as the Supreme Court of the Northwest Territories, Provisional Jurisdiction of the Yukon, even existed in July 1898 shows that the state's own categories were in disarray. The Yukon Territory was established as a separate jurisdiction in June 1898, one month after the May shootings, but by the time of the trial in July no court was yet in place. Consequently the case was heard by a court that by then had no legal jurisdiction over Yukon affairs. An appeal was launched in January requesting a writ of habeas corpus on the grounds that the prisoners had been tried in the wrong court.[59] This debate, continued in memos between Dawson City and Ottawa through the first six months of 1899, seems never to have been resolved and was concluded only when the minister of justice issued an order to proceed with the executions. The correspondence includes considerable debate on the legality of the executions as well as an independent legal opinion requested by the Department of Justice describing the trial "a hopeless nullity."[60] Questions linger about the legality of the entire proceedings — trial, verdict, and executions. Alan Grove's recent analysis of the court documents argues that the trial was "a judicial homicide of two natives who were denied the protection normally afforded to individuals tried and convicted and in circumstances that amounted to a clear defect in jurisdiction."[61]

Years later, in 1920, the case was reassessed in a different context when William McIntosh, a prospector who claimed a role in apprehending the accused, applied to the Royal Canadian Mounted Police for a pension, stating that it was owed him for his services in the case. The police requested letters from officers present at the time of the arrest — H. E. Rudd, A. G. Schwartz, and Superintendent Tucker — each of whom wrote a report recalling his own heroic involvement in the case, thick with references to personal handwritten diaries and presenting another layer of documentary evidence where both the victims and the accused are rendered invisible.[62]

This case provides a classic confrontation between customary and Western law of the kind described by Phyllis Morrow and Chase Hensel, where codified definitions rather than customary strategic manipulation of precedents become the exclusive basis for making a decision.[63] Compared with codified law, they agree, customary law may appear unregulated, poorly rationalized, and haphazard. But the consequence is that Natives are still, as they were a century ago, invariably compelled to defend their practices in a manner consistent with Western logic. In an 1898 courtroom in Dawson City, one institution was endowed with the resources and authority to carry out an act of adjudication. Ultimately the law derived its legitimacy from the silences — from the prisoners' silences in court, from the absence of witnesses for the defense, from the administrators' silences from Ottawa, from the apparent dismissal of a legal opinion on file stating that "the proceedings are a hopeless nullity," and from the deaths of men who died in prison while their case was still under appeal.

Arguably any narrative representation of reality presenting itself to us as history invokes a social system.[64] Both written and oral narratives about the deaths at Marsh Lake resonate with statements about culturally appropriate behavior. They also suggest how bureaucratic practice begins to erase local knowledge. Comparison illuminates more general issues surrounding the social life of these stories a century later, but it does *not* give us a seamless synthesis. Both kinds of records have to be understood as part of the historical, political, and cultural matrices in which they emerge. Centennial celebrations spanning 1996–98 to commemorate the Klondike gold rush will provide many opportunities to observe how the acts of constructing, remembering, and transmitting such narratives occur in a contemporary context where claims to aboriginality, collective rights, and indigenous justice now intersect with narratives of the frontier.

5

Imperfect Translations: Rethinking
Objects of Ethnographic Collection

On the cold and bleak barrenlands and mountains, many Indians lived a marginal existence. Continually in search of food, they had little time to develop colorful religious practices or art forms.

Museum exhibit label for subarctic material culture

You can go to a movie and understand what the movie represents because you are familiar with the world of the movie. Viewing a Pomo basket in a museum is like viewing a movie frame depicting a close-up of water; it could be water anywhere, or nowhere.

Greg Sarris, Keeping Slug Woman Alive

The good translation gets you far enough into the other world to begin to see what you are missing. You take your translation device . . . and you watch it run out of meaning. You watch it fall apart. That's my notion of cultural translation.

James Clifford, interviewed by Brian Wallis

In an interview several years ago, James Clifford talked about the difficulties of cross-cultural translation and told how, in art as in politics, attempts to achieve global understandings continue to be thwarted by local visions. Despite ongoing presumptions that cultural homogenization will inevitably flow from international communications networks, we continue to be confronted with discrepant meanings, and even with the possibility that frameworks of meaning are incompatible. This is an area, he suggests, where anthropologists should focus more attention.

Clifford went on to give a powerful example from a museum. The Portland Museum of Art houses the Rasmussen Collection, a series of masks, headdresses, and other objects collected from southeastern Alaska during the 1920s. When the museum made plans to reinstall and reinterpret the collection in the late 1980s, it decided to involve Tlingit elders as consultants from early stages. A dozen prominent elders, representing clans that originally owned the objects, were invited to travel to Portland, Oregon. During a planning session at the museum, objects were brought out, and elders were asked to speak about them. Clifford describes how he and the curatorial staff, focusing on the objects, waited expectantly for some sort of detailed explication about how each object functioned, who made it, what powers it had within Tlingit society. Instead, he reports, the objects acted as memory aids for the telling of elaborate stories and the singing of many songs. As these stories and songs were performed, they took on additional meanings. An octopus headdress, for example, evoked narratives about a giant octopus that once blocked a bay, preventing salmon from reaching inland rivers. By the end of the story, the octopus had become the state and federal agencies regulating the right of Tlingits to take salmon, so that what started as a traditional story took on precise political meanings in terms of contemporary struggles. "And in some sense the physical objects, at least as I saw it, were left at the margin. What really took center stage were the stories and songs." [1]

This chapter arises from my interest in juxtaposing two seemingly restricted ethnographic approaches — analysis of oral tradition and analysis of material culture. It has two purposes. At one level, it is a narrative about one woman's carvings, the stories they embody, and some meanings of those stories in her own life. In that sense it is highly specific to one individual and her retrospective account of her experiences. At another level, it is a story about ethnographic museums and their changing mandates in the late twentieth century. Contemporary studies of Native American material culture often center on highly sensitive objects — wampum belts, the sacred pole of the Omahas, Zuni war gods, Tlingit ceremonial regalia. [2] But thousands of less spectacular items, also positioned in this debate about cultural property, pass unnoticed. It is worth considering whether some of the same issues surrounding collection, documentation, exhibition, creativity, and artistic production can be focused on material objects that arrive in museums almost by chance and that might otherwise be forgotten.

The work of Kitty Smith provides such a case. Mrs. Smith, a woman of Tagish and Tlingit descent who spent her entire life in the southwestern Yukon Territory, was born about 1890 (fig. 4). Speaking years later about her life experiences, she recalled that as a young woman she used to think of wood and the stories it can tell. During the 1920s, she and her husband and their children made their headquarters at Robinson, a stop on the White Pass and Yukon Railway not far from the present community of Carcross in the Yukon Territory. They traveled regularly into the nearby Wheaton River valley to hunt and trap. Recalling one of those trips in a conversation many years later, she commented,

Ida saw that poplar tree.
"Look Mamma!"

I thought about it all night. Next day, I went to get it. That's the time I carved those things, [from] poplar. My own Daddy made silver [jewelry] — talk about fancy jobs! Jewel stuff! That's why I guess I carve, me. I did that when we were living at Robinson.[3]

Kitty Smith's carvings were experimental, and she sold them casually, she says, to various people whose names she later forgot. When arthritis eventually made it impossible for her to do detailed work with her hands, she contented herself with telling her stories in words. In 1974, when we began working together recording her narratives, place-names, and life story, I sometimes tried to ask her more about her carvings.[4] When I did so, she invariably began to tell the stories she had depicted in her carvings. One of her favorites, she said, showed Crow emerging, well fed, from the back of a whale after he had tricked Whale into swallowing him and then spent the winter living comfortably in the cavity, dining on the finest whale meat.[5]

Some of Mrs. Smith's carvings ended up in the MacBride Museum in Whitehorse, capital of the Yukon Territory. It is not entirely clear how they got there: as in many museums, the documentation for early collections is uneven. It was founded in 1952, and local residents and collectors were urged to donate memorabilia, particularly if they left the Territory when they retired. When a new curator began working there in the early 1980s, she found several wooden carvings in a glass case labeled "Carvings made by Mackenzie River Indians," referring to a region several hundred miles away (fig. 5).[6] A local artist who had known Mrs. Smith for many years suggested these carvings might have been *her* work, and he helped arrange for her to visit the museum. She was well past her ninetieth year by this time, and her eyesight was failing, but when she handled the carvings she recognized them. In a tape-recorded interview of the discussion, Mrs. Smith sounds amused by the "discovery" of her carvings but quite detached. Handling one of them, she commented, "Ah! Azanzhaya," referring back to her stories: "'Got Lost.' Just like Crow that one got lost, Azanzhaya."[7]

"WORDS," "THINGS," AND ETHNOGRAPHIC COLLECTIONS

In the short history of anthropology, analyses of spoken words and of material objects have usually been compartmentalized. In North America this dichotomy reflects the way the discipline was originally constituted. Franz Boas spent a decade of intense involvement with the American Museum of Natural History and then resigned in 1905, convinced that it was impossible to adequately represent cultural meaning on so slim a basis as physical objects.[8] He turned his attention to analysis of oral traditions, hoping to find in texts recorded directly from native speakers a more objective method of addressing the issues preoccupying the anthropology of his day — race, language, and culture.[9] Some of his followers, though, continued to argue for the superior objectivity of material culture; Alfred Kroeber, for instance, saw archaeological data as "the purest [data] there are."[10] This penchant for trying to abstract evidence about "traditional" culture from disembodied words and things, while ignoring the turmoil engulfing Native peoples at the time collections were made, has retrospectively been interpreted as a serious shortcoming of early anthropology, but it established patterns.

Regna Darnell points out how closely the history of Canadian anthropology continued to be tied to a text tradition.[11] Anthropologists based in museums — Boas, Marius Barbeau, Edward Sapir, and others — certainly did collect material culture, but they and their locally based collaborators — James Teit, Henry Tate, George Hunt, Louis Shotridge — also recorded voluminous notebooks and sometimes wax cylinders documenting oral tradition. Although spoken words and material objects have often been treated separately in anthropology — the former in journals dedicated to folklore and oral tradition, the latter in volumes associated with museum studies, they have been analyzed in remarkably similar ways. Both were originally treated as collectible objects; subsequently, attention shifted to resituating these collected words and things in their original contexts; recently both have been analyzed with reference to cultural performance, just as now they are often referred to as cultural symbols (conveying different messages to different audiences) or as cultural property.[12]

Certain arguments come full circle. If museums have long faced the challenges involved in using *things* to represent culture, an issue much discussed both in Native American communities and in contemporary anthropology is how to convey the experience of culture in *words*.[13] Increasingly, indigenous peoples in North America are making oral tradition and material objects central to their definitions of culture. In public speech, for example, performance of verbal artistry and the display of ceremonial regalia have become standard ways of demonstrating both ethnographic authority and the central place of words and things in socially reproducing culture.[14] In areas like northwestern North America, where a flourishing oral tradition continues, concerns about repatriation tend to revolve around tape recordings and transcripts of orally narrated stories and songs as much as around material culture.

Because museums collect physical objects, they preserve certain stories and ignore others. Because they collect *things*, they encourage us to evaluate cultural traditions in terms of the physical objects people made and left behind. Yukon material culture has often been compared with that of the adjacent Pacific Northwest Coast. A tradition of monumental sculpture from Northwest Coast cultures sparked a collecting frenzy during the late nineteenth century, so that beautifully carved totem poles, masks, and wooden boxes are now dispersed throughout European and North American museums. In part this tradition was enabled by the coincidence of a rich marine environment and the availability of cedar. Intensive use of coastal waters and annual salmon runs allowed sedentary communities and the kind of accumulation of wealth that permitted specialists to experiment with a wide range of techniques. Often referred to as Northwest Coast art, these works are also complex statements about the social and ceremonial workings of the communities in which they were created.

The arts of the interior are equally complex and intricate but harder to exhibit in a museum. To harvest their resources, subarctic peoples had to be mobile, so they developed a material culture based on principles that could be combined in a variety of ways. Portability was essential, and only necessities were carried from place to place. More important than the object itself was the ability to make it again when and where it was needed. Principles underlying snare construction, for instance, could be applied to hunting ground squirrels or large animals like moose and caribou. The critical issue was to learn the idea of how to construct and use a snare. Oral tradition — tools of the mind — weighs nothing and can accompany a traveler anywhere.[15]

Part of the genius of subarctic culture was the ability to take materials like bone, stone, wood, skins, and bark and transform them into necessities like clothing and shelter, tools and transportation. Archaeologists have sometimes remarked that were it not for oral tradition, remarkably little would be known about the past of subarctic peoples, because so much of their material culture perished. "It is humbling to realize how much . . . transforming trade was carried on in perishables and how scanty the archaeological record of it is in view of its documented significance. Almost invariably we will underestimate the volume of trade in the prehistoric record in this area, given the likelihood that it was also in perishable items."[16] Aboriginal people in the subarctic cordillera have had a somewhat different experience from that of many Native Americans because their material culture was never the object of such intense collecting expeditions as those experienced, for example, on the Northwest Coast or in the South Pacific.[17]

When I worked during the 1980s with Athapaskan and inland Tlingit elders on a project to develop high school curriculum materials for Yukon schools, two themes emerged repeatedly. First, elders spoke about the continuing importance of *words,* insisting that people still make use of long-standing narrative traditions to think about life. Oral tradition does not simply tell us about the past, they stated emphatically; it continues to provide guidelines for the present and to lay a foundation for thinking about the future. Second, they pointed to the continuing importance of *things* — the visible, material heritage that is steadily vanishing over time — the traps, the snares, the many strategies people used to provide a life based on hunting, fishing, and trapping. They spoke about the ceremonial clothing, the decorated tools, the small works of art that were part of everyday life. These, they say, provide the concrete examples they should be able to point to when they try to teach younger people how life should be conducted. When archaeologist Sheila Greer invited Annie Ned and me to be involved in an archaeological survey she was conducting at Kusawa Lake in the southern Yukon, Mrs. Ned was delighted to visit the field camp. After Sheila showed us the range of material culture relevant to her project, Mrs. Ned turned to me: "So now I see: they are looking for *things* and you are looking for *words.* So I'll tell you the words and you can write them down for them!" Both words and things, then, have an ongoing role in reproducing contemporary culture.

The observations of these elders suggest an approach to the spoken word and material culture subtly different from that found in museums. If museum discourse emphasizes the importance of using words to describe, interpret, and give meaning to the physical objects of collection, indigenous discourse, at least in this instance from the Subarctic, reverses this equation by suggesting that spoken words are primary and that material objects provide the essential illustrations for particularly meaningful stories. Since stories provide an important way of describing a life well lived, images can be understood with reference to what they exemplify about social relations. Both verbal arts and material representations are embedded in social life and are part of the cultural equipment used to think about and engage in reproducing or transforming complex human relationships. To the extent that objects and stories have been physically separated, these elders are concerned about reuniting the dispersed fragments.

A critical question, then, becomes how words intersect with objects in the context of social relations in which *both* are embedded. As discussed in previous chapters, one of the more useful insights of contemporary anthropology is that meaning is not fixed — that it emerges in practice. Listening to people speak about the range of meanings associated with the production of artistic work or with generations of use of handcrafted works provides glimpses of how such works shape understanding of human experience, how connections are forged between human creativity and the material world.[18] Individuals undeniably constitute, reflect on, and reconstitute themselves through words and actions — what they say and do — but they also do this through the physical objects they make and use. In Barbara Babcock's words, "Objects are used not only to represent experience but also to apprehend it and to interpret it and to give it meaningful shape. . . .Objects do speak and should be heard as significant statements of personal and cultural reflexivity." [19] How, she asks, are conceptions of personhood, social order, and cosmology articulated through handmade work? How are physical things as well as spoken words used to culturally constitute the relationship between artistry and experience? And, one might add, how can museums, which are at least partly responsible for this analytical dualism, help to reconstitute connections between object and narrative?

CONSTRUCTING LIFE STORIES IN WORDS

When I first met Mrs. Kitty Smith during the winter of 1974, she was already past her eightieth birthday and was living comfortably in a canvas wall tent fifteen miles north of Whitehorse, capital of the Yukon Territory. "The government" had built her a house in town, she said, but she found it drafty and cold and much preferred her spacious tent with its woodstove and her work space with her hides and sewing arranged as she liked them. Her granddaughter lived nearby and could give her any assistance she needed.

Her granddaughter, who was my age, had originally introduced us, suggesting that a useful task for an anthropology student would be to record her grandmother's history so that family members could have their own history booklet. I was delighted by this idea because of my interest in how women's lives had changed in the Yukon during the twentieth century. Mrs. Smith cheerfully agreed to this project, but though she responded patiently to my questions about her early life for a while, she soon shifted the focus of our afternoon conversations by asking me to record lengthy and elaborate stories that I recognized as variations on those recorded by Boas, Swanton, de Laguna, McClellan, and others. During the years we worked together she rarely talked about her own life for more than a few minutes without breaking off to tell such a story; when she returned to her personal experience, she would compose her account in a way that demonstrated the explanatory power of the narrative she had just related. In this way she provided the framework I needed to understand the complex events that had occurred during her own life.

Born about 1890 near the mouth of the Alsek River to a Tlingit father, Tàkàtà, and a Tagish mother, Tatl'èrma, she lost both parents when she was very young — her father when she was a few months old, her mother when she was six, in an influenza epidemic linked with the tragic events discussed in chapter 4. Although she never knew her father, she knew that he was well known as a literate and widely traveled man who learned to make silver jewelry, and she attributed her own interest in carving to his artistic talents.

The theme of relationships structured around matrilineal descent emerges repeatedly in her narratives. Her mother was from the south-central Yukon Territory, and her father was from the coast. Their marriage resulted from long-standing trade relationships between coastal Tlingit and interior Athapaskan peoples, and the couple took up residence with her father's maternal household. When Kitty was orphaned, her father's family "claimed her," in her words, and she was raised by her father's people — unconventional in a society where emphasis on matrilineal kinship reckoning is still very important. She was reunited with her mother's people only some twenty years later, after her first marriage ended when she took the unprecedented step of leaving an abusive husband. At that time she joined her maternal grandmother, Dúshka, and began to learn more about her Tagish ancestry. A few years later she entered a long and satisfying marriage to a Tagish man, Billy Smith, and as a mother of young children she began to carve sometimes.

When Kitty Smith talks about her childhood, she refers to stories that have as their protagonist a plucky, quick-witted orphan who invariably saves the community from unspeakable disaster. Very often in such stories, the primary relationship is between a grandmother and a loyal grandchild, and in making her points she speaks not only about her own childhood but about her contemporary relationships with grandsons. In one story, for example, an old woman is "thrown away," but her grandchild refuses to abandon her and remains with her as others move on. Together the pair kill a giant copper-clawed owl that once lived in a nearby glacier, posing grave danger to people. Their actions ultimately save the lives of the very people who had abandoned them.[20]

When she goes on to talk about her experiences as an adult, she draws on stories that explore conflicting loyalties between affines and consanguineal kin. Frequently the protagonist in such stories is a woman, and the narrative dilemma surrounds her ambiguous status if she is forced to live with her husband's people, unprotected by brothers or maternal uncles and matrilineally related women. The stories she tells allow her to dramatize examples more extreme than those normally encountered in life. For instance, in one narrative the young protagonist discovers to her horror that her husband's people have been systematically and secretly killing her brothers; with the help of her grandfather, a shaman, she is able to annihilate the perpetrators, but at great personal cost.[21]

Marriage poses an inevitable conflict for both men and women. On one hand, it is essential to retain strong links with one's own maternal kin after marriage; on the other, one partner inevitably must move away from a protective network and establish residence with affines. Although postmarital residence patterns ideally were matrilocal, this did not always happen. A story pointing out possible dire consequences depicts the plight of a man who is living with his wife's people and is betrayed by her brothers. They pretend to take him hunting and then abandon him on an island to die.[22]

Two themes emerge from Mrs. Smith's construction of her life story. First, her narratives explore tensions involved in living with affines, unprotected by one's maternal uncles and brothers. This reflects her mother's experience as well as her own: Mrs. Smith's first marriage was arranged by her father's mother in a customary alliance that placed greater value on cementing bonds between lineages than on the compatibility of the individuals involved. Her unconventional decision to leave this marriage and go live with her mother's people as a young adult woman must have been difficult not only for her but for her entire extended family. Although one of her grandchildren has referred to her as the "first feminist" because of her decision to leave, she herself rejects any suggestion that her behavior was atypical, phrasing her own decisions with reference to her maternal kinship obligations as she understands them. She stoutly maintains that she was conservative in deference to her maternal grandmother, who promulgated the view advanced in many of her own stories that marriage should strengthen, rather than weaken, ties between matrilineally related women.

At a less obvious level, her narratives explore the ambiguity surrounding her bicultural ancestry and the difficulties of reconciling her paternal Tlingit ancestry with her interior Dän (Athapaskan) matrilineage. This has been a significant question during her own life because her childhood was spent in a predominantly Tlingit family but her adult life has been spent more closely associated with Athapaskan interior traditions. Defining one's ethnicity in areas where cultural boundaries are ambiguous is a complex issue. Athapaskan speakers, now elderly, faced this dilemma with reference to Tlingits during the last century much as younger people confront it now in their dealings with Euro-Canadians.

LIFE STORIES AND CARVINGS

Mrs. Smith died in 1989 after nearly a century of active life. Three years later, when I was visiting her daughter, May Smith Hume, I asked whether she had ever seen her mother's carvings in the museum. She had not seen the carvings since her childhood, but she remembered her mother's making them and was most interested in examining them. In July 1992 we visited the MacBride Museum together. The curator provided us with a working space where we could examine and discuss each of the carvings, and she brought out several for which the museum had no documentation. May immediately identified which ones had been made by her mother and those that could not have been. "Imagine my mom's handwork here!" she commented several times as she scrutinized pieces she had not seen for more than fifty years. When I asked if she could tell me what she knew about her mother's carving techniques and materials, May, like her mother, began to tell the story underlying each carving.[23]

The stories she tells are among the ones her mother had used to illustrate *her* life story and are only summarized here. Two carvings she identified depict the story of Kaats', a man who married Bear Woman (figs. 6, 7, 8).

The narrative traces the journey of Kaats', who accidentally stumbles into Bear Woman's world. She takes him to a separate dimension of reality, where he puts his former life behind him and is permanently transformed into a bear and absorbed into bear society. Broadly, the story depicts the ambivalent relations between bears and humans, a theme common to circumpolar subarctic narratives, and how animals and humans, with their conflicting and overlapping powers, share the world.[24]

The story of Kaats' has been recorded in many versions by Swanton, Barbeau, Garfield and Forrest, Keithahn, de Laguna, and Dauenhauer and Dauenhauer.[25] Keithahn adds that the story inspired totem poles and heraldic screens in villages up and down the coast from Ketchikan to Yakutat. Sometimes published versions of the narrative are accompanied by a photograph of a carving depicting Kaats' and his Bear wife — Barbeau's photograph of a southern Tlingit Bear house post at Wrangell, Alaska; de Laguna's photo of an unpainted wooden model totem pole at Yakutat; Garfield's and Keithahn's separate photos of a totem pole at Saxman Totem Park, three miles south of Ketchikan, Alaska; and Keithahn's reproduction of a house crest originally above the entrance of Brown Bear House in Yakutat, Alaska.[26]

As May tells the story, a man, already married and with a family, was hunting. In the course of his travels, he encountered a bear disguised as a woman, who seduced him away from his human family. His human wife, deeply distressed, eventually encountered him and reproached him for abandoning her and their children. "Don't do that," he responded. "My life doesn't belong to me any more; my life belongs to them. I can't ever be with you. They spared my life because I promised I would stay with them."

In May's telling, as in her mother's, the rupture with the human wife is central to the unfolding of the story. One of her mother's carvings shows Kaats' being seduced by Bear Woman (fig. 6) and his abandoned human wife leaving with their child (fig. 7); another (fig. 8) shows him transformed and in the company of his Bear wife after he had become her partner: "He promised his life to the Bear after that Bear grabbed him."

When I returned to my earliest notes from Mrs. Smith, I discovered that she had originally told me this story in 1978 when she first talked about her carvings, then told it again in 1982 to explain certain decisions she had made in her own life.[27] Her first husband abandoned her after she was in a serious accident for which she held him responsible. He visited her in the hospital, she said, only to tell her that he was taking a second wife. She made the decision to leave him, remarkable for a woman of her background in 1912 or so, and like the human wife depicted in the carving, she left. When she was released from the hospital, she announced her decision to stay with her mother's people, matrilineally related family members she had known only at a distance to this point in her life. "So long as Grandma is living, I don't care. I'm going to sleep at my Grandma's back. Dúshka, her name," she reported years later.[28]

In an interesting juxtaposition of narrative themes, Mrs. Smith added to this carving the story she told me in 1974, when she first mentioned this work. At the top of the carving (figs. 6 and 7) appears the relentlessly innovative trickster Crow emerging from the back of a whale. Emulating her mother's storytelling style and gestures as she examined this carving, May continued,

Crow sees that whale, going like that . . . "Phewww, pheww" [imitating the whale alternately diving and blowing]. Way out there, eh? And he parked his boat and he looked at him.

"Gee," he said, "I wish I could be inside . . . I bet there's lots of fat in there."

Crow, he just loved fat. He wanted to eat fat, fat, fat all the time. So he said, "I know. When he goes . . . Pheww . . . I'll just jump in there. He'll suck me in."

Then he got his packsack, and he got lots of little wood. He breaks it all up and he put it inside his packsack. Filled it all up with wood — pitch wood, everything. Then he waits for it up there.

That whale came up just like that! Just as soon as that whale opened [his blowhole], he jumped inside! He just jumped inside that whale.

He stayed inside that whale, ate all the fat inside.
It's just like a big house!

Finally, he made a fire inside. Might as well kill it now, after I eat all the fat!

The story goes on to recount how Crow maneuvered the whale to shore, escaped through the hole in its back after people discovered the carcass and cut it open, rested in comfort while they cut up the whale and began the laborious work of rendering grease from the carcass, and then tricked them into fleeing so that he ended up in possession of all the processed grease. It is instructive to see this story, hilarious in the hands of a master storyteller, juxtaposed with the more serious narrative about Kaats', but it may convey some of the general optimism Mrs. Smith experienced after making her own decision.[29]

Moving on to other carvings, May identified another as depicting Dukt'ootl' (fig. 9). She began by telling me how surprised she had been to see this story carved on a pole installed in the entrance of the Alaska State Museum in Juneau when she visited there a few years earlier. Different though Mrs. Smith's small carving of Dukt'ootl' appears from that larger work, they tell parallel stories. The orphan Dukt'ootl', May says, was raised by an uncle but was belittled because of his low status. When a monster sea lion began to terrorize people, each adult male tried unsuccessfully to destroy him, but Dukt'ootl' was always dismissively left behind to tend the fires. He trained secretly, becoming stronger and stronger. Finally Dukt'ootl' (sometimes called "Little Blackbird" because he was covered with soot from tending the fires of others) managed to destroy the behemoth and save the camp (fig. 10).[30]

Like the story of Kaats', this narrative has been recorded by Swanton, Garfield and Forrest, Barbeau, Keithahn, de Laguna, the Dauenhauers, and Mrs. Smith herself.[31] And again, some of the same sources provide illustrations of carvings depicting this story — Barbeau's photos from Prince of Wales Island and from the Whale House at Klukwan; Garfield's photo of carved posts in Mud Bight House north of Ketchikan, and Keithahn's photos of old and new totem poles at Wrangell, Alaska.[32] This theme of the unlikely orphan hero underlies many of Mrs. Smith's narratives and mirrors her own life experience as a youngster who overcame difficult circumstances despite her very early loss of both parents.[33]

Still another carving, May says, depicts a coastal story of "the man who made Killer Whale" (fig. 11). Again, this story is well known in coastal Alaska as the story of Naatsilanéi and has been recorded by Swanton, Velten, Barbeau, Garfield and Forrest, McClellan, Cruikshank, and Dauenhauer and Dauenhauer.[34] A man goes seal hunting with his opposite moiety brothers-in-law, who abandon him on an island. The betrayal is especially deep because relations between brothers-in-law are expected to be close, and they are usually described as "partners." Alone and dejected, the protagonist begins to whittle some wood he has found, creating from his carvings the first killer whales, which become the agents of his salvation. The transformative power of carving is implicit in Kitty Smith's telling of the narrative,[35] but the theme also reflects the complexities of living in a situation where one is dependent on opposite moiety kin, as Mrs. Smith was early in her life. In telling this Tlingit story and others, Mrs. Smith draws on the coastal origins of her father's family, declares her ambivalence about the dangers of rupture from one's matriline and the difficulties of living far from one's own maternal family, and points to the transformative power of carving. The narrative parallels her own anticipation about rejoining matrilineally linked kin as an adult.

Like her orally narrated stories, then, Kitty Smith's carvings have meanings that are both culturally specific and highly personal. She tells stories in wood and in words both to reflect on crucial issues of social organization and to talk about how those issues affected her own life.[36] At the same time, they raise issues of concern both to anthropology and to museums.

OBJECTS, WORDS, AND HUMAN EXPERIENCE IN MUSEUMS

At the heart of conflicting expectations surrounding late twentieth-century museums are the narratives we tell to bring coherence to experience. Given the unruliness of human life and the difficulties of trying to create intelligible meanings, we inevitably fall back on familiar strategies. Anthropologists have demonstrated that classification systems are one strategy all humans engage in, though our typological criteria vary wildly across boundaries of gender, culture, and class. The contemporary interest in narrative practice results at least partly from the undermining of dominant taxonomies in an era of visible social fragmentation. Narratives provide a range of viewpoints from which to interpret the discrepant meanings we encounter both in human history and in daily experience. Through narrative plots, both chronological sequences and recognizable patterns are revealed.[37]

Ethnographic museums have always used narrative to convey messages about chronology and pattern in human history. Whereas historians actively debate whether narrativity clarifies or obfuscates the problems of representing history, museums are so undeniably cultural constructions that they occupy an ideal position to show the constructed nature of *all* our accounts. They provide a consistent temporal framework into which a variety of personal experiences can be inserted.[38] "The historian," says Walter Benjamin, "is bound to explain in one way or another the happenings with which he deals; under no circumstances can he content himself with displaying them as models of the course of the world. But this is precisely what the chronicler does. . . . Interpreting is not concerned with accurate concatenation of definite events, but with the way these are embedded in the great inscrutable course of the world."[39]

Historically, the narratives shaping museums have been those of mastery and classification. Science museums have exhibited mastery of nature; ethnographic and historical museums have implicitly or explicitly documented the expansion of colonialism. Conventionally concerned with the project of collection, classification, and display, museums incorporated ideas of evolutionary progress to project their messages.[40] Ethnographic museums are filled with disembodied objects, photographs, and sound recordings collected by individuals who saw their mission as salvaging a disappearing past. Underlying their endeavor was an essentialist conviction that kernels of meaning adhered to objects and could be discovered retrospectively at some time in the future through the analytical skills of a curator. One of the many problems with this nostalgic model is that it establishes an artificial historical and ethnographic baseline with reference to the time it enters a museum.[41] Another is the erasure of human initiative involved in both production and collection. Material representation is foregrounded in such narratives at the expense of any understanding of human agency.

At first hearing, the kinds of stories told by Kitty Smith's carvings sound quite familiar in a museum — narratives once carved on totem poles and house posts along the Northwest Coast. However, the conventional translation devices we inherit from museum practice do not adequately convey the range of settings and contexts in which she told them. When Kitty Smith's carvings are subsumed within a universalistic museum narrative, they inevitably invite comparison with sculptured Tlingit poles and are likely to be classified as "primitive art" or even "tourist art" or as evidence of the conventional subarctic descriptor cited in the epigraph to this chapter, about a "marginal existence . . . on the cold and bleak barrenlands and mountains." Such categories fail to do justice either to the artist's production of these carvings or to the museum's potential to adequately present the abstract ideas underlying them — kinship, marriage patterns, a range of ways to overcome adversity.

Current museum anthropology is being reformulated from different premises. A new museology, taking as its unit of analysis the entire institution, has applied sustained cultural criticism to the history and anthropology of museums.[42] One suggestion emerging from this critique is that museums of the future will need to be story driven rather than object driven.[43] "To be meaningful," says Richard Handler in a recent paper, "objects must be surrounded by other objects, by words, by human activity. Without meaningful human activity to create and recreate values, objects are meaningless."[44]

Whereas the historical tendency in museums has been to disconnect "things" from "words," Kitty Smith spent her life actively integrating these strands of tradition to construct her understanding of the changing world in which she lived for almost a century. Born less than a decade before the Klondike gold rush, she spent much of her childhood near Dalton Post, a trading post established when she was about four years old. A few years later this became a major stopping point on one of the routes used by thousands of prospectors en route to the Klondike River. When she was six years old her mother died, just as her father had a few years earlier, leaving her an orphan. Dalton Post was transformed into a Northwest Mounted Police post; conflicts between aboriginal people and police sometimes flared, and her own mother's brother was involved in the tragic altercation with prospectors discussed in the previous chapter. Within a few years, indigenous people in this region found themselves under enormous pressures from economic dislocation, illness, and death.

During her life, she would not isolate discussions of these experiences from her accounts of how the world began, how humans and animals came to coexist, and how she carved these stories in wood. Such things, she would say, simply cannot be understood separately. Her carvings contest not only the categories used to display culture in museums but also the idea that "traditional" culture exists in any static sense. Although such an observation now sounds commonplace, Kitty Smith's ways of making connections may have implications for other marginalized works in museums. They document her creative use of cultural materials at hand to construct an understanding of the human condition. They allow us to look at how culture is *made* rather than merely at its representations. The stories Mrs. Smith told to describe her work refer to the act of creation rather than to the finished object: keeping the carvings would have been highly impractical for anyone with a lifestyle as mobile as hers. Besides, they were not so much discrete "things" as one part of a tradition she used to engage with the world around her.

Following James Clifford's advice, we would do well to look at discrepant meanings if our objective is to learn about human creativity, and also at the links between the material world and the world of action. These small carvings provide a good example of Clifford's thesis that our objectivist, positivist translation devices eventually do run out of meaning. By themselves, categories like "art," "material culture," or "oral tradition" do not take us far in understanding what carvings of Kaats', Dukt'ootl', and Naatsilanéi signify, both to their maker and to viewers familiar with her metaphors. Nor do conventional cultural identifiers like "Athapaskan" or

"Tlingit" take us much further: "Any set of cultural or ethnic identifiers implies an interpretive framework external to the objects it describes."[45] If we look at meanings as emerging from human interaction with the material world rather than residing within objects, we have to wonder, with Greg Sarris, "what happened and continues to happen that allows one group of people to discuss the artifacts of another people separately from the people themselves."[46]

It is this human ability to create meanings and to reproduce culture, especially in situations of social and economic dislocation, that gives culture integrity. In a 1994 address to the Canadian Anthropology Society, Frederick Barth spoke about this issue in a way that returns us to James Clifford's concerns about translation, raised at the beginning of this chapter. Postmodernism, says Barth, presents certain challenges: it forces us to confront human life as something that is always falling apart. Yet over and over again, ethnography presents us with ways humans construct continuity and integration in the face of disorder. The compelling question, he says, is how people enmeshed in this disorderly world create an identity that has continuity, especially when there is no script. We do this by working with those strands of tradition we have at our disposal to produce and reproduce the idea that the world is still continuous, and we go on to create those continuities, often by weeding out the really incongruent portions. Culture does not produce itself; rather, images (like those of Kaats', Dukt'ootl', and Naatsilanéi) resonate because they become devices for translating new experiences that do not seem to have cultural roots. The ways humans use these images show our struggle to achieve consistency between old values and changing circumstances.[47]

Oral tradition represents present as well as past realities. In a museum context, attention to oral tradition directs us away from the idea of material, textual representations and back to the centrality of people and their social relations — from typologies that classify to narratives that connect. As museums confront the contradictions involved in "collecting" culture, one way to link discrepant meanings is to trace those meanings through cultural biographies of objects.[48] Carvings of Kaats', Dukt'ootl', and Naatsilanéi began as ancient narratives. They brought their explanatory power to the dilemmas experienced by their young female carver, who eventually sold them to buyers who probably displayed them as souvenirs. Eventually some of them arrived at their current destination as museum artifacts, where they were labeled innocuously, if inaccurately, "Carvings made by

Mackenzie River Indians." Years later they were reattributed to their now elderly maker, who lived not far from the museum.

Museums still have much to teach us about the human process of cultural construction, and many museums are struggling to tell the discrepant stories of their institutional lives and of the objects in their collections. Michael Ames's use of the metaphor of a palimpsest — a manuscript on which successive layers of thought and text have been inscribed — suggests that if our objective is to reveal these successive layers we might do well to learn from the art of storytellers like Kitty Smith.[49] In his essay "The Story-teller," Walter Benjamin makes connections between words and things explicit when he notes how "traces of the storyteller cling to the story the way the handprints of the potter cling to the clay vessel." What must not be lost, what must be retained of the storyteller's art, is "that slow piling one on top of the other of thin, transparent layers which constitutes the most appropriate picture of the way in which the perfect narrative is revealed through the layers of a variety of retellings."[50] Practicing this art in a way that acknowledges the makers of works now submerged in ethnographic collections is one of the many challenges facing museums.

6

Claiming Legitimacy:
Prophecy Narratives from Northern
Aboriginal Women

During 1992, compelling questions were raised — in the media, in museum exhibits, and in both popular and academic writings — about the construction of history. The Columbus quincentenary framed these issues on an international level. In Canada, debates were usually phrased with reference to local anniversaries. In British Columbia, for example, we heard a great deal about the bicentenary of Captain George Vancouver's visit to the west coast of North America. In the Yukon Territory, where the fiftieth anniversary of the construction of the Alaska Highway was celebrated, some aboriginal people questioned the appropriateness of eulogizing an event that had such far-reaching implications for their lives. For that year, at least, 1992 became crystallized in a metaphor grounding discussions about transition from a neocolonial world system to a postcolonial world order.[1]

All these anniversaries highlighted concerns about voice in human history — whose voices are included and whose are left out. Contesting the legitimacy of the dominant discourse is not new, of course. Certainly a concern that many voices are systematically erased from written history has been recognized for a long time now in northern aboriginal communities. As feminists have pointed out, enlarging discourse involves much more than adding and stirring in additional voices; there are fundamental methodological problems involved in rethinking familiar genres of historical narrative.

This chapter examines prophecy narratives told by aboriginal women from the Yukon Territory in the course of recording their life stories. When I first heard these narratives, I set them aside because I did not understand how they fit into the larger autobiographical project. Yet the persistence with which narratives about prophecy are told is compelling, and they provide an opportunity to frame some questions about how people use oral tradition to make connections between past and present.

One of the reasons I set these narratives aside when I heard them is that there is a large scholarly literature about prophecy — in ethnohistory, in anthropology, in sociology. Following academic convention, I wanted to spend some time reading that literature so I could locate narratives I was hearing in terms of a larger debate. The convention is not frivolous: we consult what has already been written to avoid the conceit that our interpretations are somehow original. Reading that literature, though, I was struck by how clearly our academic narratives can be seen as only one set among many. When we listen to contemporary aboriginal people draw on oral narratives to explain the ways past connects with present, we encounter other narratives that compete with academic narratives for legitimacy.

The ongoing academic debate about prophecy seems to focus on the behavior, activities, and predictions of particular prophets and to turn on two axes. In North American ethnohistory — writings by both historians and anthropologists — the central question seems to be whether prophetic movements were indigenous or a response to European contact.[2] In the more generalized sociological literature, shaped by Max Weber, the discourse concerns success or failure of specific prophets, judged in terms of their ability to transform the social and political order.

Here I want to shift the emphasis to analysis of narrative discourse, which I argue is deeply embedded in social organization. I move away from the *activities* of individual prophets and turn to oral traditions — the narratives *about* prophets that continue to be told in contemporary western subarctic communities near the upper Yukon River. Whereas much of the scholarly literature treats prophecy as exceptional behavior needing analysis and interpretation, indigenous traditions in the southern Yukon Territory discuss prophecy as consistent with the routine behavior of shamans, well within the bounds of what these specialists were expected to do. It is the retrospective consideration of prophecy stories as routine explanation for contemporary events that interests me here. My broader question is this: If these narratives are still told and understood in the 1990s as commonsense explanations, what can this contribute to our understanding of indigenous discourse about connections between past and present, particularly when local explanation heads in a direction very different from the Western scholarly debate?

The narratives I will discuss were told by elderly Yukon Athapaskan women who were involved in long-term work with the Yukon Native Language Centre. The context in which they were originally told to me is relevant, as is the question of how they are invoked in everyday conversation. The women who told these narratives were all selecting accounts they considered important to record and pass on to younger people. Some of the stories they chose to tell concern late nineteenth-century and early twentieth-century prophecies, and it was clear from their performances that they continue to take these narratives very seriously. The recurring theme is that particular shamans predicted social transformations that would accompany the arrival of Europeans, in some cases before they actually met the first whites. The inevitable point of these stories is that events that have subsequently come to pass were foretold long ago. Once again the narrators show the way narrative creates order and continuity from the disorder of experience.

Two features about the process of narration are striking; first, that prophecy accounts are singled out from a much larger body of narratives as important stories to pass on to younger listeners, and second, that they are told as though they provide a self-evident explanation, one that tellers consider routinely accessible to any listener. It is precisely at the level of explanation that the accounts clash with scholarly discourse, where their meaning is taken to be far from self-evident. I suggest that this makes them an ideal focus for ethnohistorical analysis by raising the question, What are the contexts in which these narratives continue to have meaning?

PROPHECY AND EXPLANATION: ACADEMIC NARRATIVES

The theoretical framework surrounding interpretation of prophecy has remained firmly grounded in Max Weber's analysis of Old Testament prophets. Sociological explanation stems from Weber's classic definition that portrays prophets as emerging outside routine institutional order to contest the social and political authority of established leaders. The implication is that prophets are outsiders — charismatic but marginal individuals who challenge authority yet fail to transform the political and social order. Transferred to a Native American setting, such explanations may privilege an interpretation emphasizing early Euro-American contact history or reaction to external events such as disease, population decimation, or natural disaster.[3]

This definition of prophecy as a response to external events transfers easily enough from sociological analysis to narrative analysis. Percy Cohen, for example, in an article reviewing theories of myth, proposed that prophecy is a kind of inversion of myth that develops when social organization breaks down and is no longer capable of explaining events, causing people to turn away from the past and look toward the future.[4] Given the pervasiveness of this sociological framework, the failure of nineteenth-century prophets seems inevitable.

Such explanations contrast sharply with those of subarctic aboriginal narrators, who regard stories about prophecy as evidence not of failure, but of successful engagement with change and detailed foreknowledge of events. These explanations speak directly to the issue of how one claims a legitimate voice in contemporary discussions about historical reconstruction. Despite growing scholarly interest in indigenous ethnohistory, Native Americans' views of their own history remain rare in scholarly literature. As Sergei Kan has pointed out, those that do enter this literature demonstrate that the past is regularly used to make sense of the present and to explain the current predicament of indigenous peoples in North America, and that this discourse does not develop hermetically, but arises in a dialogue with other ideologies. Subarctic prophecy narratives, for example, include elements of both the distant Plateau Prophet Dance and Christianity.[5] Kan documents how elements of such different ideologies become synthesized and absorbed into an existing narrative framework; in their attempts to defend their past against Western-imposed discourses, indigenous people can incorporate new ideas rather than being colonized *by* them.[6]

In her thoughtful discussion of narratives told by Yukon elders about the coming of the first whites to northwestern North America, Catharine McClellan has reminded us that indigenous oral traditions are not simply one more set of data to be sifted for historical veracity, and that they "can be fully understood only in relation to the total bodies of literature in which they appear."[7] For that reason, I attempt to discuss the broader indigenous narrative traditions within which prophecy stories fit on the upper Yukon River.

In the rest of this chapter, I will pose the hypothesis that if prophecy narratives provide a conventional way of making sense of dislocating change, then the relevant framework for interpreting them may be prophecy's long-term cultural consequences rather than (as Weber would direct us) its short-term political effects.[8] This approach builds directly on the work of anthropologists who suggest that prophecy may have been more widespread in early times than Spier recognized;[9] that in the western Subarctic it has long provided a routine, conventional explanation that makes sense of complex changes in familiar ways;[10] and that indigenous narrative frameworks continue to have the capacity to make sense of anomalous events.[11] Prophecy narratives provide a striking example of how southern Yukon women, at least, draw on traditional narrative as an authoritative explanation of contemporary events, an explanation that competes with Western discourse.

Prophecy Narratives from the Upper Yukon River

When I began to work with Yukon elders, I initially focused on a seemingly straightforward project of trying to help balance a documentary record that relies disproportionately on writings of traders, missionaries, and government agents, who were often poorly informed about what they were describing. The ethnographic record was growing by the mid-1970s, with works by Catharine McClellan, Richard Slobodin, John Honigmann, and Asen Balikci, available. McClellan's two-volume ethnography of the southern Yukon Territory had just appeared, and fieldwork by Robin Ridington, Roger McDonnell, and Dominque Legros was only recently under way.[12] Much of my work was done with elderly Athapaskan men and women with support from the Council for Yukon Indians, which provided honoraria for interested elders willing to record such accounts.

Frequently, elders chose to respond to questions about the past with a complex story. My initial failure to recognize the patterns undoubtedly came from the scaffolding I brought to the project — a sense that these accounts could be viewed as archival documents rather than as fully developed narrative constructions of the past. I reiterate this theme to suggest that a similar problem — an interpretive framework that predisposes us to interpret unfamiliar narratives in terms of familiar theoretical frameworks — may color our attempts to understand prophecy narratives as serious representations of the world.

The narrative structures shaping academic discourse about prophecy should also be kept in mind. Anthropologists writing about prophecy pay particular attention to the form and process of religious revitalization;[13] historians show a preference for discussing the specific circumstances in which prophets arise.[14] Ethnohistorians, drawing on both frameworks, have described their project as incorporating Native American perspectives.[15] But such a partnership, if serious, surely should turn critical attention to the symbolic and structural nature of scholarly accounts as well as indigenous accounts and to closer investigation of social systems in which all our narrative accounts are embedded.

The documentary record from northwestern North America provides us with ample evidence of early missionaries' narratives about prophecy. Most missionaries described prophets as self-interested charlatans whose primary goal was to dupe unwitting members of their own community. For instance, one of the first Anglican missionaries in the northern Yukon in the 1860s, Rev. Robert McDonald, included in his diaries regular reports of "pretensions to prophesy," with accounts of his injunctions advising Native people to stop "conjuring." [16] On 23 June 1863 McDonald reported that "some [Indians] at Peel River have pretended to divine communications in which, among other things, they say they were told it is wrong to kill foxes and martens. But I need not specify more of their delusions." Writing from down the Yukon River at Fort Yukon a few months later on 9 September he reported, "An Indian who makes pretensions to prophetic authority was present. His pretensions are as follows: that he has supernatural communication with heaven, has received a command to teach his fellow man, that those who do not receive his instructions will be punished by God, that the end of the world will be ten years hence. . . . [He] also recommended that people not set fire to the woods because visiting angels do not like the smell of smoke." [17] A few days later he claims to have encountered this same prophet, whom he identifies as "Shahoo," and reports that he "had a talk with him about making pretensions to prophesy." He notes that he was "glad to find him acknowledge that he felt he was in error, and he said he would endeavour to follow what he learnt out of the Bible." From then on, McDonald refers regularly to prophecy as "conjuring" (e.g., 18 October 1863, 6 June 1866). [18]

Although Shahoo may have responded politely to accommodate the missionary, he must surely have found the injunction odd. The ethnographic record suggests that shamans in northwestern North America were routinely expected to locate and control game, to cure the sick, to ensure success in disputes with neighboring peoples, to foretell the future, and to provide dietary rules and amulets to protect their clients — all duties enmeshed in behaviors that missionaries associated with what they called prophecy. Undoubtedly some shamans in contact with missionaries also responded by incorporating Christian concepts and making them part of their own indigenous narratives as a way of strengthening their own influence. [19] From the earliest stages of contact, then, discourse surrounding prophecy was contested.

Before introducing aboriginal narratives, it is important to locate them —

as McClellan advises — within the total body of literature in which they appear. Recent discussions about the nature of discourse in subarctic hunting societies center on ways knowledge is accumulated, maintained, and passed on, but also on ways legitimacy is claimed for particular kinds of explanations in opposition to other kinds.[20] Attention has also turned to narrative frameworks shared by narrators and their listeners and the ways shared metaphors are understood and reproduced through oral tradition.[21] Even when prophecy does not lead to short-term political and social transformations, it nevertheless may reproduce shared cultural meanings and underscore the importance of using a familiar narrative framework to explain the present, particularly as it is now invoked by indigenous people to claim authoritative interpretations of their past.[22]

Prophecy narratives in the southern Yukon seem to fit within a constellation of narratives that address a long-standing intellectual concern critical for northern hunters; that is, how humans and animals, with their overlapping and often conflicting powers and needs, can share the world.[23] A recurring metaphor in narrative presents the world as incorporating two parallel realities: one is the dimension that underlies the secular, material, temporal world of everyday life; the other is a domain that could more aptly be called superhuman and timeless. At the beginning of time, the narratives state and restate, a physical boundary — the horizon — separated these dimensions. On one side of the horizon was a snow-covered winter world where everything was white.[24] On the other side was the summer world full of color and warmth. Eventually the animals trapped on the winter side conspired to puncture the boundary so that the world as we know it could be brought into balance through its alternating seasons. In narrative, however, those dimensions remain distinct and must be negotiated repeatedly by all thinking beings and particularly by the shamans, who are more likely to travel between dimensions. Everyone has access to such journeys; the differences between the powers of a layman and a shaman are of degree rather than kind (see fig. 12).[25]

In such narratives, a protagonist meets a superhuman being who takes him or her on a journey from the secular, material, temporal world of everyday life to a supernatural, timeless domain. The two domains are marked off in some physical way. The protagonist may pass under a log, into a cave, or beyond the horizon, entering a world whose characteristics are usually the reverse of those found in the familiar world. One of the usual features of this world, for example, is that everything, including humans and animals, is white. In such a world the protagonist acquires new knowledge about proper behavior and, with great difficulty, brings that knowledge to the human world, where it can benefit the entire community. Usually this knowledge includes instructions about how people should behave to ensure proper relations with game and with other humans, as well as the injunction that if certain guidelines are followed the world will be a better place. As a consequence of this experience, the protagonist usually returns as a shaman, often with a special song learned on the journey.[26] One of the points of such narratives is to dramatize the role of powerful beings in ushering in world transformations, specifically concerning relations between the human and natural worlds.

Southern Yukon elders tell a range of narratives in which prophets figure significantly, and these stories seem to circle around related themes. Most of the prophecy narratives I have heard take the juxtaposition of these parallel worlds as a central metaphor and follow one of four distinct patterns. First, there are narratives that involve a protagonist's journey to a world where whiteness is a significant feature from which he or she returns with predictions about the coming of white people. Second, there are narratives predicting world transformation in which the other dimension, often described in terms of its whiteness, becomes the world of ordinary experience. Third are narrative journeys where the protagonist travels to heaven and returns as a shaman. Fourth are the stories commemorating shamans who foresaw and incorporated symbols and ideas from other religious cosmologies. As the twentieth century draws to a close, these narratives are retrospectively presented as ushering in the transformations that have become part of the routine experience of contemporary aboriginal peoples. Each of these four kinds of prophecy narrative is summarized below, with examples of how and where they are used in public discussion.

Foreknowledge of K'och'èn

The first kind of prophecy narrative involves a journey to a world where "whiteness" is a significant feature and where the protagonist acquires foreknowledge of the impending arrival of strangers. He or she learns about the eventual coming of white people and returns with talismans as proof, both of the journey and of the knowledge acquired.

Kitty Smith told a story she calls "The First Time People Knew K'och'èn." K'och'èn is the Tutchone and Southern Tutchone word for "white people," K'o coming from the Tutchone word for "cloud," and ch'èn from the word for "people," their fair skins implying they come from the "white" world removed from ordinary reality. In Mrs. Smith's narrative, a young boy undertakes a journey with an invisible helper who guides him. He enters the unfamiliar dimension by walking under a rainbow and receives instruction about what to eat, a bag of special (whiteman's) food, and a special song, all of which he is able to bring back with him. He returns to teach people about the habits of these strangers before white people physically arrive. He predicts that eventually "everyone will become whitemen." I pick up her story midway: [27]

This is a *story*, you know, not "story." It's *true* story.
He sees a rainbow. . . .
He stood up about this far from it, and somebody talked to him.

"Go through." He doesn't see who said that.
"Go through."

He comes, his dogs behind. Goes through.
Other side, little bit long way, he stands back.
Big sack falls down there.

"Don't eat that meat any more!
You're going to eat this grub.
This one in the sack.
Don't drink water from this ground for one week!
That many days, don't take water from this ground."
You're going to use this one, from inside your grub here, or else we're
     going to come to get you.

He took that sack.
Put it on top of his pack.
He doesn't see that man who talks to him, but he sees that rainbow.
But he talked to him.

[When he arrived home he asked his grandmother to call everyone
     together:]

"Tell those boys they got to come,
Their uncle, too, has got to come here."

Grandma goes to tell them,
"He wants you. . . . Don't know what's the matter.
He said it."

"I want you to fix that high bed for me," he said.
"I want to lay down on top."
Just quick they fix him.
"And two bridges, I want you to fix this way."
Bridge goes right there, right here, that far.
"Well, thank you," he said.
"Somebody talked to me; that's why I say that.
You come tonight before you eat: come to this bridge.
Then I'm going to tell you.
You hold your wife's hand when you come on that bridge.
I'm going to tell you. . . ."

They fix already that bed for him. On top.
He opens his sack — he doesn't know this kind of grub.
He eats something from there.
Water in there, too. He drinks water.

And he said, "They're coming now."
He sings some kind of song,
"Come on, come on my friends."

"You hold your wife's hand.
Go down, turn that way."
He tells them, "I'm going to be whiteman."
Nobody knows K'och'èn that time. That boy called them K'och'èn.
Right today they use it.

He said, "K'och'èn you, K'och'èn that one."
Turn that way, turn that way.
All that camp.

"You fellows are going to be white," that's what he said.
They don't know what he means.

"I'm not going to eat any more for seven days.
One day, this ground going to be full of K'och'èn.
You're going to be K'och'èn, you people."
Nobody knows "Going to turn whiteman."
How many whiteman grandchild have I got now?
That time, look!
I talk whiteman way, too, now.
He's honest, that boy, isn't he?

Seven days he stayed there.
And he told his grandma.
He gave her a big sack, that big one — don't know where it came from —
Anything, Indian grub, dried fish, everything is in that sack.

"Right here your grub is going to stay, Grandma.
Anything you want stays there.
It's not gone 'til you're gone.
That sack is all full of grease, everything.
No more you're going to look for grub.
Anything — fresh meat, you want it —
It's going to stay there — inside.
You want ribs? It's there.
What you wish for before you open, you say you want that one — right
    there it is.
Until you're gone, I leave this sack for you.
I'm going to stay here two days more, Grandma," he told her.
Then gone.
"Don't be sorry, nothing."

Him, he called them K'och'èn.
That's why this time Indians, nothing.
Right today, everybody calls them K'och'èn.

That time he gave them bread, nobody knows that.
"This kind of grub you fellows are going to eat."

It's true, this one.
That boy, he's gone — nobody knows where.
Now I sit down on top of that bed [like the one he asked them to make].
You sit on bed.
Before that, bed was on ground.

"You're going to be that way and you're going to turn to whiteman."
What whiteman?
That time nobody knows it.

A similar narrative was told by Rachel Dawson, a Tutchone-speaking woman who grew up at Fort Selkirk on the upper Yukon River. A protagonist whose journey takes him to the dimension inhabited by white animals and people returns as a shaman with a special song no one had ever heard. He uses his new powers to escort people to see these strangers, though he is the only one who can communicate with them. When his companions arrive, they see domestic (white) sheep wearing bells and pale people wearing "Japanese scarfs." The shaman instructs his followers that if they try to communicate with the strangers, they will be responsible for his death. Each of the white strangers ties a scarf around the neck of a Native man or woman, and then the strangers disappear. One sheep is left as evidence of the meeting, and the people return home with it, wearing their new items of clothing as further proof of the encounter. From that time on the shaman or "doctor" is able to see and communicate with white people whenever he chooses. Part of the power he acquires includes (white) swan power, conventionally a symbol of particularly powerful transformation.[28]

Predicting World Transformations

A second kind of narrative centers on a shaman's prediction of world transformation in which, with the coming of Europeans, the "other" unfamiliar world will engulf the world of ordinary reality. Angela Sidney, of Tagish and Inland Tlingit ancestry, remembered a shaman named Małal, who told people in 1912, "This ground is going to burn all over." She reported seventy years later about the time when she was ten years old:

I *saw* this old man, too: he was Indian doctor. One night he was singing: he made Indian doctor. In the morning, he told people: "This place is on fire all over." And people thought it was the flu. That flu was going to come in 1918, or whenever, when lots of people died. That's the one he talked about. That's just like fire, all. "Lots of people are going to die. But if you pray to God all the time, you are going to pass through this fire." In 1918, '19, '20, there was flu. Lots of people died.[29]

She went on to describe the impact that epidemic had on her own family. She lost her father, her aunt, and several cousins. She, her mother, and her own children became ill. Everyone was moved to the missionary's house, where they could be fed and looked after. She continues with her account, and the entire point of her story is to show the clarity of Małal's vision:

That was the old man who said, "This world is on fire." That's the sickness. He sees it like fire. And when he died, before he died, he says he is going to come back again. "Tie your dogs a long way from the camp," he tells people. But you know nowadays people don't listen to each other — he was sick, badly sick, and they thought he was crazy, I guess. "In four days I'm going to come back," he said. Here on the fourth day, those dogs started to bark all over. They heard just like somebody's singing or something. That's what the dogs were barking at — the dogs chased that spirit away again. That's what they say. That's what I heard about him, that old man. Małal, they call him.[30]

Elders are not the only members of the community who take prophecy seriously. At public hearings in 1975 on a proposed pipeline across the Yukon Territory, Joe Jack, a young Southern Tutchone man, spoke publicly about a Pelly River shaman who had foreseen tremendous changes:[31] "He said that he saw many white people coming to this land and that they will build trails to travel on. He said they will block off waterways and they will tear up the land to take out rocks . . . lastly he said they will build an iron road that will not be driven on. And, he said, when this happens . . . it will be the end of the Indian people."[32] By invoking this prophecy at a public hearing, Mr. Jack underscored the vision embodied in the prediction, a vision whose meaning is understood to be ambiguous until the event actually occurs. The very fact that he chose to make that part of his formal testimony suggests he considers it an example that speaks for itself — one that legitimizes local knowledge in the face of the scientific and bureaucratic discourse dominating these hearings.

Similarly, a Tutchone woman then involved in delivery of public health services told me about a story passed on to her by her grandmother, reporting how an early prophet predicted that strangers from the white, snowbound world would bring white material culture that would do grave danger to indigenous people: she interprets that as foreknowledge of flour, salt, and sugar, all sources of health problems, all white. Her comments reformulate the claims made by health care professionals about the dangers of excessive carbohydrates and sodium, but they do so in a locally meaningful idiom.

The contested nature of explanation is very much at issue here. Each of these accounts is told as a way of making intellectually consistent sense of disruptive changes — some past, some contemporary, some anticipated in

1. Angela Sidney, photographed in
Whitehorse in 1988. She is holding a replica
of her Deisheetaan Beaver clan crest. Photo
copyright 1988 by Jim Robb, Yukon.

2

2. Annie Ned photographed at her home in 1984. She is wearing a medal belonging to her son, Elijah Smith, who fought overseas in World War II. Photo by Julie Cruikshank.

3. Keish's sister Shaaw Tláa, also known as Kate Carmack, photographed shortly after the discovery of gold. Yukon Archives, James Albert Johnson Collection, 82/241 #21.

3

4

4. Kitty Smith photographed in Whitehorse in summer 1988. Photo copyright 1988 by Jim Robb, Yukon.

5. Three of Kitty Smith's carvings, Dukt'ootl (taller figure), Azanzhaya (smaller figure in front), and Bear Husband, (far left), stand behind a basket and a model totem pole. This is how they were displayed at the MacBride Museum, Whitehorse, for several years with the label "Carvings Made by Mackenzie River Indians." Only in the mid-1980s was Mrs. Smith identified as the carver. Courtesy of the MacBride Museum, Whitehorse, Yukon.

6   7

6. Kaats' being taken by Bear Woman. At
the top of the carving, Crow emerges from
the back of a whale. Courtesy of the
MacBride Museum, Whitehorse, Yukon.

7. The abandoned wife of Kaats' walks away
with their child as Kaats' leaves to follow
Bear Woman. Courtesy of the MacBride
Museum, Whitehorse, Yukon.

8. Kaats' and his Bear wife after he has been
transformed and integrated into the world
of Bear people. Courtesy of the MacBride
Museum, Whitehorse, Yukon.

9 10

9. Dukt'ootl', "Little Blackbird" or "Black Skin," the orphan who saved people from Sea Lion, carved by Kitty Smith. Courtesy of the MacBride Museum, Whitehorse, Yukon.

10. Carving of Dukt'ootl' in the foyer of the Alaska State Museum, Juneau, Alaska. II-B 1410, Alaska State Museum, Juneau.

1. Naatsilanéi, the man who made Killer
Whale, carved by Kitty Smith. Courtesy of
the MacBride Museum, Whitehorse, Yukon.

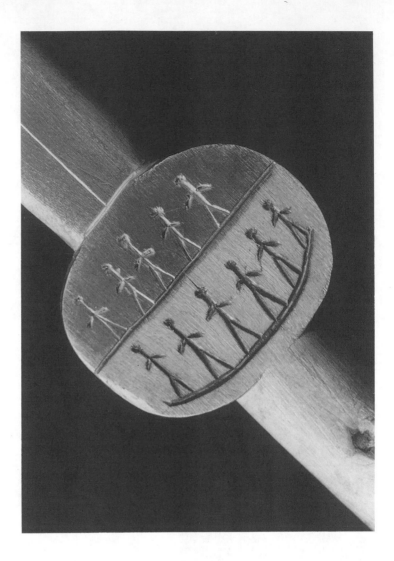

12. This medallion appears on a speaker's
staff or song stick in the MacBride Museum,
Whitehorse. The medallion's face may depict
the contrasting dimensions of reality so
prominent in stories told by Mrs. Sidney,
Mrs. Smith, and Mrs. Ned – a familiar world
of ordinary reality, a colorless winter world,
and the ability of travelers to move between
them. Courtesy of the MacBride Museum,
Whitehorse, Yukon.

the future — with reference to an authoritative narrative framework. Each is offered as evidence for the legitimacy of local knowledge and discourse, as an alternative explanation for the way things have come to be as they are that has to be taken seriously.

Travels to Heaven

A third kind of narrative involves a journey to heaven, with the protagonist returning as a prophet or shaman. Even before direct contact with Europeans, shamans visited heaven and returned with behavioral codes. In these stories, heaven often assumes the same dimensions as the "winter world," being bright or white and providing the protagonist with a new way of seeing.

A recurring theme in accounts of Yukon shamanism dramatizes how a particular shaman died, visited an upper world, and returned with new songs, new amulets, and new guidelines. Such visits, McClellan suggests, were part of an old, well-established pattern of shamanism.[33]

Narratives about journeys to heaven follow this familiar framework. Southern Yukon elders, for example, report that they first learned about Christianity from a coastal shaman named Nasq'a who had traveled to heaven. An old blind man, mistreated by his young wife, wandered off by himself in great distress. He was summoned by a stranger who restored his sight and led him on a journey from the world of ordinary reality (which is portrayed as appearing "blue") up a long ladder to a bright and shining place, heaven: "Half of the earth was dark, and Heaven was shining everywhere. There was no dark anywhere there. All the time there was sunshine and there were green leaves."[34] There he met Jesus, learned powerful songs, mastered new behavioral codes, and brought back physical evidence of his journey — a magical gunnysack. From then on, according to John Joe, the elderly Southern Tutchone man who told me this story in the mid-1970s, he was able to tell his story by preaching like Christian missionaries.[35]

A more detailed account of such a journey comes from Annie Ned when she was close to one hundred years old. We are able to compare the narrative structure of her version with a brief account left by a missionary in 1917, echoing the conviction McDonald expressed during the 1860s, that prophecy must be eradicated. Mrs. Ned's husband, Johnny, is remembered by many elders as a powerful shaman who was widely known as a prophet. Reportedly he made a journey to heaven, where he met God and returned able to speak and preach in English, and with a song that sounded very much like a Christian hymn:

> I can't talk about Johnny: it might be we'd make a mistake. I can't speak for other people. I can't show my husband's song.[36] I can tell you what *happened*, though. To start with, he got [an] Indian song. That man doesn't know anything, doesn't talk [English]. How come he talked [English] that time? He started to talk. I thought he's gone crazy! So I got Mr. Young [the missionary], and he said, "Don't bother Annie. I think he's going to go somewhere [to heaven?]. He's believing [he's experiencing conversion]." My husband took control all over: Carmacks, Dawson, all over. He took it around, that control. . . . After he got power, he can heal people.[37]

In fact, the missionary, possibly the same "Mr. Young," left his own impressions about Johnny Ned's prophecies in an unsigned letter on file in the Anglican Church records, advising an incoming missionary about the delicacy of the situation. His frame of understanding is quite different from that provided by Mrs. Ned, and if he understood her interpretation of those events, that interpretation has certainly been marginalized in *his* competing narrative:

> There is a cult in existence in the Champagne district under the leadership of Johnny Ned. For the most part, his teaching is alright. However, he has some fantastic ideas and has mixed on [*sic*] some native superstition to Christianity. I think that it is better to recognize everything that is good in his teaching than to attempt to antagonize him. After a while, when you get to know him you may be able to steer him along the right lines. A great many Indians throughout the country have been more or less worked up over his teachings and some of them believe his story regarding visions that he has had. Mr. Swanson [another missionary] and I talked over the subject and agreed that it was better to approve of his teachings as far as they agreed with Christian and to emphasize the fact that what he is teaching is the religion of Christ as practised and taught for hundreds of years.[38]

Mrs. Ned and I have discussed this letter, and she explicitly rejects this interpretation of her husband's powers, situating him firmly in aboriginal shamanic understanding: "It didn't come from God! He got it himself!" Her claim to authority comes from a framework she considers more encompassing than that provided by an Anglican missionary, whom she remembers as a short-term visitor at best. Once again, these accounts underscore the contested nature of prophecy narratives. On one hand, Johnny Ned seems to be incorporating Christian concepts to his own advantage.

On the other, missionaries are adopting a kind of bureaucratic pragmatism in their attempts to incorporate and subsume local knowledge as a way of extending their influence.

Foreknowledge of Religious Symbols

A final set of prophecy narratives centers on how shamans incorporated unfamiliar religious symbols in ways subsequently interpreted as transformative. Shamanic prophets are now said to have foretold the coming of new religious ideas, specifically Christianity and Baha'i.

Angela Sidney, who lived for eighty-nine years, engaged in a continuing intellectual struggle to integrate traditional understandings with modern ideas. As a young woman, she became extremely interested in and involved with the Anglican Church, and during the final years of her life she became very active in the Baha'i faith. She devoted a great deal of attention to reconciling her present beliefs with the shamanistic ideas she learned from her parents, uncles, and aunts, and she provided a splendidly coherent account of the connections between past ideas and present understandings. She took the ability of prophets to communicate with a higher being as a given. In the course of recording her life history, she asked, "What about Oral Roberts? He got messages from God. What about Father Divine? Well, that's why I think Indians are like that . . . [able to communicate directly with superhuman beings]. But we call it Indian doctor." [39]

In her narratives about the shaman Małal and the Pelly River shaman remembered as Major, she demonstrated that she, like the younger people cited above, continued to struggle with the issue of how traditional paradigms inform contemporary understanding. Her vehicle for linking these ideas centered on prophecy, as demonstrated in two stories she told about the Pelly River shaman. One story links his predictions to Christianity; the other links them to Baha'i. For some years the question of conflicting loyalties to such different institutional religions troubled her, but near the end of her life she reconciled any conflict between these two religious frameworks by showing how Major demonstrated foreknowledge of them both.

When Angela Sidney was nine years old, she says, she learned about Major from her mother. Years later, she claimed her own authority to tell about this prophet with reference to her mother's words. Major reportedly named a particular day Łinday, or "Sunday," before anyone knew that days might have special names, and he designated the day before Sunday as Łinday K'esku, or "little Sunday."

They tell about that old man — his name was Major — there were no English people in this country, that time. My mother saw him when she went to Pelly, a long time ago. And she said nobody knows about Sunday, Saturday, or anything like that. But he used to call it Łinday, that means "Sunday." Łinday K'esku means "little Sunday." That means "Saturday." But I guess he can't say it very good and he said Sunday as "Łinday," Łinday Tlein, that means "Big Sunday." I guess that was a white man name, but he can't say it.[40]

He encouraged his followers to make crosses out of golden eye eagle feathers and to wear them when they went hunting.

Year 1910, I see everybody's got crosses made out of golden eye eagle feathers. They made crosses, and everybody wore them if they were going out hunting, anything like that. And they say that's what Major told them to do. I was about nine years old and I asked my mother, "What's that for?"

And she said that's what Old Major told them to wear, to use when they go out hunting so they would get their game easily and things like that. Nothing would bother them. That's what she told me at that time. I just thought of that now! I guess it was a cross. I guess that's what it was. At that time I never thought of it, see?

. . . That's why I go to anybody that's praying. Don't care what kind of people they are. I was a good Anglican. I used to go to W.A., go to Easter Sunday, go to World Day of Prayer.[41]

Catharine McClellan, who heard similar accounts from Mrs. Sidney's mother, Maria, and her contemporaries in the 1940s and 1950s, wrote about the use of crosses by shamans but pointed out that this same shaman, Major, also urged people to put the sign of the cross in charcoal on their legs and arms. The symbol may be borrowed, she notes, but the emphasis on the four limbs and on the ceremonial use of charcoal are very old in the interior. She also points out the utility of designating a special day when people would be called together for meetings. The missionaries' "Sunday" worked to the advantage of shamans, whose efficacy was enhanced by the participation of an audience. The idea of Sunday was fortuitous because it brought people together for regular meetings. According to McClellan, these sessions were usually described as "prayer meetings," and attendance was heavy. The head shaman laid his hands on people's heads, foretelling sickness or death, expelling menstruating women from the group, and singing songs that were later remembered as "hymns." She concludes that "in brief, holding the seance on Sunday did little to change its essentially aboriginal nature."[42] Shamans, then, were able to incorporate Christian symbolism and to use Christian narrative in ways that enhanced their own authority.

In the late 1980s, as her own ideas continued to change, Mrs. Sidney had given more thought to the role of Major's prophecies in foreshadowing new ideas. Rethinking them, she found his words prophetic with reference to the coming of Baha'i to the Yukon. Major, she says,

tells about how it's going to be the last day, someday. So he said, "It's not going to happen right away. It's going to be long time yet," he said. "And," he said, "that animal is going to have nine legs. A nine-legged animal is going to be our food," he said.

And that's the one us Indians think maybe that's Baha'i. That Baha'i assembly has nine points. That's what we think. That's what it is. And he said, "If the people believe and live my way, I'm going to be very, very old. But if people don't accept me, God will take me away." . . .

Well, nothing like that happened until Baha'i people started coming here, telling about things like that. That's why we think — my family — we think that's what he meant. Because there's no animal got nine legs. And he said, "That's going to be your food, isn't it?" It's just *like* food. So there's lots of us joined in. I think I was the last one joined in because I'm Anglican. All of my kids joined the Baha'i. That's why I joined in, me too.[43]

By juxtaposing these two prophecy narratives, Mrs. Sidney establishes that intellectually there is no necessary conflict between Anglicanism, Baha'i, and indigenous shamanism. She is able to use this framework to provide an entirely satisfactory explanation of her ability to integrate ideas that others might find contradictory. Pleased with this reconciliation, she asked that the longer orally recorded tape from our interview be duplicated as her "teaching tape." She then requested that her daughter take it to Baha'i meetings to play for other members of the Baha'i faith so they could understand the linkages between the Baha'i prophet and indigenous prophets.

The prophecy narratives summarized above work within a familiar narrative framework where teller and listener share an understanding of the relation between parallel dimensions of reality. Knowledge from one dimension can be brought to the other by a shaman, who can then draw on his or her experience to dispense prophetic advice. These prophecies are evaluated by contemporary narrators not in terms of whether they altered social circumstances, but in terms of their ability to forge legitimate links between knowledge experienced by past prophets and events experienced by present tellers.

Underscoring all the narrators' accounts is the view that this is a conventional, routine, self-evident way of explaining the linkages between past and present. As has been suggested for neighboring Dene Dhaa prophets, prophecy long has been a normal part of experience. "Stories provided the landscape in which visions could occur, and songs provided the trail through the landscape."[44] Competing with this, we have the scholarly analysis of prophecy and prophetic movements that interprets such accounts as unusual, extraordinary, problematic, and in need of a different foundational explanation.

CLAIMING LEGITIMACY

In conclusion, it is worth returning to questions raised at the outset of this chapter. Elderly Athapaskan women tell prophecy narratives in the 1980s and 1990s as though these narratives speak for themselves — as though their message is a self-evident, commonsense explanation. What can this contribute to understandings about how connections between past and present are formulated and publicly presented? What do these narratives tell us about the construction, performance, and communication of knowledge? Why do elders specifically select these narratives as important ones to pass on to younger people in the 1990s?

Much of the academic debate surrounding prophecy concerns historical reconstruction of past events. Historians may treat oral traditions as one kind of source among many and approach them as "evidence" of "what really happened." Tellings by contemporary Athapaskan elders raise different questions. Oral traditions are presented not as evidence but as fully developed narrative constructions. Their tellings may cause us to reexamine the scholarly debate about prophecy.

To review that debate briefly: Ethnohistorians pose the question whether prophetic movements were indigenous or a response to external crises. Certainly the archaeological and documentary record for the upper Yukon River shows no shortage of disruptive events.[45] Prophecy narratives, at least in the western Subarctic, may have provided a way to explain changing circumstances long before the disruptions associated with contact, by embedding unfamiliar events within a familiar narrative framework. If this is the case, the relevance of "indigenous" versus "contact" distinctions may blur, leaving questions about their origins unanswerable.

The sociological literature emphasizes the short-term success or failure of particular prophets' attempts to transform the social and political order. Yet narrators seem to pay more attention to the explanatory power of words than to when individual prophets arose or what they achieved. Shamans like Major, Małal, or Johnny Ned can foretell Christianity, Baha'i, or apocalypse, and their prophecies are reinvoked years later not with reference to their short-term efficacy but to give meaning to events. In other words, following Renato Rosaldo's insight that narratives *shape* rather than *reflect* human conduct,[46] telling a prophetic narrative may give a storied form to proper relations. Such narratives may provide listeners with ways to think about how they should respond to external events.

Told now, prophecy narratives seem to establish meaning for events that have come to pass during narrators' own lifetimes — events as diverse as arrival of newcomers, cataclysmic epidemics, the expansion of state control, and the introduction of religious orthodoxies. Meanings of oral narratives are not fixed: they have to be understood in terms of how they are used. By explaining events in ways intellectually consistent with the framework oral tradition has long provided, prophecy narratives establish a complex relation between words and events. Words are not merely evidence for events (as they might be in a formulation where written documents are analyzed): events legitimize the words. Words have power to foretell events, and in this way, as Annie Ned, puts it: "Old time words are just like school." The words provide food for thought, but their meaning becomes clear only after the event has come to pass.

Scott Rushforth has recently written two thoughtful papers about knowledge, authority, and legitimation of beliefs among Dene hunters at Bear Lake, Northwest Territories.[47] Based on lengthy conversations with Dene men in the Mackenzie Valley, Rushforth discusses how, in Dene society, knowledge comes to be seen as legitimate when it is based on what he calls primary experience. He provides examples of Dene men who spoke to the Mackenzie Valley Pipeline Inquiry from their own personal experience about land-based activity and how they place far greater value on that knowledge than on the information provided by "expert witnesses" several steps removed from direct experience. He proposes that for Dene hunters, primary experience is the epistemological foundation of knowledge and is given far greater weight than secondary experience. Using the Mackenzie Valley Pipeline Inquiry as a case in point, he shows how expert systems invoked in hearings are resisted precisely because they threaten local authority. Indigenous people repeatedly assert the authority of their own local knowledge and reject the validity of those expert systems, which they see as derived from secondhand information rather than from direct experience.

Accounts about prophecy told by Yukon women add an additional dimension to Rushforth's thesis, one that I suspect is related to gender. These narratives suggest that a woman's knowledge and her right to speak come not only from her own experience but also from experiences conveyed directly to her by her mother, her grandmother, or other elders. Until recently, aboriginal people in the Subarctic acquired knowledge in two ways: one of those ways was by direct experience and observation; the other was through oral tradition — the narratives and instruction passed from one generation to the next. A woman's own knowledge and her right to speak derive from her direct connection with those words and with the experience of hearing those words from grandmothers, grandfathers, mothers, and aunts.[48] The purpose of these narratives is evaluated not in terms of whether shamans effected changes, but in terms of how words give meaning to events and how events, in turn, legitimize the words.

Increasingly, we understand that histories are interpretations that change in relation to changing circumstances. As others have pointed out, however, this ideology coexists with a competing ideology of history as "just the facts."[49] Ironically, historical relativism gets invoked more frequently for indigenous history than for mainstream history: in the Yukon Territory, for example, the gold rush and the Alaska Highway are taken for granted as reference points for local history and juxtaposed with aboriginal narratives "about" the gold rush or the highway. Thus constituted, relativism reinforces the legitimacy of mainstream history by making it seem more "real" or more "truthful."

At an obvious level, indigenous prophecy narratives have always been contested by the dominant ideology. But the context is less about facts or causality than about legitimacy. If they are taken to be fully developed narratives, they can be understood not just as evidence, or as one interpretation among many, but as an explanation competing for legitimacy, performed in a way that invokes ethnographic authority.

The enduring tradition of storytelling in the southern Yukon Territory suggests that narratives continue to address important questions during periods of social upheaval. Rather than prophecy narratives' being seen as evidence of failure to cope or of social breakdown, they may be viewed as successful engagement with changing ideas. Social sciences conventionally make a distinction between behaviors that might be characterized as adap-

tive strategies and those identified as expressive forms; the former are usually located with reference to the business of making a living and the latter
with reference to literary and artistic pursuits. Such a distinction, I suggest,
is inappropriate in situations where people see storytelling as central to ongoing reproduction of their culture. Yukon storytellers demonstrate the
critical intelligence embedded in oral narrative by showing how contemporary events are discussed with reference to traditional narrative, how an
understanding of the past informs our comprehension of the present.
Prophecy narratives are one more instance of the continuing use of tradition as a resource to frame explanations about the contemporary world.
They offer a competing form of historical consciousness that deserves to be
taken seriously.

7

Negotiating with Narrative: Establishing Cultural Identity at the Yukon International Storytelling Festival

Arctic and subarctic peoples have long been portrayed to distant audiences through museum exhibits, school textbooks, photographs, and films. "By their things we shall know them" remains one premise underlying images of ingenious technology, marginal economies, and the unremitting tedium of life at high latitudes.[1] Such depictions collide with indigenous expressions of attachment to place and constructions of the North as a homeland, rendered forcefully through land claims negotiations in northern North America, Home Rule in Greenland, Saami parliaments in Scandinavia, and nationalist aspirations among Siberian northern minorities.[2]

More complicated imagery is emerging at cultural performances in circumpolar regions from Greenland to northern Europe and Siberia, and across northern North America.[3] Superficially, these public presentations appear both to invert museological conventions and to occupy a climate different from deliberate speechmaking. Whereas views about transfer of land and power are deeply contested in northern communities, events like festivals supposedly occur in a climate where emphasis is on children, on celebration, on time out of time.[4] Any investigation of the history of cultural festivals, though, leads to literature documenting long-standing tensions between local initiatives to bolster cultural autonomy and pragmatic efforts by states to incorporate diversity.[5] The more successful a festival, the more probable is tension between emerging political aspirations and official ceremony, making these sites vivid experimental spaces for defining identity.

This chapter examines intercultural transactions at one public festival in northern Canada — the Yukon International Storytelling Festival. The question that interests me has recently been raised by Fred Myers, who suggests that public performances of indigenous culture should be understood as tangible forms of social action rather than as texts or representations standing outside the real activity of participants. He points to a dramatic shift in popular discourse during the past two decades. Once an oppositional model, the idea that indigenous people should represent themselves (rather than be represented by others, such as anthropologists) now meets widespread, commonsense approval. Yet Myers notes that contemporary critical theorists tend to treat performances of cultural identity as social texts for predictable kinds of analyses. They correctly discern inequality but then focus on the ideological interests such productions serve within the dominant system, emphasizing incorporation of colonial influences, commoditization of culture, or perceived "inventions of tradition." Such analyses, he argues, erase the ways indigenous peoples confer meaning on circumstances that confront them, having the effect of a double erasure of agency — first by colonial forces, then by postcolonial analyses. "Translation," Myers states concisely, "*is* the ethnographic object" in the late twentieth century.[6]

Anthropologists can no longer claim a privileged role as translators of culture,[7] but we are trained to provide ethnographic analysis of the translation process — to observe how ideas about culture are publicly produced and conveyed in intercultural transactions. We should be competent to compare ways of communicating about different epistemologies and to analyze the difficulties of translating between the specific and the general, the particular and the universal, the practical knowledge of cultural insiders and the theoretical concerns of anthropology.[8] James Clifford also suggests that as local visions increasingly thwart attempts to achieve global understandings, we should focus ethnographic investigation on the dynamics of translating discrepant meanings.[9]

Growing attention to dialogue in ethnographic fieldwork during recent decades, especially evident in work rooted in Native American narrative traditions, reminds us that questions about intercultural translation have long intrigued scholars attentive to the subtleties of conversational storytelling. This connection is evident, for instance, in Regna Darnell's investigation of Cree narrative performance; in Dennis Tedlock's analysis of an emerging dialogical model in anthropology; in Dell Hymes's work with storytellers who, despite concern that their work may be in vain, persist in trying to communicate with their listeners; in Greg Sarris's reflections about conversations that accompany oral storytelling processes; and in Keith Basso's close attention to the relation between storytelling and the meanings of place.[10] Such work reminds us that this translation project is situated in a long ethnographic tradition that pays increasing attention to dialogue.

Questions about cultural translation, central to much of late twentieth-century anthropology, were also asked decades ago by previous critics of modernity. Mikhail Bakhtin, Walter Benjamin, and Harold Innis independently struggled with ideas about the relation between storytelling, cultural translation, and social action — Bakhtin from Stalinist Russia, Benjamin fleeing Nazi Germany, Innis returning to Canada shaken by his experiences in the trenches of World War I. Each was concerned about the role of oral storytelling in human history, yet each based his research on ancient and medieval texts rather than on exposure to practicing storytellers. The relevant intersection lies in their shared commitment to the potential of oral storytelling and our opportunity to investigate ethnographically what this may mean now, when similar positions are so vigorously advocated by indigenous peoples. Bakhtin's fascination with human artistry as communicative behavior and his optimism about the transformative potential of folk culture to destabilize official culture had their broadest explication in his investigation of medieval carnival.[11] Harold Innis, writing about Canada's relations with its western and northern territories, advanced a thesis about cultural translation that began with economics and moved toward an exploration of how oral tradition challenges imperialist conceptions of time and space.[12] Walter Benjamin was concerned about deteriorating dialogue in modern society. He attributed this loss to the marginalization of oral narrative forms that once held the power to interweave information, moral content, and philosophical guidance. I will return to their individual insights later, while letting their questions about oral narrative help frame the issues raised here.

The Yukon International Storytelling Festival, held since 1988, attracts audiences each summer to a Whitehorse park on the Yukon River. A growing theme has been its circumpolar emphasis: indigenous performers from Greenland, Norway, Sweden, Siberia, and Alaska as well as from Arctic and Subarctic Canada are regular guests. Northern peoples have made concerted efforts to collaborate in recent years because of shared concerns about a deteriorating land base, erosion of subsistence economies, and submersion in larger nation-states. Their representatives have forged international alliances, developing comparative and global perspectives on issues surrounding political autonomy and building networks of support that include Dene, Tlingit, Inuit, Yupiit, Inupiat, Saami, Greenlandic, and other northern peoples.[13]

Although festival promotion underscores its international nature and the circumpolar origins of performers, most of the storytellers come from small communities in northwestern Canada, and the stories they tell concern intensely local issues. Land claims agreements between the Canadian government and individual Yukon First Nations are now being completed after twenty-five years of protracted negotiations, and they have profound implications for administration of land, resources, and social institutions. On 14 February 1995, the Yukon First Nations Land Claims Settlement Act (Bill C-33), and the Yukon First Nations Self-Government Act (Bill C-34) were proclaimed as law by the government of Canada. The major challenge facing indigenous leaders as they work out practical implications of binding legal obligations is how to move ahead in ways that will both satisfy their constituents and promote partnerships with nonindigenous Yukoners, who outnumber First Nations two to one.

Not only do divergent perspectives arise between indigenous Yukoners and newcomers, but Native Yukoners come from fourteen dispersed communities and speak eight distinct languages belonging to two different families. Despite cultural, linguistic, historical, and material disparities, these groups recognized the strategic importance of presenting a collective public voice in negotiating the overall agreement framing their settlement. But any idiom developed to do two things at once — to mark ethnicity to outsiders and to create internal cohesion — must necessarily be simple and inevitably becomes too restrictive to provide a meaningful metaphor for organizing personal behavior over the long term.[14] Since enactment of legislation, views about how to make land claims settlements work locally are becoming internally contested, mirroring larger discussions about identity emerging across northern Canada.[15]

Simultaneously, individuals are being recruited from communities to participate on legally mandated boards administering resources, education, health care, and heritage.[16] Self-government agreements enshrine provisions for joint management of specific programs by First Nations, federal, and territorial levels of government. After generations of exclusion from decisions affecting their social institutions and resources, this seems to connote remarkable progress. Yet there are risks: conceptual categories gaining legal and political force have become conventional during two decades of land claims negotiations, framed by Western concepts in the English language as "aboriginal rights," "self-government," "comanagement," "cultural heritage," and the ubiquitous "TEK," discussed at length in chapter 3. Even when they share terminology, indigenous people may understand these terms to have meanings very different from those attributed to them by government negotiators for whom such language has become routine.[17]

Public storytelling in the Yukon occurs in a context where indigenous peoples are struggling to defend their autonomy. They are deliberating among themselves whether to work within the terms of the dominant society, using the language of policymaking that increasingly dominates public transactions between indigenous Yukoners and non-Natives, or to reject those terms and insist on asserting positions using their own paradigms. In the following pages I discuss how this process unfolds at the Yukon International Storytelling Festival, where I have been a participant for several years. The analysis is based on my continuing research documenting oral tradition with Yukon Athapaskan (Dän) and Tlingit elders since the 1970s, regular attendance at the festival from 1989 until 1994, participation as an instructor at a festival-sponsored Elderhostel in 1993, and discussions with performers, festival organizers, and audience members in 1992, 1993, and 1994. After providing some background, I summarize four performances by elders from Alaska, northern British Columbia, and the Yukon at the 1993 and 1994 festivals, commenting on how each frames issues of identity. I selected these performances because of my familiarity with the narrators' work during the past two decades. I suggest that each speaker structures his or her narrative in a way meant to convey themes of identity by linking social institutions, land, and social history.

The issue of audience is critical. Audiences include local indigenous people, international indigenous visitors, families from the local white community, and tourists visiting the Yukon at the summer solstice and eager to attend local cultural events. Some listeners know the speakers well, are intimately familiar with the context they speak from, and bring understandings learned in communities where stories would conventionally be told, songs sung, and dances danced. Others are hearing the performers for the first time and may bring expectations gained from popular festivals. Expectations, then, reflect both regional and universalistic criteria, and often a mixture of both. How do competing local and global frameworks complicate the issues framed by Bakhtin, Benjamin, and Innis and the audience reception of contemporary performances? And what messages does the language of indigenous narrative convey to multicultural audiences?

BACKGROUND

The 1988 Northern Storytelling Festival was launched in Whitehorse, with funding from the Yukon Arts Council, a nongovernmental agency supporting local artists. Registered as a nonprofit society, the festival now has a board of directors, a newsletter called *Ts'étlaw Hunday,* and an energetic network of volunteers. Each year, efforts are made to schedule the festival to coincide roughly with the summer solstice, and most events occur in two enormous tents, with additional performances in smaller outlier tents. With up to three thousand visitors attending annually, ticket sales have been as high as sixteen thousand dollars. Core organizers have always included indigenous women and men, but most of the volunteers working on the mechanics of administration, fund-raising, advertising, and mounting the festival have been non-Native.[18] In 1994, for the first time, the festival was cosponsored by the Kwanlin Dan First Nation, formally acknowledging the centrality of local indigenous storytellers to the festival's ongoing stability.

Since its inception, references to authenticity (often phrased in terms of linguistic diversity) have figured prominently in festival promotion. Newspaper reports from 1988 noted that participants would come from six countries speaking twenty languages, adding that "the storytelling festival is an especially strong tool for northerners to preserve their culture."[19] That year participants came from Cape Dorset, Hudson Bay, Iceland, Greenland, and the Yukon. The following year more countries were represented: Greenland, Russia, northern Japan, Iceland, Denmark, Alaska, northern Canada, and Zimbabwe. Again, the newspaper reported the languages spoken: "English, French, Ukrainian, Han, Tagish, Tlingit, Northern Tutchone, Southern Tutchone, Kaska, Loucheux, Cree, Finnish, Japanese, Danish, Icelandic to name a few."[20] The third Northern Storytelling Festival brought Tukaq Theater from Greenland,[21] as well as groups from Iceland, Sweden, Finland, Canada, and the United States, and the fourth brought "sixty-four storytellers from around the world."[22]

By 1992 the name had been changed to the Yukon International Storytelling Festival, and for the first time visitors were able to attend from Chukotka in northeastern Siberia. The Hooper Bay Traditional Dance group, including more than a dozen energetic elders ranging from their early sixties to their late eighties, also came that year, making their first public appearance outside Alaska. They returned in 1994 accompanied by Roy Bell, grandson of the ninety-year-old group leader, who was interviewed about his work documenting Yup'ik song, dance, and stories and his plans to study performance art in Seattle the following year.[23]

Public projections of authenticity are balanced by local concerns of First Nations, who increasingly view the festival as a vehicle for translating cultural axioms to broad audiences. Over the years, local performers have become familiar with and confident about the venue — large tents and milling crowds in an open-air park — and have been able to assess the competence of their audiences. They have watched audiences grow, expand, and change in composition. They have experimented with storytelling strategies, noting which kinds of stories elicit the most engaged responses. They are all aware that performing in large tents in a downtown city park differs dramatically from the cultural context of storytelling in their own homes, but they accommodate their audiences, weighing the seemingly decontextualized setting against the opportunity to speak to receptive listeners. Whereas visiting performers sometimes bring translators and speak in indigenous languages, most local storytellers prefer to address their audiences in English rather than working through an intermediary.

Performers' adaptability was impressively evident during the summer of 1994, when organizers were forced to move the entire festival indoors on the second day as violent winds ripped through the site, toppling sound equipment and tearing tents. Being relocated across town to a formal stage at the newly built Yukon Arts Centre with its state-of-the-art lighting, sound system, and sloped seating for several hundred people did not inhibit the performers, and elders carried on telling stories much as they might have in tents. The only noticeable difference was that audience members who usually move casually from tent to tent were more likely to remain seated politely from the beginning to the end of each performance in the theater.

Indigenous storytelling assumes a relationship between speaker and listener. A listener becomes knowledgeable by hearing successive tellings of stories and may mull over, reinterpret, and absorb different meanings with each hearing. One dilemma facing performers at this festival is that predominantly urban audiences have limited familiarity with indigenous narrative styles. Even when stories are told in English, listeners hearing them for the first time often have great difficulty understanding them at more than a superficial level. Yet many visitors are attending the festival precisely to experience "authenticity," "cultural distinctiveness," "cultural preservation" — and to listen for such messages even when they are hard to understand. With more indigenous participants attending each year, performers can sometimes work on two levels. On one hand, they recognize the limitations of a diverse audience unlikely to notice subtleties of the stories and songs; on the other, members from their own communities have heard the stories before, are present as knowledgeable and critical listeners, and are attentive to nuances. This ability to address dual audiences is especially apparent when songs are sung in indigenous languages, and some listeners hear levels of humor or pathos opaque to others. It becomes more sharply focused when a performer publicly addresses issues contested within his or her own community but not easily grasped by the larger audience.

CONNECTING STORY TO LAND

Four storytellers performing in 1993 and 1994 illustrate the distinct ways messages are presented and received. A Tlingit elder established clear links between land, story, and ceremonial objects. A Tutchone-speaking couple made connections between land, songs, and past events. An Inland Tlingit elder linked land with clan histories that she has recently published in collaboration with a linguist. And an elder from the First Nation cosponsoring the 1994 festival unexpectedly read newspaper clippings and letters documenting the forcible removal of indigenous people from the site where the storytelling festival was being held. If the first three performances met universalistic expectations of broad audiences even when we might not fully understand the content, the fourth illustrates the process of control and resistance inherent in any festival, the inability of festival organizers to stage-manage all performances, and the unwillingness of tellers to be restrained by tidy regulations. Collectively, the four performances speak to issues of intercultural transaction connecting storytellers with audiences.

****

Connections between story, object, and land were posed by Austin Hammond, senior elder of the Łukaax̱.ádi Tlingit clan, who spoke at the festival on 27 June 1993. At eighty-two years of age, he had traveled by car almost two hundred miles from his coastal home in Haines, Alaska. Accompanied by the Tlingit theater group he founded and instructs, Naa Kahidi, he entered the large tent to address an audience of several hundred people. First he established the relevance of his story for a Yukon audience by stating why he had traveled so far, by reminding listeners of the long-standing trading relations and kinship ties binding coastal Tlingit and interior Athapaskan peoples, and by naming his own classificatory brothers and sisters from the Yukon interior.

He then asked his assistants to bring forward a hammered copper shield and a Chilkat blanket. Both had originally belonged to his ancestor Daanawaak, a Chilkat chief referred to as "about sixty years old" when Aurel Krause met him in 1885.[24] The name Daanawaak, which passed to

Mr. Hammond, is etched on the copper, the inscription reading simply "Donawock, Chief of the Chilkats, Died Feb 12, 1904."[25] Noting connections between the copper he was holding and the ancient Tlingit-Athapaskan trade in inland native copper, he said that Daanawaak's copper was "not going to tear down like that paper you have," adding, "My father told me, 'Pass that story on. Everyone will need it. Don't die with that story. . . . It's got to be up to you.'"

Next, indicating Daanawaak's Chilkat robe depicting the Łukaax̱.ádi sockeye salmon crest, he told its story. Some young men were paddling on the lake when their boat capsized and one disappeared in the water. Despite his companions' efforts to pull him to safety, the young man was swallowed by a giant sockeye salmon, whose image is woven into the blanket. "This is our paper," he reminded his attentive audience, making the point that history inscribed on ceremonial objects is always present, not archived in books.[26]

Austin Hammond was a powerful speaker, and his audience listened attentively as he spoke. Even those unfamiliar with the Tlingit clan histories could understand that he was establishing visually striking ceremonial objects as authoritative points of reference for his narratives and making further parallels between those objects and items of material culture valued by members of the audience, specifically paper and the written word. To many this masterful incorporation of story, visual imagery, and Tlingit language represented a high point of that year's festival. This became all the more poignant when Austin Hammond unexpectedly became ill and died one week later on 3 July 1993, making the Whitehorse festival his last public performance — his final attempt to translate precise meanings associating narrative with visual images.

At the end of Mr. Hammond's life, Richard and Nora Dauenhauer were engaged in writing biographies of Tlingit elders, and their account of his experiences helps to contextualize some of the things he was saying.[27] As Łukaax̱.ádi clan leader, Austin Hammond was both custodian of his clan house and steward of clan property, called at.óow in the Tlingit language and translated literally as "an owned or purchased thing or object." At.óow, a concept underlying all dimensions of Tlingit social and ceremonial life, refers broadly to the tangible and intangible property owned by the clan — songs, stories, artistic designs, personal names, and land.[28] Daanawaak's shield and robe are among the most important Łukaax̱.ádi at.óow, and the sockeye salmon crest is replicated on staffs, grave markers, blankets, and tunics.[29] The sockeye Chilkat robe that Austin Hammond brought to the festival encapsulates the history of the Łukaax̱.ádi clan and is understood by Tlingit people to be "a fiber deed to land along the Chilkat River from Sockeye Point on Chilkoot Lake to the beach along Lutak Inlet and from the tidelands to Mt. Ripinski." [30] In a 1981 film titled *Haa Shagóon* and made to discuss concepts of land ownership, Austin wore this robe and stated, "To those who come asking, 'Where is your history?' I answer, 'We wear our history.' " [31]

During the 1980s, Austin Hammond testified at public hearings on such issues as Native fishing rights, clear-cutting at Chilkoot Lake, and commercial development on tribal lands in Haines, Alaska. Central to his struggle to retain clan-owned lands has been a concern to demonstrate clan ownership in the absence of paper deeds and titles. Key to the project of cultural translation in which he was so deeply involved is the paradox that paperwork is as alien to Tlingit tradition as clan ownership is alien to Western law. [32] Austin Hammond's final public performance was a powerful statement of the relation between material and narrative traditions, but it was also a statement about landownership, a point I will return to after considering three other performances.

****

Connections between story and place were framed differently by Roddy and Bessie Blackjack from the central Yukon Territory. As Tutchone language teachers at the school in their community, they have grown comfortable with public performance, usually to audiences familiar with their stories and competent to appreciate renditions of narratives "everyone knows." Listeners growing up in homes where they hear these stories learn narrative frames and come to recognize how individual storytellers experiment with themes to reflect on their own life experiences. [33] On 26 June 1994, after the festival had been driven indoors by strong winds, the Blackjacks were among the first to speak in the Yukon Arts Centre to a mixed audience of several hundred people, some familiar with their narratives and others hearing them for the first time.

Roddy Blackjack began with an excerpt from a story cycle tracing the adventures of two brother-transformers who made the world suitable for human habitation at the beginning of time. [34] Recognizing that many listeners would not know that this narrative fits within a larger cycle of related stories, he shifted to a shorter, self-contained one about Mountain Man, who inhabits a subterranean world, quipping "and I guess that's why we should have subsurface rights!" The reference to this controversial land claims issue was immediately apparent to everyone in the audience, even those who might not follow more subtle parts of the story. More experienced listeners may have noticed that he tells this story differently than female storytellers do: women typically emphasize the intelligence and competence of Mountain Man's wife,[35] whereas Mr. Blackjack makes Mountain Man the protagonist, relegating the wife to a minor role. He concluded with a short story about Camprobber and his wife that may have alarmed those members of his audience paying close attention, because it features a murder-suicide in which the husband kills his wife, whom he suspects of betrayal, and then kills himself when he realizes his error. The editing of sex and violence from narratives told to children is a convention that seems peculiar to some indigenous Athapaskan storytellers.

He then introduced his wife, Bessie Blackjack, who sang four songs in the Tutchone language, each expressing intimate personal connections between people, season, and place. Such songs commemorate personal experiences and are remembered and sung years later, with the context always foregrounded: who "made" the song and on what occasion, where it was composed, when it was sung, and what the song meant to its composer. Roddy explained the context for each song in English, then briefly translated key passages.

The first, he said, was "her dad's song" about the loneliness of separation from his wife in autumn. Mrs. Blackjack's father had taken a job as a lineman on a riverboat one spring and spent the summer "up in Mayo." When he saw leaves falling in autumn, he realized how much he missed his wife, so he composed a song to her. "The leaves are falling down without seeing my wife yet," Roddy translated, and then Bessie sang in a clear, powerful voice. He introduced her second song as "her grandpa's song" — a farewell to a woman friend. This grandfather had traveled upriver to Lake Laberge, Mr. Blackjack explained, adding, "There were lots of good-looking girls at Lake Laberge. When he came back up north, he sang that song to her." A third song, he said, was "her grandma's song" about a trip from Little Salmon village (Tánintsę́ Chú Dachäk) to the Pelly River during the dangerous time after spring breakup when rivers are swollen. "One bunch from Little Salmon went to Pelly River and just about drowned in the river. It was right after breakup. When they got home, the leaves were starting to grow so they sang a song to those leaves, 'If we [had] drowned at Pelly River, we would never see leaves again.'"

Athapaskan traditions of storytelling differ markedly from Tlingit narratives like Austin Hammond's. The stories Roddy Blackjack told and the songs Bessie Blackjack sang are not clan property, but they convey an immediate connection to place.[36] His narratives recall original relations between human and nonhuman worlds; her songs convey the experiences of hudé dän, "long ago people" transported to the present through their songs. For listeners familiar with their repertoire, both signal connection to place — Roddy's stories retelling how people came to be in the Yukon at the beginning of time, Bessie's songs commemorating deep connections with place and the stubborn particularity of voices that continue to be heard in the present.

****

A third series of connections between story and place was posed by Elizabeth Nyman, a Tlingit elder from Atlin, northern British Columbia. She spoke on 26 June 1994, following Roddy and Bessie Blackjack, and told stories about the origins of landscape features on the Taku River and how those stories connect her Yanyeidí clan with those places. Born in 1915, she has recently completed a bilingual book recording Yanyeidí clan history in Tlingit and English, prepared during a fifteen-year collaboration with linguist Jeff Leer.[37]

Phrasing her account tactfully that day, in terms of what children (rather than her audience) need to know, she pointed to sources from which she takes guidance — the land, her elders, her clan. She began, "This is how I show what little I know," including herself with her audience as a learner to avoid openly challenging the competence of her listeners. This inversion of the more common narrative in Canadian history in which indigenous people are assigned the role of children, needing tutelage, is worth noting.[38]

The name T'àkhú, she reported, comes from the sound geese make when they rest at the mouth of the Taku River during their annual Arctic migration. Two giants once battled at the mouth of the Taku River. The winner decapitated his rival, throwing the loser's head across the river, where it remains a mountain known as Łkudasêts'k Shàyí, and his heart and windpipe into the river, where each became an island.[39] She spoke about Taku Glacier, which periodically surges, forming an impassable barrier across the river. During one surge, Tlingit people first discovered neighbors living across the glacier when they lost a stone adze and heard voices responding to their cries of distress. She recounted Yanyeidí clan origins and history, telling how people traveled on that river, paying respectful attention to the glacier and recalling how her own father, who understood glaciers to be sentient beings, used to remind the Taku Glacier, "We don't want trouble. We want to go [travel] back and forth [on the river]."

She emphasized her need to reconfirm, through her words, Yanyeidí claims to the Taku River: "I'm glad to see everyone understands it, understands every word we say. When I see they don't believe it, I think they *should* believe it, like my dad, like my stepmother. Now it is my turn to tell. The Taku River hears me, and if I say anything bad, he hears me." Giving only the slightest hint that what she was saying might be contested by others, she continued: "The new generation think we want to claim Taku, but we don't! We just want people to respect it, like the old generation. It's not that I want to take Taku River and pack it around!"

As she spoke that day, she conveyed the impression of a quiet, gracious elder patiently recounting uncontroversial history as a way of publicly restating her clan's connection to place, echoing the style used by Austin Hammond a year earlier. The complexity of her speech became more apparent two weeks later, on 9 July, when she addressed a group of Tlingit elders among whom Yanyeidí claims *are* contested, at Brook's Brook, ninety miles south of Whitehorse. There she began by acknowledging that she faced challenges about her right to prepare her book. "People say I wrote that book because I want to make a name for myself. That's not true. I did it so I could tell them our history." But as she retold her Yanyeidí history, this time speaking in Tlingit, translated into English for the benefit of younger people, it became clear that her audience included many who support a competing version of clan history, one that challenges specific Yanyeidí claims. Such claims are not simply part of past history — they continue to play a critical role in contemporary politics because each version has implications for the implementation of land claims agreements. Recording clan histories does not freeze them in a static state, as some might argue; on the contrary, it generates fresh debates about conflicting and competing versions.[40]

At the Storytelling Festival with its mixed audience, such controversy was masked as Mrs. Nyman stated again that her primary purpose in telling clan history is to bequeath this legacy to her descendants in a form they can understand clearly.[41] As she phrased it in her book,

I will not live forever,
but those who come after you will read it.
If only you were taken by boat along the Taku River,
you could write down the whole story in a book.[42]

****

Superficially, a fourth example departs radically from the indirect story-telling styles discussed above. In 1994 the Kwanlin Dan First Nation, whose territories fall within the municipality of Whitehorse, volunteered to cosponsor the Storytelling Festival. From their perspective, the festival offers untested ground to publicly challenge the formal Yukon land claims negotiation process. They encouraged their elders to speak about their memories of the waterfront, now in the downtown city center.[43]

One elder who spoke on the same day as the Blackjacks and Mrs. Nyman was Jessie Scarff, a long-term resident of Whitehorse and an astute observer of Indian-white relations with lengthy experience interacting with people from all sectors of the community. Mrs. Scarff used her performance time to outline the forcible removal of indigenous people from the Yukon River waterfront between 1915 and the mid-1960s. She began by stating where she was born and when she had moved to Whitehorse, pointing out that her first Whitehorse home had been very close to the present site of the Storytelling Festival. She told us that she had recently been "doing research in the archives" (an ironic pronouncement from an elder in her seventies) and had come upon some documents she wanted to read to us. She went on to talk about how indigenous people living on the waterfront had been classified as "squatters" — a pointed contrast with the contemporary convention of referring to "First Nations" — and then read from documents that had been duplicated in a pamphlet being distributed to festivalgoers at that very moment.

The first document was a letter written to the Department of Indian Affairs on 14 October 1915, by an Indian agent, John Hawksley. She read:

Sir: The White Pass & Yukon Transportation Co. have ordered the Indians at White-horse to move from their land where they are now squatted. While at Whitehorse, in company with Inspector Bell of the R.N.W.M.P. [Royal Northwest Mounted Police] and two of the White Pass Officials I have selected a piece of land (160 acres) about two miles north of the town for an Indian Reserve. It is situated on the bank of the river, there is good water and wood supply.

I hereby apply to you for permission to have these two pieces of land surveyed and duly recorded as Indian Reserves.

John Hawksley
Indian Superintendent

The second document recorded the response from the local newspaper, the *Whitehorse Star*, a week later, reminding the by now uncomfortable audience of the history of racism in the town. She read,

The Star congratulates Indian Superintendent Hawksley on his wisdom in moving Indians, houses, tents, bags and baggage from the swamp above town to a point below town on the left limit of the river. Ever since the Indians founded a village above the town three years ago this paper has waged a campaign to have them removed but it never received a word of encouragement either from the authorities or from the citizens. Now that the Indians are gone it is hoped any future move to establish a village so near town will promptly be nipped in the bud. It is better for the Indians that they should be away by themselves and it is certainly better for the town that they be not camped so close to the source of public water supply. (*Whitehorse Star*, 22 October 1915)

The third document, reminding audiences that this was no mere episode from ancient history, was a letter written by a former Yukon commissioner to the Whitehorse mayor on 21 February 1962:

Commencing immediately, the Department of Northern Affairs and National Resources and the Government of the Yukon Territory will be removing buildings located on Crown land in Whiskey Flats, Moccasin Flats, Sleepy Hollow, West of Eighth Avenue and on Two Mile Hill. At present, we will be moving only those buildings which are not being used for residential purposes. Later in the season, when the cold weather moderates, we will undertake the removal of buildings which are occupied as residences.

Yours sincerely,
F. H. Collins, Commissioner

The tone of her presentation was clear, didactic, and uncompromising: these removals had affected her, her family, and her friends. "What we have got, we like to share, but we don't like to be stepped on." Although the audience response was tepidly polite following her performance, people could be overheard expressing discomfort or even hostility as they left. The clear consensus of several visitors I spoke casually with afterward was that "politics" had no place at a storytelling festival.

What was the larger context for Mrs. Scarff's comments? They emerge from discussions among members of the Kwanlin Dan First Nation about lands claimed in ongoing negotiations with the federal government. Although Yukonwide Land Claims and Self-Government Agreements were virtually in place by summer 1994, awaiting ratification by the government of Canada, those agreements now require individual communities to negotiate the details of specific claims directly with federal negotiators. At the time of this festival, only four Yukon First Nations had completed the specific negotiations that will allow them to proceed with the implementation phase; the remaining twelve were still preparing to do so.[44] Claims made by adjacent First Nations inevitably overlap, forcing communities into competition with one another. Kwanlin Dan members, engulfed by an urban community, see themselves as particularly disadvantaged because waterfront lands they might otherwise select have been alienated by territorial, municipal, and industrial interests and also because their urban setting draws a membership from throughout the Yukon, giving them a less cohesive constituency than some other First Nations. Now that an overall agreement has been completed, the urgency for governments to settle claims with individual communities is decreasing, and Kwanlin Dan members have expressed concern that as one of the most complex claims, theirs may receive low priority. Mrs. Scarff's comments underscore material disparities that are growing among Yukon communities.

The Kwanlin Dan tactic startled its audience but achieved its intended effect — conveying a clear message that the land claims process does not satisfy everyone. In the following days, newspaper and radio coverage, though not necessarily supporting their position, featured presentations by Kwanlin Dan members about their claims to waterfront lands. A cartoon in a local newspaper showed a child being dragged into the Storytelling Festival by a mother urging, "Come on, it will be fun!"[45] Yet Jessie Scarff's message was not so different from the more oblique storytelling strategies used by Austin Hammond, Roddy and Bessie Blackjack, and Elizabeth Nyman — it just fit more clearly within dominant paradigms and hence violated shared perceptions of many audience members about the kind of storytelling appropriate at a cultural festival.

THE SOCIAL LIFE OF STORIES

Questions about the vitality of storytelling have intrigued students of human behavior for generations, just as they animate social action from the

Arctic to the South Pacific. In the 1930s, 1940s, and 1950s, with some urgency, Bakhtin, Benjamin, and Innis independently imagined the power of oral tradition to destabilize commonsense categories, to promote non-confrontational ways of reevaluating hegemonic concepts, to encourage dialogue rather than monologue. Drawing on classical and medieval texts, they were concerned primarily with what they saw as the diminishing power of oral dialogue in human affairs. But at the end of the twentieth century there is growing evidence that orality remains a powerful force in the world and that its consequences are open to investigation. In the mid-1990s, as shock waves reverberated around the world following the execution of Nigerian writer and activist Ken Saro-Wiwa, we were reminded how deeply threatening autocratic regimes still find the spoken words of storytellers.

Bakhtin, with his energetic appreciation of the destabilizing possibilities of folk humor, struggled in 1930s Russia to imagine subversion in totalitarian states. Any adequate reading of contemporary culture, in his view, required an understanding of how ordinary people have used oral communication strategies to resist arbitrary power. Bakhtin's reference point was Russian peasant culture, and his target the increasingly authoritarian Soviet state where he lived. He drew his examples from how medieval French peasants used ribald, satirical humor to challenge authority through carnivals, yet he never, in any of his translated writings, directly discusses ordinary, everyday, contemporary folk storytelling.[46]

A decade later, Walter Benjamin grappled with similar issues engulfing Europe during the early years of Hitler's ascendancy. He noted the insidious consequences of deteriorating dialogue in modern society, attributing this at least partly to the diminishing role of the storyteller. As communications technology proliferates, he argued, information becomes fragmented and detached from the moral philosophical guidance we think of as knowledge and might once even have called wisdom. The power of narrative storytelling lies in its capacity to interweave such elements by combining drama and practical experience with moral content. Storytelling, in his view, is open ended rather than didactic, allowing listeners to draw independent conclusions. Medieval storytellers recounted events without imposing interpretation, and their practice had equally important consequences for the art of telling and the art of listening. By the very act of telling stories, narrators explore how their meanings work; by listening, audiences can think about how those meanings apply to their own lives. Stories allow listeners to embellish events, to reinterpret them, to mull over what they hear, and to learn something new each time, providing raw material for developing philosophy.[47] Once interactive storytelling is replaced by mechanical communication, he alleged, human experience becomes devalued.

Writing from Canada, Harold Innis proposed that Arctic and subarctic regions provide a visual template for the modernist tendency to conceptualize time as spatially laid out, mechanically segmented, and linear. Colonial projects, he observed, move forward by devising and reinforcing categories — objectivity, subjectivity, space, time — that encourage the annexation of territories and the subjugation of former inhabitants.[48] Gradually, those at the center monopolize what comes to be considered rational discourse and marginalize those who speak in a different idiom. Innis admired the structural characteristics of oral tradition and recognized its potential to balance spatial with temporal concepts by reinjecting an appreciation for the importance of qualitative time in human affairs. Oral tradition permits continuous revision of history by actively reinterpreting events and then incorporating such constructions into the next generation of narrative. Its flexibility allows a gifted storyteller to adapt a given narrative to make sense of a confusing situation. Like Benjamin, Innis believed that orally transmitted narratives develop in their hearers a capacity to listen, a deteriorating skill in an age of ever-fragmenting information.[49]

The concept of storytelling as communication-based social action seems particularly germane in the contemporary Yukon. During a generation of land claims negotiations, indigenous Yukoners have become increasingly attentive to international perspectives on their political struggles. The global stage on which their settlement is now evaluated seems very different from the village meetings that led to slow, steady consensus building during the early 1970s. Since then, opportunities to attend international workshops, conferences, and meetings have allowed them to compare experiences with other indigenous peoples and to bring back narratives about what they have learned. Simultaneously, the larger world has become increasingly aware of northern peoples. If the first wave of enthusiasm for Arctic and subarctic territories was generated by demands for resources — furs, gold, minerals, oil, gas, hydroelectric power — the second focuses on addressing the social and ecological crises caused by casual extraction procedures. But interest groups enmeshed in these debates seem unable to devise unambiguous models to evaluate competing urban demands for hydroelectric power, requirements of tundra ecosystems, or indigenous peoples' claims to rights of self-determination. With increasing numbers of qualitative variables, the translation process grows confrontational.

Given the range of ongoing policy decisions being made about northern land claims, local government, industrial expansion, and militarization of the Arctic, the issue of how depictions of culture translate across cultural boundaries becomes critical.[50] One current avenue for claiming legitimacy in liberal democracies is demonstrating distinctive culture. Yet this creates new problems for indigenous people if the larger world essentializes indigenous voice, expecting all people from one community to say the same thing. The stakes for effective translation — often by diverse performers for heterogeneous audiences — become higher in a world where culture is a marker of authenticity in political negotiations and where conflicting folk models of culture operate simultaneously. A stereotype-filled setting like a subarctic storytelling festival held at the summer solstice seems an appropriate location to investigate public, intercultural transactions as forms of serious social action.

Following Benjamin and Innis, a model of social action foregrounding communication makes audiences central to performance, participating by inscribing meaning on what they see and hear. Contemporary studies of cultural performance too often belittle the role of audiences, criticizing the power of the spectators' gaze to transform performers into victims of subjectivity, or implying that audiences are vulnerable to duplicitous inventions and incapable of understanding what they see.[51] Performers at this festival take their audiences extremely seriously, as witnesses. Broad endorsement of First Nations claims is critical, and speakers are aware that audiences at the festival, like those hearing land claims, include both distant and local supporters and critics.[52]

Minimally, performers at this festival must address four audiences. First there are international visitors, mostly indigenous guests from other northern countries who come to meet Yukoners and to compare personal, political, and artistic experiences. Second, tourists visiting the Yukon for the summer solstice attend the festival to experience an event that seems to typify local culture. Third are non-Native Yukoners, some who know performers personally and others whose experience of indigenous people comes largely through the rhetoric of land claims negotiations that has dominated formal interactions between Natives and newcomers for more than two decades. Fourth, indigenous Yukoners come as appreciative and critical listeners to applaud family and friends, to compare local stories with those told by visitors, and to evaluate the impact of Yukon storytelling on this very mixed audience.

The contemporary explosion of cultural festivals adds ideological freight — expectations of pedagogical instruction or aesthetic experience, nostalgia for lost spirituality and search for sacred tradition, or pure entertainment. Identities, as Friedman notes, are carved out not in a vacuum but in a world already defined.[53] Despite substantial agreement about hearing perspectives on controversial issues directly from those affected rather than through intermediaries, audiences historically demonstrate preference for varying characteristics of voice. In the 1970s, the role of spokesperson was usually claimed by political activists involved in such negotiations as the Mackenzie Valley Pipeline Inquiry in northwestern Canada, Saami protests surrounding the Kautokeino-Alto dam in northern Norway, settlement of Alaska land claims in the face of oil development, and the formulation of Home Rule in Greenland.[54] But the paradigm that indigenous peoples should portray their own cultures to a larger world has come to prominence within a pronounced global ideological shift to conservative values. Increasingly, it is Native artists who are now invited to speak to non-Native audiences. Ironically, indigenous people are once again indexed by artistic production, reviving the legacy discussed at the outset by objectifying culture through objects, photographs, and ethnographic films.[55] Currently we are more likely to hear indigenous political leaders described in the popular press as "out of touch," while visual artists, writers, and storytellers (especially when they deal with environmental themes) are identified as providing more "authentic" projections of indigenous voice. When people understand Austin Hammond, Bessie Blackjack, and Elizabeth Nyman as performing authentic indigenous artistic tradition and Jessie Scarff as talking about politics, that inscription of meaning comes from audiences rather than from performers.

The storytellers whose work is discussed here make it clear that they do not necessarily speak with one voice, that they do not consider themselves victims, and that their traditions, though actively mobilized in intercultural transactions, are not invented except insofar as cultural understandings are always creatively reinterpreted. They resolutely persist in connecting large issues to local contexts. They also connect categories in ways that Bakhtin might see as undermining conventional understandings, Innis as reinjecting a temporal dimension into discussions of place, and Benjamin as providing a coherent conceptual framework.

Austin Hammond links material culture with narrative to illustrate that an ancient copper shield, a fiber robe, and a story are all deeds to land. Audience members were moved to see ceremonial regalia usually separated from the world by glass in metropolitan museums transported in suitcases by car from coastal Tlingit homes to illustrate the words of a narrative in the manner of Benjamin's storyteller. This challenges the familiar museum paradigm that objects are primary and words illustrative. Spectators familiar with the Tlingit claims negotiations during his tenure as clan leader recognize that Mr. Hammond's story documents the alienation of Łukaax̱.ádi clan lands — by the Presbyterian Church in the late nineteenth century, by government in the early twentieth century, and by forestry companies in the 1990s.

Bessie and Roddy Blackjack frame their presentation with reference to genealogy and place. The transition from Roddy's stories to Bessie's songs underscores Innis's idea that a sound-based paradigm can contribute to cultural remembrance.[56] Mrs. Blackjack's songs anchor history to land and make place central to her understanding of the connections between present and past as she maps events on the rivers, lakes, and trails connecting the territories in which she, her parents, and her grandparents traveled.

Elizabeth Nyman uses geographical features to map family and clan histories that she learned as a child and now transmits in terms applauded by some, contested by others, and opaque to most members of her audience. Her story, told to three distinct audiences — readers of her book, listeners at the Storytelling Festival, and elders at their own meetings two weeks later — illustrates Benjamin's principle that narrative frames "facts" differently for different audiences.

Jessie Scarff speaks to us in more directly accessible language, but she inverts conventional categories — making a performance of performance in a way that Bakhtin would surely find carnivalesque — posing archival research as the source of an elder's ethnographic authority, by reminding us that "First Nations" were defined not long ago as "squatters," and by challenging our preconceptions about storytelling with her hard-hitting narrative.

Using stories, regalia, place-names, and songs, each performer signals the importance of land and kinship as attachment points for memory. Following Innis, we see how annexation of territories, extraction of minerals, and layers of bureaucratic administration have exerted pressures both on land and on long-standing institutions associated with kinship. Genealogy, place, and the ceremonial objects associated with both become focal points by which cultural memory resists faceless bureaucracy. Land has been central to ongoing public discussions in the Yukon for more than two decades, but conceptions of place conveyed in these performances differ from the precise legal language in which they are articulated in legislation now known as Bill C-33 and Bill C-34.

A story now heard in the Yukon describes how a visitor invited to a primary school classroom in the early 1990s asked children what they hoped to do when they finished school. One youngster waved his hand enthusiastically. His occupational choice? "A land claims negotiator!" Although usually told to illustrate the inertia accompanying a generation of negotiations, the story has a more optimistic side. The Umbrella Final Agreement is in no way a finite bounded solution and is more like the unfinished and unfinishable projects Harold Innis once referred to as "the breath of cultural life." [57] As the hard work of implementing land claims settlements continues, daily exchange of stories in everyday conversation allows those who feel marginalized by the process to disrupt commonsense understandings of just how "settled" such settlements are. Sites like the Yukon Storytelling Festival provide locations for engaged exposure to different perspectives and opportunities to investigate how local knowledge and social action are mediated by dialogue. We cannot know the outcomes of such transactions, nor can we expect them to be tidy, but we can learn a great deal if we take seriously the social agency of the participants.

Epilogue

Anyone involved in long-term ethnographic research confronts the irony that work conducted during one period, within one set of guidelines, will inevitably be evaluated differently a generation later. Ethnographic research is an interactive business and a humbling one. As students, we begin knowing very little, listen closely to the stories we are told, and learn soon enough that communities everywhere are diverse and complex and that stories told by one person or one sector of the community may seem naive or wrongheaded to others — if not at the time they are told, then probably sometime in the future. We also learn that anthropological narratives we have absorbed share the same characteristics. The theoretical perspectives that animate one generation of scholars are frequently reinterpreted by the next as the dead hand of history.

The energetic thesis inspiring community-based oral history projects in the Yukon Territory during the 1970s and 1980s was that gender, age, class, ethnicity, and locale influence the ways people think and talk about their experiences. Collaborative projects seemed to offer unlimited opportunities for documenting such varieties of remembered history. If classic ethnographies written during the 1940s and 1950s, with titles like *The Tanana Indians* or *The Kaska Indians,* seemed to erase any sense of human agency and were often unrecognizable to members of the communities where they were set, our optimistic objective was to show the complexities of life lived during the turbulent decades of the early twentieth century. Our adversary was positivism, and our goal was documenting multiplicity. And the elder storytellers I worked with certainly taught me to think about those issues in more complex ways than I had imagined. In academic scholarship during the same period, emphasis in the study of verbal arts shifted from text to performance, from ideas of stability toward lack of closure, from concepts of orderliness to appreciation of variety, from imperial history to critical examination of hierarchies of narratives. But changing theoretical questions led anthropologists to particular conclusions about social construction just about the time that indigenous organizations began to recognize the strategic value of using such concepts as "tradition" and "boundedness" as a framework to present their claims to collective rights and distinctive identity. If our 1970s criticism of earlier anthropology centered on its confident assertion of objective truths, emerging preferences for deconstruction may now be viewed as offensive or even as harmful to indigenous peoples' struggles. As disciplines like anthropology and history become more comfortable with ideas about social construction of the past, we may disappoint audiences who are asking different questions and searching for clearer depictions of history more consistent with notions of objectivity than with the apparent ethical barrenness of postmodern relativism. Increasingly, indigenous communities facing legal battles require authoritative versions of metanarratives we hoped to make problematic. If the unified discourse required for political mobilization sometimes tends to essentialize voice, where are the possible intersections of indigenous paradigms with scholarly theory at the end of the twentieth century?

Narratives arguably connect analytical constructs with the material conditions of people's daily lives, leading in directions quite different from postmodern relativism. In this book I have spoken of narrative as fluid, transformative, and intersubjective, and as situated in process and performance. But I nevertheless hear and understand these stories as being told thoughtfully and purposefully, as being grounded in everyday life, and as having political consequences. Anthropology has emerged from a decade of self-scrutiny less confident about both objectivist and constructivist claims, but aware that throughout the world boundaries of culture, race, gender, class, and religion are drawn ever more firmly as positions to speak from — whether to assert different truth claims or to deny humanity to those who seem unfamiliar. Verena Stolcke, for instance, shows how in parts of Europe the mirage of liberalism is fading as cultural fundamentalism becomes constructed in global political arenas with fixed, firm, and increasingly "naturalized" boundaries.[1] Anthropology's project of analyzing how translation occurs across such boundaries has never seemed more important.

For two decades in the Yukon, such translation has centered on clarifying relations between past and present and their contemporary collisions. Ray Fogelson coined the term "epitomizing" to characterize dramatic incidents that condense complex forces and make them easy to grasp in an icon or a symbol, a theme explored elsewhere in this book.[2] If the discovery of Klondike gold in August 1896 has long constituted a key epitomizing event in Yukon history, passage of comprehensive land claims legislation a century later in February 1995 abridges intricate processes that we will undoubtedly hear encapsulated in key phrases for years to come. Both "gold rush" and "land claims" signify far-reaching structural changes in relations between indigenous peoples and the state — gold, the arrival of strangers, land claims, the settlement of debt. But gold was not just accidently "discovered" on an August evening — its general location had been known for decades, and its consequences for state expansion have resonated for a century. Land claims were not "settled" with the signing of legal documents. The first formal claim was filed by Chief Jim Boss in 1901; negotiations with the Canadian government got seriously under way in the 1970s; the proceedings have absorbed the lives of a generation of indigenous leaders just as the real negotiations about what this legislation means are likely to dominate economic and political discussions into the next century.

Modern agreements reached between indigenous people in northern Canada and the Canadian government involve complex transfers of land, money, and constitutionally guaranteed rights to self-governance, framed as *comprehensive* land claims agreements. While self-evidently about reallocating land and political power, they are also rooted in broader issues of restructuring everyday, commonsense, taken for granted categories and practices. The issue of who controls images and representations of First Nations portrayed locally and to the larger world remains at the core of land claims negotiations. Although the outcomes of these settlements are uncertain and are the subject of much speculation, two decades of successful negotiations have already rearranged the conventions within which First Nations history and culture are depicted in the Yukon. Control of narrative representation, like transfers of land, carries material consequences.

In her recent analysis of cultural colonialism in a medium-sized rural British Columbia town where land claims negotiations have not yet begun, Elizabeth Furniss argues that Canadian colonialism is shaped simultaneously by two pervasive narratives — one of frontier, the other of benevolence — blended and transformed into a cherished national icon. Canadians are quick to differentiate the history of Native-white relations in this country from the Indian wars by which the American West was won. Ours is a polite colonialism, and our frontier narratives ring with peculiar combinations of individualism and benevolent paternalism. Furniss demonstrates how the logic of colonialism's culture is reproduced in each generation through commonsense symbols that dominate public presentations of local identity. Analyzing written texts, museum exhibits, land claims forums, and public festivals, she contends that the material consequences of those stories can be seen in the legacy of unequal power relations. Inequality in these communities cannot be explained just by racism or by economics, she argues. It is maintained and reproduced through manipulation of symbols and by the power to control representations that allows one sector of society (settlers who define themselves as "pioneers") to control the images and the public identities of others (whom they collectively lump as "Indians") without their input. This process is reinforced in taken for granted public representations of epitomizing events (like a gold rush or a land claims settlement) used to amplify and to project the community's relationship to the larger world.[3]

The narratives discussed in this book work to destabilize epitomizing narratives and to address multiple audiences, some local and some global. One consequence of having two decades of land claims negotiations behind, rather than ahead, may be a shift in local understanding about how interpretations of the past serve social ends and how narrative and history reciprocally shape one another. Indigenous Yukon storytellers are experimenting, as they have always done, with shifting social and political contexts. In so doing, they engage a long tradition of narrative strategies for translating stories, symbols, and meanings. Angela Sidney's masterful telling of the adventures of Ḵaax̱ach'góok, Annie Ned's account of the Man Who Stayed with Caribou, and Kitty Smith's carvings of Duk'tootl and Naatsilanéi all demonstrate how a master storyteller can make century-old stories relevant in a variety of contemporary circumstances. Their performances demonstrate how a story can reframe both vexing issues and commonsense categories by providing a larger context.

In the wake of land claims negotiations in the Yukon, there has been a virtual explosion of community-based oral history projects. The Yukon International Storytelling Festival projects an increasing First Nations presence. Locally produced plays and films are being written and performed by aboriginal writers and actors. Indigenous Yukoners with training in anthropology are taking a central role in cultural documentation projects, and they place significant emphasis on the role of oral tradition.[4] The process whereby young people take on, reembody or reincorporate stories during successive hearings over the course of their lives, making them their own, is one that long preceded writing but that may be extended by writing, film, and other artistic production when elders are no longer living to tell the stories themselves. The efforts of a new generation of adults to transform familar, everyday categories and to forge new connections in global contests will continue to raise important questions about cultural translation.

In anthropology, as in any other form of storytelling, theory is tremendously helpful when it generates new questions and is utterly constraining when it predetermines answers. The work we do is grounded in talk, in dialogue, in interactive relationships. What too often are missing from scholarly studies, as Greg Sarris reminds us, are interruption and risk. Academics too often frame the experiences of others with reference to scholarly norms. Yet unless we put ourselves in interactive situations where we are exposed and vulnerable, where these norms are interrupted and challenged, we can never recognize the limitations of our own descriptions. It is these dialogues that are most productive, because they prevent us from becoming overconfident about our own interpretations.

Notes

PREFACE

1. Clark and Holquist, *Mikhail Bakhtin*, 11, 14.

2. Sidney, Smith, and Dawson, *My Stories Are My Wealth*; Sidney, *Place Names, Tagish Tlaagú*, and *Haa Shagóon*; Smith, *Nindal Kwädindür*; Ned, *Old People in Those Days*. A comprehensive account appears in Cruikshank and others, *Life Lived Like a Story* (hereafter, *Life*).

3. Johnson, *Body in the Mind*, 171–72.

4. I am indebted to Judith Stamps's *Unthinking Modernity* for pointing me to parallels in the work of Harold Innis and Walter Benjamin.

5. Dauenhauer and Dauenhauer, "Oral Literature," 102.

6. Under the direction of linguist John Ritter, the Centre targets language instruction in the schools, but it also produces a substantial list of publications.

7. Issues of how narrators "edit" their narratives in performance are elaborated in Rice and Murray, *Talking on the Page*.

8. Anderson, "National Identity"; Nuttall, *Arctic Homeland*.

9. Sarris, *Keeping Slug Woman Alive*, 7.

1. "MY ROOTS GROW IN JACKPINE ROOTS"

1. De Certeau, *Practice of Everyday Life*, 123.

2. See overviews in Strathern, *Shifting Contexts*; Miller, *Worlds Apart*; Kearney, "Local and the Global"; Marcus, "Ethnography in/of the World System."

3. Borneman, *Belonging in the Two Berlins*, writing about postwar Berlin (see especially 18–19), and Anderson, "National Identity and Belonging in Arctic Siberia," discussing post-Soviet reassessment in extreme northern Siberia, both provide insightful analyses of categories of belonging following political upheavals.

4. McClellan, "Culture Change" (1950); McClellan, *My Old People Say*..

5. See, for example, Ned, in Cruikshank and others, *Life*, 280–81, 298–301, 308–10.

6. Moore, "Story of Tes Ni'a"; see also McClellan, "Indian Stories."

7. Duncan, *Northern Athapaskan Art*.

8. For further examples see Cruikshank, *Dan Dhá Ts'edenintth'é/Reading Voices* (hereafter, *Reading Voices*), 107–15.

9. Cruikshank and others, *Life*, 340–44.

10. Urquhart, *Historical Statistics*, 304.

11. The most thorough accounts come from ethnographic research conducted by Catharine McClellan during five decades, especially *My Old People Say*, "History of Research," "Intercultural Relations," "Inland Tlingit," "Tagish," "Tutchone," and McClellan and others, *Part of the Land.*.

12. For an excellent discussion of Yukon languages, see McClellan and others, *Part of the Land*, chapter 6. Overviews of contemporary language issues appear in *Speaking Out*, by Southern Tutchone linguist Daniel Tlen and in Moore, "Ethnonyms and the Kaska."

13. Angela Sidney, a trilingual speaker of Tlingit, Tagish, and English, worked with me and linguist Jeff Leer documenting Tagish and Tlingit place-names during the summer of 1980. Her work provides evidence of the range of loan traditions. For example, there are direct borrowings, as in the conversion of the Athapaskan Deslin, "flowing out," to the Tlingit Deslin Áayi (appending the Tlingit word for "lake"), now Teslin Lake. There are also more complicated borrowings, like the present Tlingit place-name Nilaseen, translated as "telling someone to hide something" but more likely a case of sound switching where an Athapaskan *s* is elided to a Tlingit *l*, converting the Athapaskan name Nisaleen, or "flowing out," to the more euphonious Tlingit pronunciation. A third kind of borrowing is illustrated by the conversion of Athapaskan Taghahi (with its distinctive Athapaskan *gh* to Tlingit Tahyaahi (personal communication, Jeff Leer).

14. These terms are cognate with the more familiar term Dene, the term of self-reference used by speakers of Athapaskan languages in the Mackenzie River drainage of western subarctic Northwest Territories.

15. Smith, in Cruikshank and others, *Life*, 251, 252. Significantly, Kitty Smith's granddaughter, Judy Gingell, was appointed commissioner of the Yukon in 1995. She is the first woman and the first person of First Nations ancestry to hold this position as the federal government's representative in the Yukon.

16. Sidney, *Place Names;* Sidney, in Cruikshank and others, *Life,* 71, 79; Cruikshank, "Getting the Words Right."

17. Ned, in Cruikshank and others, *Life,* 328–31.

18. Sidney, in Cruikshank and others, *Life,* 44–48, and in Cruikshank, *Reading Voices,* 29–31.

19. For the full text of this story, see Sidney, in Cruikshank and others, *Life,* 86–88.

20. For fuller versions of her glacier stories, see Smith, in Cruikshank and others, *Life*, 205–8, 258–62.

21. Ned, in Cruikshank and others, *Life*, 296–97.

22. I thank members of the Champagne-Aishihik First Nation for inviting me to attend some of the negotiations dealing with the heritage agreement.

23. Borneman, *Belonging in the Two Berlins*, 19, 28. See also Pine, "Naming the House."

24. Easterson, *Potlatch*.

25 McDonnell, "Kasini Society," describes this system in detail for the eastern Yukon Territory.

26. Cruikshank, "Gravel Magnet."

2. "PETE'S SONG"

1. I had already been living in the Yukon for several years by 1974 and had heard about Mrs. Sidney from her children, grandchildren, and numerous friends. Consequently we already knew we shared an interest in oral history when we first met.

2. Sidney, Smith, and Dawson, *My Stories Are My Wealth;* Sidney, *Place Names, Tagish Tlaagú,* and *Haa Shagóon.*

3. Swanton, *Tlingit Myths and Texts,* nos. 67 and 101, p. 225 and n. 321.

4. Dauenhauer and Dauenhauer, *Haa Shuká,* 82–107 and notes on 323–33.

5. McClellan, in an unpublished manuscript and in personal communication, points to shamanic overtones in both versions she has recorded.

6. Robin Ridington, personal communication, 1996. I am indebted to Ridington's advice about both the navigational techniques and the metaphorical meanings this story evokes.

7. Sidney, Smith, and Dawson, *My Stories Are My Wealth,* 109–13.

8. Dauenhauer and Dauenhauer, *Haa Shuká,* 82–107. In the version told by Andrew P. Johnson, Ḵaax̱'achgóok relied on his knowledge of the stars and planets to find his way home; see especially 95, 330.

9. Ricoeur, "Model of the Text," 98.

10. To appreciate how she incorporated this narrative into her life story, see Cruikshank and others, *Life*, 135–36, 139–45.

11. Oral copyright for songs, as for stories and artwork, remains vested in clans; however, issues surrounding ownership of songs continue to be particularly sensitive. In their 1987 publication, the Dauenhauers note that Mr. Johnson specifically asked that the words to Ḵaax̱'achgóok's song not be transcribed.

12. Compiled from discussions on 4 June 1981 (tape 387), 22 June 1981 (tape 390), and 6 July 1985 (tape 559). These tapes are stored with the Yukon Native Language Centre in Whitehorse.

13. Sidney, "Story of Ḵaax̱'achgóok."

14. Portelli, *Death of Luigi Trastulli,* 54–55.

15. See Siikala, "Understanding Narratives," for discussion of similar concerns surrounding oral traditions from Asia and the South Pacific.

16. Hymes, "Language, Memory, and Selective Performance"; Sanjek, "Anthropology's Hidden Colonialism."

17. See Cruikshank, 21–36, and Sidney, 21–158, in Cruikshank and others, *Life.*

18. See Sidney, in Cruikshank and others, *Life,* 35, 136, 139–45.

19. Bauman, *Verbal Art as Performance* and *Story, Performance, and Event.*

20. Abrahams, "Past in the Presence," 48; Siikala, "Understanding Narratives," 212.

21. Abrahams, "Past in the Presence," 47.

3 . YUKON ARCADIA

1. Skookum Jim's accomplishments, evaluated differently in the historical literature and in his own community, are discussed in chapter 4.

2. The bibliography was commissioned by the Canadian Polar Commission and was compiled by Lynda Howard, Ross Goodwin, and Lynne Howard in 1994 at the Arctic Institute of North America in Calgary. It has been an invaluable resource in preparing this chapter.

3. See, for instance, Labrador Inuit Association, *Our Footprints Are Everywhere;* Nungak, *Northern Quebec Inuit Elders;* Barnaby, "University Research and the Dene Nation"; Inuit Cultural Institute, *Recollections of Levi Iqalujjuaq;* Council for Yukon Indians, *Voices of the Talking Circle;* Inuit Circumpolar Conference, *Comprehensive Arctic Policy.*

4. Several Canadian conferences were held in 1996 on the topic of indigenous knowledge, including the Inuit Studies conference in St. Johns, Newfoundland, an Aboriginal Science and Technology conference in Winnipeg, and one titled Sacred Lands: Claims and Conflicts, also held in Winnipeg, Manitoba.

5. This literature is enormous: overviews include Posey and Overall, *Ethnobiology;* Freeman, "Ethnoscience"; Brush, "Indigenous Knowledge"; Hansen, *Arctic Environment;* Davis and Ebbe, *Traditional Knowledge;* Kuhn and Duerden, "Review of Traditional Environmental Knowledge."

6. Cited in Hansen, *Arctic Environment,* 35–36.

7. See Richards, "Cultivation," 61–62.

8. Kalland, "Indigenous Knowledge," 152–53; see also Dyck, *Indigenous Peoples and the Nation State.*

9. See, for example, the work by Saami sociolinguist Elena Helander, "Role of Saami Traditions."

10. Bourdieu, *Language and Symbolic Power,* 12.

11. See Bielowski, "Inuit Indigenous Knowledge," and Hobson, "Traditional Knowledge Is Science." Elsewhere, the acronym IPR (indigenous property rights) frames parallel discussions in South America and elsewhere; see, for example, Posey, "Intellectual Property Rights."

12. See Ridington, "Tools in the Mind," for an extended discussion of this issue.

13. From a visit to Berlin in February 1996.

14. Berger, *Northern Frontier, Northern Homeland.*

15. See Feit, "Self Management and State Management," for a broad discussion of this issue.

16. Hobson, "Traditional Knowledge Is Science," 2.

17. *TEK Talk* (UNESCO), 1, no. 1 (1992): 1.

18. Quoted in Freeman, "Ethnoscience," 87.

19. See, for example, Johnson, *Lore;* Richardson, "Harvesting Traditional Knowledge"; Keskitalo, "Integration of Indigenous Peoples' Knowledge"; Etylen, "Preservation, Transmission and Utilization of Indigenous Knowledge."

20. Huntington, "Traditional Ecological Knowledge of Beluga Whales" (1994), 87.

21. Okrainetz, "Towards a Sustainable Future."

22. Keskitalo, "Integration of Indigenous Peoples' Knowledge," 38.

23. Huntington, "Traditional Ecological Knowledge of Beluga Whales" (1995), 20 (my emphasis).

24. See Bourdieu, *Language and Symbolic Power,* 134−35, for a discussion of this approach.

25. McClellan, *My Old People Say,* 108; Workman, *Prehistory of the Aishihik-Kluane Area,* 16.

26. See Sidney, in Cruikshank and others, *Life,* 75−78, and Smith, in the same volume, 208−13, for versions of this narrative.

27. Morrow and Hensel, "Hidden Dissension."

28. Kapferer, "Bureaucratic Erasure," 84.

29. See Ellen, "What Black Elk Left Out"; McClusky, "Black Elk Speaks but So Does John Niehardt"; Kaiser, "Chief Seattle's Speeches"; Low, "Contemporary Reinvention of Chief Seattle."

30. Bruun and Kalland, *Asian Perceptions of Nature.*

31. Ellen, "What Black Elk Left Out."

32. Fienup-Riordan, "Original Ecologists?"; Burch, "Rationality and Resource Use among Hunters."

33. See, for example, Tanner, *Bringing Home Animals;* Ridington, *Trail to Heaven;* Feit, "Hunting and the Quest for Power."

34. See, for example, Brightman, *Grateful Prey*.

35. See Pederson, "Nature, Religion and Cultural Identity," for a discussion of this issue with reference to the environmental movement.

36. Wenzel, *Animal Rights, Human Rights*, 6. For a Greenlandic perspective see Lynge, *Arctic Wars, Animal Rights*.

37. Cited in Trigger, "Archaeology and the Integrated Circus," 330.

38. Balzer, "From Ethnicity to Nationalism," 80.

39. Vitebsky, "From Cosmology to Environmentalism," 188–91, and personal communication, 1996.

40. Jackson, "Preserving Indian Culture."

41. Passerini, *Memory and Totalitarianism*.

42. Posey and Overall, *Ethnobiology*, 3, estimates that the annual world market for such plant-based medicines is U.S.$43 billion.

43. Strangely titling his article "Anthropology's Terrible Triumph," the report's author, John Richards, summarized its content in the newspaper *Vancouver Sun,* 21 December 1995.

44. Howard and Widdowson, "Traditional Knowledge Threatens Environmental Assessment," 34.

45. McEachern, *Reasons for Judgment*, 45–52.

46. A house is a matrilineage of people who can trace common ancestry, whereas members of a clan know they are related but may not be able to identify all the genealogical links.

47. McEachern, *Reasons for Judgment*, 75. For critical discussion of this judgment, see Miller, "Anthropology and History in the Courts"; Mills, *Eagle Down Is Our Law*.

48. Hansen, *Arctic Environment*, 21. Signatories to the AEPS are Canada, Denmark, Finland. Greenland, Iceland, Norway, Sweden, and the United States.

49. Okrainetz, "Towards a Sustainable Future in Hudson Bay"; Richardson, "Harvesting Traditional Knowledge."

50. Huntington, "Traditional Ecological Knowledge of Beluga Whales" (1994, 1995).

51. Brooke, "Experiences Gained by the Inuit."

52. Vitebsky, "From Cosmology to Environmentalism," 199.

53. Okrainetz, "Towards a Sustainable Future in Hudson Bay," 15.

54. Sissons, "Systematization of Tradition"; see also Thomas, "Inversion of Tradition."

55. I was not present at this session, but the exchanges were summarized not long afterward both by a speaker and by a member of the audience. Because they characterize the kinds of exchanges I have observed in similar settings, I summarize them here.

56. Giddens, *Consequences of Modernity.*

57. Latour, *We Have Never Been Modern.*

58. Strathern, *Shifting Contexts,* 155, 162.

4. CONFRONTING CULTURAL ERASURE

1. Innis, *Fur Trade in Canada, Cod Fisheries,* and *Essays in Canadian Economic History.*

2. Innis, *Empire and Communications* and *Bias of Communication.*

3. Innis, *Empire and Communications,* 68–69, 81–82, and *Bias of Communication,* 43–45.

4. Innis, *Bias of Communication,* 8–9.

5. Stamps, *Unthinking Modernity,* 11.

6. Innis, *Bias of Communication,* 190. Stamps, *Unthinking Modernity,* 51, notes that this speech was first delivered in 1948.

7. Bakhtin, *Rabelais and His World* and *Dialogic Imagination;* Clark and Holquist, *Mikhail Bakhtin,* 1–15.

8. Innis, *Bias of Communication,* 8–9.

9. Innis, *Essays in Canadian Economic History,* 314, 335–36; Stamps, *Unthinking Modernity,* 47, 57–58.

10. Cruikshank, "Oral Traditions and Written Accounts" and "Images of Society."

11. The Yukon Native Language Centre has been involved in extensive placename documentation throughout the Yukon; see, for example, Tom, *Èkeyi.*

12. Boyd, "Demographic History," 144; de Laguna, "Tlingit," 205.

13. The term "discovery" is problematic because it describes a discrete, bounded incident, and Fogelson's paper "Ethnohistory of Events and Nonevents," 143, is instructive. Fogelson identifies what he calls "epitomizing events . . . in narratives that condense, encapsulate, and dramatize longer term historical processes." The existence of gold had been known for decades. Robert Campbell referred to gold near Fort Selkirk in his journals in 1850. The missionary Robert McDonald noted traces in Birch Creek near the Yukon-Alaska border in the 1870s. In 1887 the geologist George Dawson named prospectors who were making a reasonable living panning gold on the Pelly River; see Dawson, *Report,* 133. Yet the term is always used to commemorate 17 August 1896, celebrated annually as Discovery Day in Dawson City, Yukon.

14. Ogilvie, *Early Days on the Yukon,* 125–30; Berton, *Klondike,* 42–43; Zaslow, *Opening of the Canadian North,* 101–3; Wright, *Prelude to Bonanza,* 125–30; Coates and Morrison, *Land of the Midnight Sun,* 70–81.

15. Ogilvie, *Early Days on the Yukon,* 133.

16. Berton, *Klondike,* 42, 43.

17. Ogilvie, *Early Days on the Yukon,* 127–29; Zaslow, *Opening of the Canadian North,* 101–3; Wright, *Prelude to Bonanza,* 287–89, 295; Carmack, *My Experiences in the Yukon.*

18. Berton, *Klondike,* 400.

19. Skookum Jim's lawyer, W. L. Phelps, kept detailed notes and copies of correspondence between himself, Jim, Jim's daughter Daisy, and Daisy's guardian Percy R. Peele. Much of the correspondence deals with Jim's will, but it also contains comments about the changes occurring in Jim's and Daisy's lives. Copies of the papers and an inventory of contents are stored in the Yukon Archives manuscript collection.

20. McClellan, "Avoidance between Siblings" and *My Old People Say,* 414–15, 432–33.

21. See Cruikshank and others, *Life.* Angela Sidney's account appears in her own words on 57–65, Kitty Smith's on 186–87.

22. Swansdown has transformative properties and is associated with shamans and with curing, making it a suitable gift for an animal helper.

23. There was a later, smaller gold rush at Atlin, British Columbia.

24. McClellan, "Wealth Woman and Frogs" and "Indian Stories."

25. See Cruikshank and others, *Life,* throughout, and summarized on 339–46.

26. For examples from very different kinds of works, see, for example, Longstreth, *Silent Force,* 209, and Coates, *"Best Left as Indians,"* 310.

27. Robert Berkhofer, *White Man's Indian,* and Daniel Francis, *Imaginary Indian,* have both analyzed the mutability of such stereotypes in fine detail.

28. The account here comes from sworn testimony at the trial and from first-person accounts later compiled by some of the participants. They are filed at the National Archives of Canada in Royal Canadian Mounted Police Records RG 18, ser. A1, vol. 154, files 391–498 (1898), and RG 18, ser. F1, vol. 3153, file 8596 (1920); and also in Department of Justice Records, RG 13, ser. C1, vol. 1434, file "Nantuck Brothers." Significantly, the details (though not the substance) differ considerably from Annual Northwest Mounted Police Reports of Superintendents Steele (1898), Wood (1899), and Primrose (1900), which seem to have been compiled from a distance.

29. Dickey, "Letter," 72.

30. Boillot, *Aux mines d'or,* 88–89.

31. One photo is in the Yukon Archives collection, no. 807. Another is printed in Price, *From Euston to Klondike,* 127.

32. Report of Superintendent S. B. Steele, Upper Yukon District for June 1898, Northwest Mounted Police Records, National Archives of Canada, RG 18, ser. A1, vol. 154, files 445–98.

33. There is also considerable correspondence about this over a period of two months in National Archives of Canada, RG 18, ser. F1, vol. 3153, file 8596 (1920).

34. These men are named in court documents as J. A. Peterson and W. H. Lear.

35. Letter from Justice Thomas McGuire to the secretary of state, Ottawa, dated 3 August 1898, National Archives of Canada, RG 13, ser. C1, vol. 1434.

36. Ibid.

37. These and following quotations come directly from transcripts of *Queen v. Jim Nantuck,* National Archives of Canada, RG 13, ser. C1, vol. 1434, file "Nantuck Brothers." Page numbers refer to the hand-numbered pages of the transcript.

38. This definition comes from the transcript of *Queen v. Frank Nantuck,* National Archives of Canada, RG 13, ser. C1, vol. 1434, file "Nantuck Brothers," 15.

39. *Klondike Nugget* (Dawson City, Yukon), 3 August 1898, 3.

40. Letters to the minister of justice, one carrying the names of W. C. Bompas, T. H. Canham, James Turner, R. M. Dickey, Wm. H. Judge, R. J. Bowen, and Andrew S. Grant, dated 1 August 1898. Bompas also wrote two other letters outlining his views in greater detail to Major Walsh, commissioner of the Northwest Mounted Police, dated 1 August and 3 August 1898 (National Archives of Canada, RG 13, ser. C1, vol. 1434). Although Bompas's letters contained self-interested requests for more funding to spread missionary teachings that would prevent such incidents, this one still suggests that he was attentive to local issues, and it remains the only letter on file presenting an alternative explanation to that given by witnesses, newspapers, and the judge.

41. These appeals were made to C. A. Dugas, the newly appointed judge of the Yukon Territorial Court, by H. C. Lisle, advocate for the accused. Reprieve was granted by Judge Dugas, and the execution was postponed first to 2 March 1899 and then, after the second appeal, to 4 August 1899 (National Archives of Canada, RG 13, ser. C1, vol. 1434).

42. Letter from Frank Harper, sheriff of the Yukon Territory, to the secretary of state, 7 March 1899 (National Archives of Canada, RG 13, ser. C1, file 1434).

43. A similar incident was recorded on the Yukon River at Fort Reliance in 1877. In his memoirs, trader Leroy McQuesten noted that his partner, Mayo, had prepared a mixture of arsenic and grease to kill mice in his store. Some women mistook the arsenic for flour and used it for cooking. Three elderly women died, and a sixteen-year-old-girl was blinded. See McQuesten, "Life in the Yukon," 7.

44. See Smith, in Cruikshank and others, *Life,* 176–78.

45. Mrs. Sidney's account appears in Cruikshank, "Life," 356–59.

46. McClellan, *My Old People Say,* 497.

47. Her fuller account is recorded in Cruikshank, "Life," 357–59.

48. Chief Jim Boss was responsible for initiating the first official land claim on behalf of Yukon Indians, a document filed by a local lawyer, T. W. Jackson, in 1902

(on file, Yukon Archives). Boss was widely regarded by other Native people as someone who knew how to deal with "whitemen," so it is not surprising that the fugitives took his advice.

49. See Berkhofer, *White Man's Indian*, and Francis, *Imaginary Indian*.

50. Longstreth, *Silent Force*, 209.

51. Clark and Holquist, *Mikhail Bakhtin*, 9.

52. Saris, "Telling Stories."

53. Bourdieu, *Language and Symbolic Power*, 42, 134. His editor, John Thompson, expands on Bourdieu's definition of "institution" in the introduction to the book, 8.

54. Bourdieu, *Language and Symbolic Power*, 131.

55. Correspondence is in National Archives of Canada, Royal Canadian Mounted Police Records, RG 18, ser. F1, vol. 3153, file 8596 (1920).

56. Telegram from A. Bowen Perry to the comptroller, Northwest Mounted Police in Ottawa, dated 24 September 1898 (National Archives of Canada, RG 18, ser. F1, vol. 3153, file 8596 [1920]).

57. Letter from Joseph Pope, undersecretary of state, with copies to the missionaries who cosigned the bishop's letter, 28 October 1898 (National Archives of Canada, RG 13, ser. C1, vol. 1434).

58. Letter from E. Newcombe, deputy minister of justice, to both Fred White, comptroller, and Superintendent Steele, dated 4 January 1899 (National Archives of Canada, RG 13, ser. C1, vol. 1434, file "Nantuck Brothers").

59. Grove, "'Where Is the Justice, Mr. Mills?'" 101.

60. Correspondence in National Archives of Canada, RG 13, ser. C, vol. 1434, file "Nantuck Brothers."

61. Grove, "'Where Is the Justice, Mr. Mills?'" 87–88.

62. Correspondence and reports, National Archives of Canada, RG 18, ser. F1, vol. 3153, file 8596 (1920), part 2. McIntosh's pension claim was denied.

63. Morrow and Hensel, "Hidden Dissension."

64. See White, *Content of the Form*, 14.

5. IMPERFECT TRANSLATIONS

1. Clifford, "Interview with Brian Wallis," 153.

2. See, for example, Fenton, "Keeping the Promise"; Ridington, "Sacred Object as Text"; Merrill, Ladd, and Ferguson, "Return of the Ahayu:da"; Dauenhauer and Dauenhauer, *Haa Tuwunáaga Yís*.

3. Smith, in Cruikshank and others, *Life*, 248.

4. These stories were later published in Sidney, Smith, and Dawson, *My Stories*

Are My Wealth; Smith, *Nindal Kwädindür;* Cruikshank, *Athapaskan Women* and *Stolen Woman;* and Cruikshank and others, *Life.*

5. See Cruikshank, *Athapaskan Women,* 75–77.

6. Personal communication, Joanne Meehan, 1992.

7. Jim Robb, a local artist who had known Mrs. Smith for many years, first suggested these carvings might be hers. He helped to arrange for her to visit the museum. A tape recording (and my transcript) of a discussion between Mrs. Smith, her granddaughter Judy Gingell, curator Joanne Meehan, and First Nations heritage adviser Louise Profeit LeBlanc in 1985 is on file at the MacBride Museum. Mrs. Smith also talked about Azanzhaya in a story she told me in March 1979 (Yukon Native Language Centre tape 333; in Cruikshank, *Stolen Woman,* 39). There she identified Azanzhaya as the Yukon man who killed the Bear sons of Kaats' after they killed their father. The story is discussed later in this chapter.

8. Boas, "Some Principles of Museum Administration," cited in Jacknis, "Franz Boas and Exhibits," 108.

9. Darnell, "Boasian Text Tradition."

10. Kroeber, *Nature of Culture,* cited in Handler, "On the Valuing of Museum Objects," 21.

11. Darnell, "Boasian Text Tradition."

12. Cruikshank, "Oral Tradition and Material Culture."

13. For a discussion of the complexities of representing culture through objects, see, for example, Kirshenblatt-Gimblett, "Objects of Ethnography," and Pearce, *Objects of Knowledge.* For a parallel discussion of problems of conveying culture through words, see Dauenhauer and Dauenhauer, "Oral Literature Embodied and Disembodied."

14. See, for example, Fowler, *Shared Symbols;* Kan, "Sacred and the Secular"; and again, Dauenhauer and Dauenhauer, *Haa Tuwunáagu Yís.*

15. See Ridington, "Technology," "Knowledge," and "Tools in the Mind."

16. Workman, *Prehistory of the Aishihik-Kluane Area,* 94.

17. See Cole, *Captured Heritage,* but also Krech and Hail, "Art and Material Culture of the North American Subarctic."

18. See Babcock, "Modeled Selves" and "'At Home, No Women Are Storytellers'"; Zolbrod, "When Artifacts Speak"; and Ljungstrom, "Narratives of Artefacts," for a range of perspectives on these issues.

19. Babcock, "Modeled Selves," 317–18.

20. Smith, in Cruikshank and others, *Life,* 258–62. There are a number of surging glaciers in this region of the Yukon. People understood that such glaciers were once the dens of giant animals that periodically emerged to terrorize humans. Whenever one of these animals could be killed, elders say, its glacier (den) would retreat.

21. Smith, in Cruikshank and others *Life*, 190–93.

22. Smith, in Cruikshank and others *Life*, 193–200.

23. May agreed that our conversation should be recorded, and the tapes and transcripts are on file at the McBride Museum in Whitehorse, Yukon.

24. McClellan, *Girl Who Married the Bear.*

25. See Swanton, *Tlingit Myths and Texts,* nos. 19, 69; Barbeau, *Totem Poles,* 215; Garfield and Forest, *Wolf and the Raven,* 29–37; Keithahn, *Monuments in Cedar,* 156; de Laguna, *Under Mount St. Elias,* 879–80; and Dauenhauer and Dauenhauer, *Haa Shuká,* 218–43 and notes on 390–406.

26. These photos appear in Barbeau, *Totem Poles,* 214; de Laguna *Under Mount St. Elias,* plate 168; Garfield and Forest, *Wolf and the Raven,* fig. 11, p. 30; and Keithahn, *Monuments in Cedar,* 6, 13, 160.

27. Cruikshank, *Stolen Woman,* 37–39.

28. Smith, in Cruikshank and others, *Life,* 228.

29. Mrs. Smith's own version of this narrative appears in Cruikshank, *Athapaskan Women,* 75–77.

30. Dukt'ootl' is also sometimes referred to as "Black Skin" on the coast, where Swanton noted that this figure was a crest of the Gaanax̱teidí and Gaanax̱.ádi clans. I too was intrigued to recognize Mrs. Smith's narrative in the carving erected in the foyer of the Alaska State Museum in Juneau when I visited there in summer 1992, shortly after I heard May tell the story several hundred miles inland in the Yukon.

31. See Swanton, *Tlingit Myths and Texts,* no. 93; Garfield and Forest, *Wolf and the Raven,* 73–77; Barbeau, *Totem Poles,* 298–302; Keithahn, *Monuments in Cedar,* 143–48; de Laguna, *Under Mount St. Elias,* 890–92; Dauenhauer and Dauenhauer, *Haa Shuká,* 138–51 and notes on 348–59; and by Mrs. Smith in Cruikshank, *Stolen Woman,* 37–39.

32. Barbeau, *Totem Poles,* 297, 303; Garfield and Forrest, *Wolf and the Raven,* fig. 33, p. 74; Keithahn, *Monuments in Cedar,* 118, 119, 120.

33. Smith in Cruikshank and others, *Life,* 254–62.

34. See Swanton, *Tlingit Myths,* nos. 4, 71; Velten, "Three Tlingit Stories," 168–80; Barbeau, *Totem Poles,* 290; Garfield and Forrest, *Wolf and the Raven,* 81–83, 122–25; McClellan, *My Old People Say,* 449–53; Cruikshank, *Stolen Woman,* 62–65; Dauenhauer and Dauenhauer, *Haa Shuká,* 108–137 and notes on 334–47.

35. Other stories from the southern Yukon also show the power of carving: Crow created the first humans by carving them from poplar.

36. For an illuminating discussion of similar issues in the life of Cochito Pueblo artist and potter Helen Codero, see Babcock, "Modeled Selves" and "At Home, No Women Are Storytellers," esp. 226.

37. Carr, *Time, Narrative and History,* 59; Ricoeur, "Value of Narrativity," 171.

38. Ames, *Cannibal Tours and Glass Boxes*, 143; Gable, Handler, and Lawson, "On the Uses of Relativism"; Crang, "Spacing Times, Telling Times," 42.

39. Benjamin, "Storyteller," 96.

40. Jordanova, "Objects of Knowledge," 32; Crang, "Spacing Times, Telling Times," 30.

41. Welsh, "Repatriation and Cultural Preservation," 843.

42. Lumley, *Museum Time Machine;* Vergo, *New Museology;* Ames, *Cannibal Tours and Glass Boxes.*

43. Durrans, "Future of the Other," 156–57; Crang, "Spacing Times, Telling Times," 33.

44. Handler, "On the Valuing of Museum Objects," 21.

45. Handler, "On the Valuing of Museum Objects," 23.

46. Sarris, *Keeping Slug Woman Alive*, 53.

47. Barth, "Production and Reproduction of Society."

48. See especially Kopytoff, "Cultural Biography of Things."

49. Ames, *Cannibal Tours and Glass Boxes*, 141.

50. Benjamin, "Storyteller," 92, 93.

6. CLAIMING LEGITIMACY

1. Hill, "Contested Pasts and the Practice of Anthropology," 809.

2. Spier, *Prophet Dance of the Northwest;* Wallace, "Revitalization Movements"; Suttles, "Plateau Prophet Dance among the Coast Salish"; Aberle, "Prophet Dance and Reactions to White Contact"; Walker, "New Light on the Prophet Dance"; Ridington, *Swan People;* Miller, *Prophetic Worlds;* Abel, "Prophets, Priests and Preachers"; Peterson, "Review of *Prophetic Worlds.*"

3. See, for example, Walker, "New Light on the Prophet Dance."

4. See Cohen, "Theories of Myth," 351–52. Spier's monograph on the Plateau Prophet Dance originally posed the related question of whether this was an aboriginal or a contact phenomenon. It is worth noting that subsequent analyses focusing on the Plateau, including Aberle, "Prophet Dance and Reactions to White Contact," Walker, "New Light on the Prophet Dance," and Miller, *Prophetic Worlds,* seem to favor a contact thesis, while studies with a more northerly geographical focus favor aboriginal origins — for instance, McClellan, "Shamanistic Syncretism in Southern Yukon"; Suttles, "Plateau Prophet Dance among the Coast Salish"; Ridington, *Swan People;* and Moore and Wheelock, *Wolverine Myths and Visions.* It may also be significant that publications emphasizing aboriginal origins seem to rely on indigenous concepts, whereas those elaborating a contact hypothesis emphasize the broad historical and ecological context in which those ideas emerged.

5. Spier documented the spread of the Prophet Dance from the Columbia Plateau as far as southern Alaska and the Mackenzie River by the early 1800s. Although certain diagnostic features of the Prophet Dance (world renewal, a special dance, structured community ritual) were not incorporated into Yukon prophecy narratives, McClellan suggests that news of the Prophet Dance undoubtedly reached the Yukon River and contributed to the activities of early prophets in this region. See her "Shamanistic Syncretism," 136.

6. Kan, "Shamanism and Christianity."

7. McClellan, "Indian Stories," 128.

8. Long, "Prophecy, Charisma and Politics."

9. McClellan, "Shamanisic Syncretism in Southern Yukon" and *My Old People Say*, 577; Suttles, "Plateau Prophet Dance among the Coast Salish"; Ridington, *Swan People*.

10. McClellan, "Wealth Woman and Frogs"; Moore and Wheelock, *Wolverine Myths and Visions*, 59–60.

11. McClellan, "Indian Stories"; Cruikshank, "Images of Society"; Cruikshank and others, *Life*.

12. Ethnographies that became available during this period include Honigmann, *Culture and Ethos of Kaska Society* and *The Kaska Indians;* Slobodin, "Kutchin Concepts of Reincarnation"; Osgood, *Han Indians;* McClellan, *My Old People Say;* McDonnell, "Kasini Society"; Ridington, *Swan People;* Legros, "Wealth, Poverty and Slavery."

13. Wallace, "Revitalization Movements"; Aberle, "Note on Relative Deprivation Theory."

14. Miller, *Prophetic Worlds.*

15. Axtell, "Ethnohistory"; Jennings, "Growing Partnership"; Trigger, "Ethnohistory."

16. Born near the Red River to an Ojibwa mother and a Scottish trader, McDonald came to the northern Yukon in the early 1860s. Although he shared the church's enthusiasm for collecting converts, he was less zealous than his contemporaries in the Church Missionary Society about trying to modify the local indigenous cultures. Prophecy, though, seemed to trouble him, perhaps because he interpreted its manifestations as competing with Christian teachings.

17. McDonald, "Journals, 1862–1913."

18. As an indication of how prevalent prophecy was on the upper Peel and upper Yukon Rivers at this time, the following notes can be gleaned from McDonald's diaries. On 3 January 1864, he refers to "an Indian pretending to prophesy at Peel River but Mr. A. Flett [the trader] has prevented him from going too far with it." More references appear in 1865: on 11 January he refers to a man who "pretends to receive divine revelations," and the next day he names "Tiujito, a Mackenzie

River Tukudh who has been making extravagant pretensions to prophesy, and to being favoured with divine revelations." On 5 February he spoke with people on the Bonnet Plume River about their Peel River neighbors, noting that "there is still one among them pretending to divine authority to teach the Indian religion, but he is not attended to." On 25 May he spoke against "delusions of the Indians led astray by those making pretensions to prophesy"; on 25 June he spoke directly to one of the nuk-kut (*sic*) "who makes pretensions to prophesy." Several years later, on 27 July 1874, he referred by name to the prophet Larion and his wife, who told their followers that they would die if they were baptized. Larion's wife, especially, claimed direct communication with and advice from supreme beings. The general tone of McDonald's notes suggests that it was missionaries who saw themselves as competing with shamans, rather than the reverse.

19. McClellan, "Shamanistic Syncretism," 136–37.

20. See especially Rushforth, "Legitimation of Beliefs" and "Political Resistance."

21. Ridington, *Little Bit Know Something*.

22. There is, of course, a difference between *explaining* the local meaning of events and publicly *legitimizing* local discourse or knowledge. One dilemma faced by indigenous people trying to convince outsiders of the legitimacy of their perspective may be that within any one community, interpretations based on oral tradition are inevitably contested and debated in daily conversation. Yet in publicly presenting an authoritative stance to outsiders, in arguing for the legitimacy of oral tradition as a valid historical perspective, claimants sometimes feel compelled to present oral tradition as though it were uncontested "truth."

23. This is discussed in detail in McClellan, *My Old People Say*, and in McDonnell, "Kasini Society."

24. Yukon narratives tell how, at the beginning of time, the trickster Crow was white "like a seagull" before he was blackened trying to escape through a smoke-hole in one of his escapades; see Cruikshank and others, *Life*, 274, 313. Ridington, in *Swan People*, suggested that for Prophet River Dunne-za, prophets were specifically the people with swan power, swans belonging to that separate dimension of whiteness. Moore and Wheelock, *Wolverine Myths and Visions*, 60, note that this separate dimension is the home for seagulls and snow geese, also white.

25. McClellan, "Shamanistic Syncretism."

26. A clear example is "Moldy Head," told by Angela Sidney, 75–78, and by Kitty Smith, 208–13, in Cruikshank and others, *Life*.

27. The fuller version of Mrs. Smith's narrative appears in Cruikshank and others, *Life*, 254–58.

28. Fieldnotes with Mrs. Rachel Dawson, 1974; see also Ridington, *Swan People*, on the special characteristics of swan power among Dunne-za.

29. Sidney, in Cruikshank and others, *Life*, 155.

30. Sidney, in Cruikshank and others, *Life,* 156.

31. This Pelly River shaman was one of the most widely remembered in narrative and is mentioned by McClellan, "Shamanistic Syncretism," and also by Mrs. Sidney in Cruikshank and others, *Life,* 154, 158.

32. Alaska Highway Pipeline Inquiry, transcript of public hearings, J. Jack Carcross, vol. 44 (1976), 5967.

33. McClellan, *My Old People Say,* 556. See also Brown, "Track to Heaven" and "Abishabis," and Brown and Brightman, *"Orders of the Dreamed,"* for parallel experiences in the eastern Subarctic.

34. McClellan, *My Old People Say,* 554.

35. Fieldnotes, 13 December 1978.

36. By saying this, she is indicating her understanding of the power of spoken words, that if used inappropriately they might bring harm to speaker and listener. An essential component of a shaman's power was his song, which came to him as a result of his contact with an animal spirit helper. Earlier, Mrs. Ned made a similar statement about her father's power. She has sung her husband's song for me several times, but it would be inappropriate to make a recording of it, because once recorded, it could be used out of context.

37. Ned, in Cruikshank and others, *Life,* 326.

38. This letter is on file in the Anglican Church records, Yukon Territorial Archives, and is dated 25 April 1917.

39. Sidney, in Cruikshank and others, *Life,* 154.

40. Sidney, in Cruikshank and others, *Life,* 154.

41. Sidney, in Cruikshank and others, *Life,* 158. She refers here to the Women's Auxiliary of the Anglican Church.

42. McClellan, "Shamanistic Syncretism," 135.

43. Sidney, in Cruikshank and others, *Life,* 154–55.

44. Moore and Wheelock, *Wolverine Myths and Visions,* 59.

45. An enormous volcanic eruption on the Alaska-Yukon border more than eight hundred years ago undoubtedly displaced human populations on the upper Yukon. The so-called Little Ice Age between 1600 and 1800 had a dramatic effect on people living in this region, not only because of deteriorating climatic conditions but also because of the building and draining of glacier-dammed lakes and the shifting drainages cause by surging glaciers in the southwest Yukon. The arrival of fur traders first from the Northwest Coast and then from the eastern Subarctic in the nineteenth century was closely followed by the arrival of competing Roman Catholic and Anglican missionaries. The Klondike gold rush at the beginning of the twentieth century brought thirty to forty thousand would-be prospectors to the upper Yukon. The expansion of the Canadian state into northwestern North America im-

ported governing and legal infrastructures, with serious long-term consequences for indigenous people. The imposition of residential schools, the growing pressures on wildlife, the economic dislocations after the introduction of gold, silver, lead, and zinc mines, the construction of the Alaska Highway in the 1940s, projected pipeline developments in the 1970s, the ongoing disruptions associated with the negotiation of a land claims agreement in the Yukon — certainly all these changes support the hypothesis that prophets could have arisen in response to externally induced stresses.

46. Rosaldo, *Culture and Truth,* 129.

47. Rushforth, "Legitimation of Beliefs" and "Political Resistance."

48. See also Binney, "Maori Oral Narratives," for parallel observations from New Zealand.

49. Gable, Handler, and Lawson, "On the Uses of Relativism," raises this with reference to the current appetite for public presentations of history.

7. NEGOTIATING WITH NARRATIVE

1. This imagery has been challenged by Brody, *Living Arctic;* Fitzhugh and Crowell, *Crossroads of Continents;* Balikci, "Anthropology, Film and Arctic Peoples" (1989); and Fienup-Riordan, *Eskimo Essays* and *Freeze-Frame.* Nevertheless, the Inuit continue to be portrayed, in Brody's words, as the "kindergarten culture" suitable for discussion in the earliest grades of school.

2. Minority Rights Group, *Polar Peoples.*

3. In Greenland see, for example, Hanson, "The Tukaq Theater"; in northern Scandinavia see *Dichtogiisa* (newsletter of the Nordic Sami Institute, 1990–92, international edition); and on the Kola Penninsula, Huttenen, "Encountering Ethnic Groups." In Siberia these issues are discussed by Fryer and Lynn, "National State Formation" (1995); on Sakhalin by Grant, *In the Soviet House of Culture* (1995), 160–63; and as a note in *Ts'étlaw Hunday* (newsletter of the Yukon International Storytelling Festival) 2, no. 2 (1993): 6. Erich Kasten (Frei Universität, Berlin) reports similar events from his ongoing research in Kamchatka (personal communications, 1994–95).

4. See, for example, Stoeltje, "Festival."

5. These issues are thoroughly discussed in Wilson, *Folklore and Nationalism in Modern Finland;* Lass, "What Keeps the Czech Folk 'Alive'?" Linke, "Anthropology, Folklore, and the Government of Modern Life"; Tuohy, "Cultural Metaphors and Reasoning"; Bauman and Sawin, "Politics of Participation in Folklore Festivals"; Dow and Luxfield, "National Socialist Folklore"; Karp, "Festivals," 281; and more generally in Hutchinson, *Modern Nationalism.*

6. Myers, "Culture-Making," 679.

7. Asad, "Concept of Cultural Translation."

8. Hastrap, "Native Anthropology," 155; Kuper, "Culture, Identity, and the Project of a Cosmopolitan Anthropology."

9. Clifford, "Interview with Brian Wallis."

10. See Darnell, "Correlates of Cree Narrative Performance"; Tedlock, "Analogic Tradition" and *Spoken Word,* part 4; and Basso, *Wisdom Sits in Places.*

11. Bakhtin, *Rabelais and His World.*

12. Innis, *Fur Trade in Canada, Empire and Communications,* and *Bias of Communication;* Stamps, *Unthinking Modernity,* 41–96.

13. Inuit Circumpolar Conference, *Principles and Elements for a Comprehensive Arctic Policy;* Minority Rights Group, *Polar Peoples.*

14. See Stordahl, "How to Be a Real Sami," for discussion of parallel problems in northern Scandinavia.

15. See, for example, Dorais, "Inuit Identity in Canada"; Hedican, "On the Ethno-politics of Canadian Native Leadership"; Levin, *Ethnicity and Aboriginality.*

16. Canada, *Umbrella Final Agreement.*

17. This problem is thoroughly discussed by Dyck, "Negotiating the Indian 'Problem'"; Feit, "Self Management and State Management"; Rushforth, "Legitimation of Beliefs"; Morrow and Hensel, "Hidden Dissension"; Keesing, "Colonial and Counter-colonial Discourse."

18. Initially, organizers described their goal as emulating storytelling festivals in Chartres, France; Jonesboro, Tennessee; and Toronto, Ontario. Retrospectively, and with growing First Nations participation on the board of directors, they attribute inspiration for the festival to Angela Sidney, who attended the Toronto Storytelling Festival in 1984 and returned eager to hold a similar event in the Yukon. Her role is described in a booklet published by the Yukon International Storytelling Festival and the Northern Research Institute, "'Become a World.'"

19. *Yukon News* (Whitehorse), 15 June 1988, 1.

20. *Yukon News,* 9 June 1989, 15.

21. See Hanson, "Tukaq Theater."

22. *Yukon News,* 12 June 1991, 12.

23. *Whitehorse Star,* 29 June 1994, 3.

24. Krause, *Tlingit Indians,* 94.

25. See also Dauenhauer and Dauenhauer, *Haa Kusteeyí,* 209. When I visited Mr. Hammond in his home a year earlier, he showed me a framed letter written to Daanawaak in 1885 by Henry Nichols, lieutenant commander in the United States Navy, during tense negotiations between the United States Army and Tlingit chiefs. Following Daanawaak's example, Mr. Hammond acted as an intermediary between Tlingits and non-Tlingits.

26. Dauenhauer and Dauenhauer, *Haa Kusteeyí*, 227.

27. Dauenhauer and Dauenhauer, *Haa Ḵusteeyí*, 207-50.

28. Dauenhauer and Dauenhauer, *Haa Ḵusteeyí*, 13-15.

29. Dauenhauer and Dauenhauer, *Haa Ḵusteeyí*, 229.

30. Dauenhauer and Dauenhauer, *Haa Ḵusteeyí*, 242, 244.

31. Dauenhauer and Dauenhauer, *Haa Ḵusteeyí*, 244.

32. Dauenhauer and Dauenhauer, *Haa Ḵusteeyí*, 241, 242, 247.

33. McClellan, *Girl Who Married the Bear;* Cruikshank and others, *Life,* 339-56.

34. This narrative is also recorded in Sidney and others, *My Stories Are My Wealth,* 39-44.

35. See, for example, Smith, in Cruikshank and others, *Life,* 233-38.

36. See Basso, "'Stalking with Stories'"; Kari, *Tatl'ahwt'aenn Nenn';* Tom, *Èkeyi: Gyò Cho Chú;* Cruikshank, "Getting the Words Right."

37. Nyman and Leer, *"Gágiwdul.at."*

38. Dyck, *Tutelage.*

39. Nyman and Leer, *"Gágiwdul.at,"* 2-7.

40. This point is discussed at length with reference to oral history in Africa by Cohen, "Undefining of Oral Tradition."

41. Nyman and Leer, *"Gágiwdul.at,"* xxii.

42. Nyman and Leer, *"Gágiwdul.at,"* 23.

43. Another strategy, not discussed here, was to invite Ellen Gabriel, a prominent Mohawk activist from eastern Canada who played an important role during the confrontation between Mohawks, Quebec police, and the Canadian army during 1992. They advertised her appearance as one by a "children's writer and artist" but anticipated, correctly, that she would use her time to restate publicly her opposition to any land claims negotiations with the Canadian government.

44. Three years later, in 1997, Kwänlin Dän First Nation is still negotiating its claim with federal and territorial governments.

45. *Whitehorse Star,* 30 June 1994, 10.

46. Bakhtin, *Rabelais and His World.*

47. Benjamin, "Storyteller"; Stamps, *Unthinking Modernity,* 23-40.

48. Innis, *Essays in Canadian Economic History,* 12-14.

49. Innis, *Empire and Communications;* 64-100, 215-17. Stamps, *Unthinking Modernity,* 48-51, 65-96.

50. Flaherty, "Freedom of Expression."

51. See Myers, "Culture-Making," 693, for a discussion of this.

52. See also Brennais, "Shared Territory."

53. Friedman, "Past in the Future," 837.

54. Berger, *Northern Frontier, Northern Homeland;* Paine, *Dam a River, Damn a People?* Nuttall, *Arctic Homeland.*

55. This point is also made by both Karp, "Festivals," and Myers, "Culture-Making."

56. See Stamps, *Unthinking Modernity*, 66.

57. Canadian Broadcasting Corporation, "Legacy of Harold Innis."

EPILOGUE

1. Stolcke, "Talking Culture," elaborated in her seminar "Transatlantic Connections," in the Department of Social Anthropology, Cambridge University, 17 May 1996.

2. Fogelson, "Ethnohistory of Events and Nonevents."

3. Furniss, "In the Spirit of the Pioneers."

4. Carlick, "Girl and the Grizzly"; Jensen, "Yukon Elders' Documentation Project"; Johnson, "Southern Yukon Beadwork Traditions" and "Southern Yukon Beadwork Objects."

Bibliography

Abel, Kerry. 1986. "Prophets, Priests and Preachers: Dene Shamans and Christian Missions in the Nineteenth Century." In *Historical Papers, Communications Historiques: A Selection from the Papers Presented at the Canadian Historical Association Annual Meeting, Winnipeg,* ed. Donald Avery, 211–24. Ottawa: Tanamac International.

Aberle, David. 1959. "The Prophet Dance and Reactions to White Contact." *Southwestern Journal of Anthropology* 15 (1): 74–83.

———. 1972. "A Note on Relative Deprivation Theory as Applied to Millenarian and Other Cult Movements." In *Reader in Comparative Religion: Anthropological Approaches,* 3d ed., ed. William Lessa and Evon Z. Vogt, 537–41. New York: Harper and Row.

Abrahams, Roger D. 1992. "The Past in the Presence: An Overview of Folkloristics in the Late Twentieth Century." In *Folklore Processed: In Honour of Lauri Honko on His Sixtieth Birthday,* ed. Reimund Kvideland, 32–51. Studia Fennica Folkloristica 1. Helsinki: Suomalaisen Kirjallisuuden Seura.

Ames, Michael. 1992. *Cannibal Tours and Glass Boxes: The Anthropology of Museums.* Vancouver: University of British Columbia Press.

Anderson, David. 1995. "National Identity and Belonging in Arctic Siberia: An Ethnography of Evenkis and Dolgans at Khantaiskoe Ozero in the Taimyr Autonomous District." Ph.D. diss., Cambridge University.

Asad, Talal. 1986. "The Concept of Cultural Translation in British Social Anthropology." In *Writing Culture: The Poetics and Politics of Ethnography,* ed. James Clifford and George E. Marcus, 141–64. Berkeley: University of California Press.

Axtell, James. 1981. "Ethnohistory: An Historian's Viewpoint." In *The European and the Indian: Essays in the Ethnohistory of Colonial North America,* ed. James Axtell, 3–15. New York: Oxford University Press.

Babcock, Barbara. 1986. "Modeled Selves: Helen Codere's 'Little People.'" In *The Anthropology of Experience,* ed. Victor W. Turner and Edward M. Bruner, 316–43. Urbana: University of Illinois Press.

———. 1993. "'At Home, No Women Are Storytellers': Potteries, Stories, and Politics in Cochiti Pueblo." In *Feminist Messages: Coding in Women's Folk Culture,* ed. Joan N. Radner, 221–48. Chicago: University of Illinois Press.

Bakhtin, Mikhail. 1984a. *The Dialogic Imagination.* Austin: University of Texas Press.

———. 1984b. *Rabelais and His World.* Trans. Helene Iswolsky. 1968. Bloomington: Indiana University Press.

Balikci, Asen. 1989. "Anthropology, Film and Arctic Peoples." *Anthropology Today* 5 (2): 4–10.

Balzer, Marjorie Mandelstam. 1994. "From Ethnicity to Nationalism: Turmoil in the Russian Mini-empire." In *The Social Legacy of Communism,* ed. James R. Millar and Sharon L. Wolchik, 56–88. Cambridge: Cambridge University Press.

Barbeau, Marius. 1990. *Totem Poles.* 1950. New ed. with foreword by George F. MacDonald. Ottawa: National Museums of Canada.

Barnaby, Joanne. 1987. "University Research and the Dene Nation." Summary of presentation to the ACUNS meetings in Yellowknife. In *Education, Research, Information Systems and the North,* ed. W. P. Adams, 27. Ottawa: Association of Canadian Universities for Northern Studies.

Barth, Frederick. 1994. "Production and Reproduction of Society." Plenary Address to Canadian Anthropology Society, Vancouver, British Columbia, 6 May 1994.

Basso, Keith. 1984. "'Stalking with Stories': Names, Places and Moral Narratives among the Western Apache." In *Text, Play and Story: The Construction and Reconstruction of Self and Society,* ed. Stuart Plattner, 19–55. Washington DC: American Ethnological Society.

———. 1996. *Wisdom Sits in Places: Landscape and Language among the Western Apache.* Albuquerque: University of New Mexico Press.

Bauman, Richard. 1977. *Verbal Art as Performance.* Prospect Heights IL: Waveland.

———. 1986. *Story, Performance, and Event: Contextual Studies of Oral Narrative.* Cambridge: Cambridge University Press.

Bauman, Richard, and Patricia Sawin. 1991. "The Politics of Participation in Folklife Festivals." In *Exhibiting Cultures: The Poetics and Politics of Museum Display,* ed. Ivan Karp and Steven D. Lavine, 288–314. Washington DC: Smithsonian Institution Press.

Benjamin, Walter. 1969. "The Storyteller." In *Illuminations,* ed. Hannah Arendt, 83–109. New York: Schocken.

Berger, Thomas R. 1977. *Northern Frontier, Northern Homeland: The Report of the Mackenzie Valley Pipeline Inquiry.* 2 vols. Ottawa: Minister of Supply and Services.

Berkhofer, Robert F., Jr. 1978. *The White Man's Indian: Images of the American Indian from Columbus to the Present.* New York: Knopf.

Berton, Pierre. 1958. *Klondike: The Life and Death of the Last Great Gold Rush.* Toronto: McClelland and Stewart.

Bielowski, Ellen. 1992. "Inuit Indigenous Knowledge and Science in the Arctic." *Northern Perspectives* 20 (1): 5–8.

Binney, Judith. 1987. "Maori Oral Narratives, Pakeha Written Texts: Two Forms of Telling History." *New Zealand Journal of History* 21 (1): 16–28.

Boas, Franz. 1907. "Some Principles of Museum Administration." *Science* 25: 921–33.

Boillot, Leon. 1899. *Aux mines d'or du Klondike — Lac Bennett à Dawson City.* Paris: privately published.

Borneman, John. 1992. *Belonging in the Two Berlins: Kin, State and Nation.* Cambridge: Cambridge University Press.

Bourdieu, Pierre. 1991. *Language and Symbolic Power.* Ed. John B. Thompson. Cambridge: Polity.

Boyd, Robert T. 1990. "Demographic History, 1774–1784." In *Handbook of North American Indians,* vol. 7, *Northwest Coast,* ed. Wayne Suttles, 412–21. Washington DC: Smithsonian Institution.

Brenneis, Donald. 1987. "Shared Territory: Audience, Indirection and Meaning." *Text* 6 (3): 339–47.

Brightman, Robert. 1993. *Grateful Prey: Rock Cree Human-Animal Relationships.* Berkeley: University of California Press.

Brody, Hugh. 1987. *Living Arctic.* London: Faber and Faber.

Brooke, Lorraine F. 1994. "Experiences Gained by the Inuit of Nunavik, Canada: Working with Indigenous Knowledge." In *Arctic Environment: Report on the Seminar in Integration of Indigenous Peoples' Knowledge,* ed. Bente V. Hansen, 72–85. Copenhagen: Ministry for the Environment (Iceland), Ministry for the Environment (Denmark), and Home Rule of Greenland (Denmark Office).

Brown, Jennifer. 1982. "The Track to Heaven: The Hudson Bay Cree Religious Movement of 1842–1843." In *Papers of the Thirteenth Algonquian Conference,* ed. William Cowan, 53–63. Ottawa: Carleton University Press.

———. 1988. "Abishabis." In *Dictionary of Canadian Biography,* 7:3–4. Toronto: University of Toronto Press.

Brown, Jennifer, and Robert Brightman. 1988. *"The Orders of the Dreamed": George Nelson on Northern Ojibwa Religion and Myth, 1823.* Winnipeg: University of Manitoba Press.

Brush, Stephen B. 1993. "Indigenous Knowledge of Biological Resources and Intellectual Property Rights." *American Anthropologist* 95:653–86.

Bruun, Ole, and Arne Kalland. 1995. *Asian Perceptions of Nature: A Critical Approach*. Richmond, Eng.: Curzon.

Burch, Ernest S. 1994. "Rationality and Resource Use among Hunters." In *Circumpolar Religion and Ecology: An Anthropology of the North,* ed. Takashi Irimoto and Takaho Yamada, 163–85. Tokyo: University of Tokyo Press.

Canada, Minister of Indian and Northern Affairs. 1993. *Umbrella Final Agreement between the Government of Canada, the Council for Yukon Indians and the Government of the Yukon*. Ottawa: Minister of Supply and Services.

Canadian Broadcasting Corporation. 1994. "The Legacy of Harold Innis." *Ideas,* 6, 13, 20 December.

Carlick, Alice. 1995. "The Girl and the Grizzly: Bringing Traditional Narratives into Yukon Classrooms." *Northern Review* 14:34–47.

Carmack, George. 1933. *My Experiences in the Yukon*. Seattle: privately published.

Carr, David. 1986. *Time, Narrative and History*. Bloomington: University of Indiana Press.

Chapman, William Ryan. 1985. "Arranging Ethnology: Pitt Rivers and the Typological Tradition." In *Objects and Others: Essays on Museums and Material Culture,* ed. George Stocking, 15–48. Madison: University of Wisconsin Press.

Clark, Katerina, and Michael Holquist. 1984. *Mikhail Bakhtin*. Cambridge: Harvard University Press.

Clifford, James. 1989. "Interview with Brian Wallis." In "The Global Issue: A Symposium." *Art in America,* July, 86–87, 152–53.

Coates, Kenneth S. 1991. *"Best Left as Indians": Native-White Relations in the Yukon Territory, 1840–1973*. Montreal: McGill-Queen's University Press.

Coates, Kenneth S., and William R. Morrison. 1988. *Land of the Midnight Sun*. Edmonton: Hurtig.

Cohen, David. 1989. "The Undefining of Oral Tradition." *Ethnohistory* 36 (1): 9–18.

Cohen, Percy. 1969. "Theories of Myth." *Man* 4 (3): 337–53.

Cole, Douglas. 1985. *Captured Heritage: The Scramble for Northwest Coast Artifacts*. Vancouver: Douglas and McIntyre.

Council for Yukon Indians. 1991. *Voices of the Talking Circle: Yukon Aboriginal Languages Conference, 1991*. Ottawa: Department of Secretary of State.

Crang, Mike. 1994. "Spacing Times, Telling Times and Narrating the Past." *Time and Society* 3 (1): 29–45.

Cruikshank, Julie. 1979. *Athapaskan Women: Lives and Legends*. National Museum of Man Mercury Series 57. Ottawa: National Museums of Canada.

———. 1983. *The Stolen Woman: Female Journeys in Tagish and Tutchone Narra-*

tive. National Museum of Man Mercury Series 87 Ottawa: National Museums of Canada.

———. 1985. "The Gravel Magnet: Some Social Impacts of the Alaska Highway on Yukon Indians." In *The Alaska Highway: Papers of the Fortieth Anniversary Symposium,* ed. Kenneth Coates, 172–87. Vancouver: University of British Columbia Press.

———. 1987. "Life Lived Like a Story: Cultural Constructions of Life History by Tagish and Tutchone Women." Ph.D. diss., University of British Columbia.

———. 1989. "Oral Traditions and Written Accounts: An Incident from the Klondike Gold Rush." *Culture* 9 (2): 25–34.

———. 1990. "Getting the Words Right: Perspectives on Naming and Places in Athapaskan Oral History." *Arctic Anthropology* 27 (1): 52–65.

———. 1991. *Dan Dhá Ts'edenintth'é/Reading Voices: Oral and Written Interpretations of the Yukon's Past.* Vancouver: Douglas and McIntyre.

———. 1992a. "Images of Society in Klondike Gold Rush Narratives: Skookum Jim and the Discovery of Gold." *Ethnohistory* 39 (1): 20–41.

———. 1992b. "Oral Tradition and Material Culture: Multiplying Meanings of 'Words' and 'Things.'" *Anthropology Today* 8 (3): 5–9.

Cruikshank, Julie, in collaboration with Angela Sidney, Kitty Smith, and Annie Ned. 1990. *Life Lived Like a Story: Life Stories of Three Yukon Elders.* Lincoln: University of Nebraska Press; Vancouver: University of British Columbia Press.

Darnell, Regna. 1974. "Correlates of Cree Narrative Performance." In *Explorations in the Ethnography of Speaking,* ed. Richard Bauman and Joel Scherzer, 315–36. Cambridge: Cambridge University Press.

———. 1992. "The Boasian Text Tradition and the History of Anthropology." *Culture* 12 (1): 39–48.

Dauenhauer, Richard, and Nora Dauenhauer. 1987. *Haa Shuká/Our Ancestors: Tlingit Oral Narratives.* Seattle: University of Washington Press; Juneau: Sealaska Heritage Foundation.

———. 1990. *Haa Tuwunáagu Yís/For Healing Our Spirit: Tlingit Oratory.* Seattle: University of Washington Press; Juneau: Sealaska Heritage Foundation.

———. 1994. *Haa Kusteeyí/Our Culture: Tlingit Life Stories.* Seattle: University of Washington Press; Juneau: Sealaska Heritage Foundation.

———. 1995. "Oral Literature Embodied and Disembodied." In *Aspects of Oral Communication,* ed. Uta M. Quasthoff, 91–111. New York: de Gruyter.

Davis, Shelton, and Katrinka Ebbe, eds. 1995. *Traditional Knowledge and Sustainable Development: Proceedings of a Conference Held at the World Bank, Washington, September 27–28.* Environmentally Sustainable Development Proceedings, series 4. Washington DC: World Bank.

Dawson, George M. 1898. *Report on an Exploration in the Yukon District, North-*

west Territories and Adjacent Northern Portion of British Columbia, 1887. Ottawa: Geological Survey of Canada.

de Certeau, Michel. 1984. *The Practice of Everyday Life.* Trans. Stephen Rendall. Berkeley: University of California Press.

de Laguna, Frederica. 1972. *Under Mount St. Elias: The History and Culture of the Yakutat Tlingit.* 3 vols. Smithsonian Contributions to Anthropology 7. Washington DC: Smithsonian Institution Press.

––––––. 1990. "Tlingit." In *Handbook of North American Indians,* vol. 7, *Northwest Coast,* ed. Wayne Suttles, 203–28. Washington DC: Smithsonian Institution.

Dickey, R. M. 1898. Letter to the editor. In *Westminster: A Paper for the Home,* 16 July, 72. Sinclair Collection, Victoria, British Columbia Provincial Archives.

Dorais, Louis-Jacques. 1988. "Inuit Identity in Canada." *Folk* 30:23–31.

Dow, James, and Haanjost Luxfield. 1991. "National Socialist Folklore and Overcoming the Past in the Federal Republic of Germany." *Asian Folklore Studies* 50: 117–53.

Duncan, Kate. 1989. *Northern Athapaskan Art: A Beadwork Tradition.* Seattle: University of Washington Press.

Durrans, Brian. 1988. "The Future of the Other: Changing Cultures on Display in Ethnographic Museums." In *The Museum Time Machine: Putting Cultures on Display,* ed. Robert Lumley, 114–69. New York: Routledge.

Dyck, Noel. 1986. "Negotiating the Indian 'Problem.'" *Culture* 6:31–41.

––––––. 1991. "Tutelage and the Politics of Aboriginality: A Canadian Dilemma." *Ethos* 56:39–52.

Dyck, Noel, ed. 1985. *Indigenous Peoples and the Nation State.* St. John's: Memorial University, Institute for Social and Economic Research.

Easterson, Mary. 1992. *Potlatch: The Southern Tutchone Way.* Burwash Landing YT: Kluane First Nation.

Ellen, Roy. 1986. "What Black Elk Left Out." *Anthropology Today* 2 (6): 8–12.

Etylen, V. M. 1994. "Preservation, Transmission and Utilization of Indigenous Knowledge in the Industrial Epoch." In *Arctic Environment: Report on the Seminar on Integration of Indigenous Peoples' Knowledge,* ed. Bente V. Hansen, 146–49. Copenhagen: Ministry for the Environment (Iceland), Ministry for the Environment (Denmark), Home Rule of Greenland (Denmark Office).

Feit, Harvey. 1988. "Self Management and State Management: Forms of Knowing and Managing Northern Wildlife." In *Traditional Knowledge and Renewable Resource Management in Northern Regions,* ed. Milton M. R. Freeman and Ludwig N. Carbyn, 72–91. Edmonton: Boreal Institute for Northern Studies.

––––––. 1995. "Hunting and the Quest for Power: The James Bay Cree and Whitemen in the Twentieth Century." In *Native Peoples: The Canadian Experience,* ed.

R. Bruce Morrison and C. Roderick Wilson, 181–223. Toronto: McClelland and Stewart.

Fenton, William. 1988. "Keeping the Promise: Return of the Wampums to the Six Nations Iroquois Confederacy, Grand River." *Anthropology Newsletter,* October, 3, 25.

Fienup-Riordan, Ann. 1990a. *Eskimo Essays: Yup'ik Lives and How We See Them.* New Brunswick: Rutgers University Press.

———. 1990b. "Original Ecologists? The Relationship between Yu'pik Eskimos and Animals." In *Eskimo Essays: Yup'ik Lives and How We See Them,* 167–91. New Brunswick: Rutgers University Press.

———. 1995. *Freeze-Frame: Alaska Eskimos in the Movies.* Seattle: University of Washington Press.

Fitzhugh, William W., and Aron Crowell, eds. 1988. *Crossroads of Continents: Cultures of Siberia and Alaska.* Washington DC: Smithsonian Institution Press.

Flaherty, Martha. 1995. "Freedom of Expression or Freedom of Exploitation?" Address by the president, Inuit Women's Association, to the Association of Canadian Universities for Northern Studies Fourth National Student Conference, Ottawa.

Fogelson, Raymond. 1989. "The Ethnohistory of Events and Nonevents." *Ethnohistory* 36 (2): 133–47.

Fowler, Loretta. 1987. *Shared Symbols, Contested Meanings: Gros Venture Culture and History, 1778–1984.* Ithaca: Cornell University Press.

Francis, Daniel. 1993. *The Imaginary Indian.* Vancouver: Arsenal Pulp.

Freeman, Milton M. R. 1988. "The Significance of Animals in the Life of Northern Foraging Peoples and Its Relevance Today." Paper presented at International Symposium on Human-Animal Relationships in the North, 23–25 February, Hokkaido, Japan.

———. 1992. "Ethnoscience, Prevailing Science, and Arctic Co-operation." In *Arctic Alternatives: Civility or Militarism in the Circumpolar North,* ed. Franklin Griffiths, 79–99. Toronto: Samuel Stevens.

Freeman, Milton, and Ludwig Carbyn. 1988. *Traditional Knowledge and Renewable Resource Management in Northern Regions.* Edmonton: Boreal Institute for Northern Studies.

Friedman, Jonathan. 1992. "The Past in the Future: History and the Politics of Identity." *American Anthropologist* 94 (4): 837–59.

Fryer, Paul, and Nicholas J. Lynn. 1995. "National State Formation among the Republics of the Russian Federation: Sakha (Yakutia) and Komi Republics." Unpublished manuscript, Scott Polar Research Institute.

Funston, Frederick. 1896. *Over the Chilkoot Pass to the Yukon.* New York: Scribner's.

Furniss, Elizabeth. 1997. "In the Spirit of the Pioneers: Historical Consciousness, Cultural Colonialism and Indian/White Relations in Rural British Columbia." Ph.D. diss., University of British Columbia.

Gable, Eric, Richard Handler, and Anna Lawson. 1992. "On the Uses of Relativism: Fact, Conjecture and Black and White Histories at Colonial Williamsburg." *American Ethnologist* 19 (4): 791–805.

Garfield, Viola, and L. Forrest. 1961. *The Wolf and the Raven*. 1948. Seattle: University of Washington Press.

Giddens, Anthony. 1990. *The Consequences of Modernity*. Cambridge: Polity.

Grant, Bruce. 1995. *In the Soviet House of Culture: A Century of Perestroikas*. Princeton: Princeton University Press.

Grove, Alan. 1995. "'Where Is the Justice, Mr. Mills?' A Case Study of R. v. Nantuck." In *Essays on the History of Canadian Law*, vol. 6, *British Columbia and the Yukon*, ed. Hamar Foster and John McLaren, 87–127. Toronto: Osgood Society for Canadian Legal History.

Handler, Richard. 1991. "Who Owns the Past? History, Cultural Property, and the Logic of Possessive Individualism." In *The Politics of Culture*, ed. Brett Williams, 63–74. Washington DC: Smithsonian Institution Press.

———. 1992. "On the Valuing of Museum Objects." *Museum Anthropology* 16 (1): 21–28.

Hansen, Bente V., ed. 1994. *Arctic Environment: Report on the Seminar on Integration of Indigenous Peoples' Knowledge*. Copenhagen: Ministry for the Environment (Iceland), Ministry for the Environment (Denmark), Home Rule of Greenland (Denmark Office).

Hanson, Kirsten Thonsgaard. 1986. "The Tukaq Theater: A Cultural 'Harpoon Head.'" *Arctic Anthropology* 23 (1–2): 347–57.

Hastrap, Kirsten. 1993. "Native Anthropology: A Contradiction in Terms?" *Folk* 35:147–61.

Hedican, Edward J. 1991. "On the Ethno-politics of Canadian Native Leadership and Identity." *Ethnic Groups* 9:1–15.

Helander, Elena. 1993. "The Role of Saami Traditions in Sustainable Development." In *Politics and Sustainable Development in the Arctic*, ed. Jyrki Kakonen, 67–79. Aldershot, Eng.: Dartmouth.

Hill, Jonathan. 1992. "Contested Pasts and the Practice of Anthropology." *American Anthropologist* 94 (4): 809–36.

Hobson, G. 1992. "Traditional Knowledge Is Science." *Northern Perspectives* 20 (1): 2.

Honigmann, John J. 1949. *Culture and Ethos of Kaska Society*. Publications in Anthropology 40. New Haven: Yale University Press.

———. 1954. *The Kaska Indians: An Ethnographic Reconstruction.* Publications in Anthropology 41. New Haven: Yale University Press.

Howard, Albert, and Frances Widdowson. 1996. "Traditional Knowledge Threatens Environmental Assessment." *Policy Options* 17 (9): 34–36.

Howard, Lynda, Ross Goodwin, and Lynne Howard, eds. 1994. "Indigenous Knowledge in Northern Canada: Annotated Bibliography." Draft prepared for Canadian Polar Commission by Arctic Science and Technology Information System, Arctic Institute of North America, University of Calgary.

Huntington, Henry. 1994. "Traditional Ecological Knowledge of Beluga Whales: A Pilot Project in the Chukchi and Northern Bering Seas." In *Arctic Environment: Report on the Seminar in Integration of Indigenous Peoples' Knowledge,* ed. Bente V. Hansen, 86–106. Copenhagen: Ministry for the Environment (Iceland), Ministry for the Environment (Denmark), Home Rule of Greenland (Denmark Office).

———. 1995. "Traditional Ecolological Knowledge of Beluga Whales." *World Wildlife Fund Bulletin* 4 : 20.

Hutchinson, John. 1994, *Modern Nationalism.* London: Fontana.

Huttenen, Arja. 1995. "Encountering Ethnic Groups and Their Identities in Sports: Reindeer Races on the Kola Peninsula as an Example." In *Encountering Ethnicities,* ed. Teppo Korhonen, 118–27. Helsinki: Suomalaisen Kirjallisuuden Seura.

Hymes, Dell. 1981. *In Vain I Tried to Tell You.* Philadelphia: University of Pennsylvania Press.

———. 1985. "Language, Memory and Selective Performance: Cultee's 'Salmon Myth' as Twice Told to Boas." *Journal of American Folklore* 98 : 391–434.

Innis, Harold Adams. 1930. *The Fur Trade in Canada.* Toronto: University of Toronto Press.

———. 1940. *The Cod Fisheries: The History of an International Economy.* Toronto: University of Toronto Press.

———. 1950. *Empire and Communications.* Oxford: Clarendon.

———. 1951. *The Bias of Communication.* Toronto: University of Toronto Press.

———. 1956. *Essays in Canadian Economic History.* Toronto: University of Toronto Press.

Inuit Circumpolar Conference. 1992. *Principles and Elements for a Comprehensive Arctic Policy.* Montreal: Centre for Northern Studies and Research.

Inuit Cultural Institute. 1988. *Recollections of Levi Iqalujjuaq: The Life of a Baffin Island Hunter.* Eskimo Point: Inuit Cultural Centre.

Jacknis, Ira. 1985. "Franz Boas and Exhibits: On the Limitation of the Museum Method of Anthropology." In *Objects and Others: Essays on Museums and Material Culture,* ed. George Stocking, 75–111. Madison: University of Wisconsin Press.

Jackson, Jean. 1995. "Preserving Indian Culture: Shaman Schools and Ethno-education in the Vaupes, Colombia." *Cultural Anthropology* 10 (3): 302–29.

Jennings, Francis. 1982. "A Growing Partnership: Historians, Anthropologists and American Indian History." *Ethnohistory* 29 (1): 21–34.

Jensen, Marilyn. 1995. "The Yukon Elders' Documentation Project: A Yukon First Nations Oral History Project." *Northern Review* 14:21–27.

Johnson, Ingrid. 1995. "Southern Yukon Beadwork Traditions: An Inland Tlingit Perspective." *Northern Review* 14:28–33.

———. 1996. "Southern Yukon Beadwork Objects: A Narrative of Reclaiming Culture." Master's thesis, University of British Columbia.

Johnson, Mark. 1987. *The Body in the Mind.* Chicago: University of Chicago Press.

Johnson, Martha, ed. 1992. *Lore: Capturing Traditional Ecological Knowledge.* Ottawa: Dene Cultural Centre and International Development Research Centre.

Jordanova, Ludmilla. 1989. "Objects of Knowledge: A Historical Perspective on Museums." In *The New Museology,* ed. Peter Vergo, 22–40. London: Reaktion.

Kaiser, Rudolf. 1987. "Chief Seattle's Speeches: American Origins and European Reception." In *Recovering the World: Essays on Native American Literature,* ed. Brian Swann and Arnold Krupat, 497–536. Berkeley: University of California Press.

Kalland, Arne. 1994. "Indigenous Knowledge — Local Knowledge: Prospects and Limitations." In *Arctic Environment: Report on the Seminar on Integration of Indigenous Peoples' Knowledge,* ed. Bente V. Hansen, 150–67. Copenhagen: Ministry for the Environment (Iceland), Ministry for the Environment (Denmark), Home Rule of Greenland (Denmark Office).

Kan, Sergi. 1990. "The Sacred and the Secular: Tlingit Potlatch Songs outside the Potlatch." *American Indian Quarterly* 14 (4): 355–66.

———. 1991. "Shamanism and Christianity: Modern Day Tlingit Elders Look at the Past." *Ethnohistory* 38 (4): 363–87.

Kapferer, Bruce. 1995. "Bureaucratic Erasure: Identity, Resistance and Violence — Aborigines and a Discourse of Autonomy in a North Queensland Town." In *Worlds Apart: Modernity through the Prism of the Local,* ed. Daniel Miller, 69–90. London: Routledge.

Kari, James. 1986. *Tatl'ahwt'aenn Nenn': The Headwaters People's Country; Narratives of the Upper Ahtna Athapaskans.* Fairbanks: Alaska Native Language Center.

Karp, Ivan. 1991. "Festivals." In *Exhibiting Cultures: The Poetics and Politics of Museum Display,* ed. Ivan Karp and Steven D. Lavine, 279–87. Washington DC: Smithsonian Institution Press.

Kearney, M. 1995. "The Local and the Global: The Anthropology of Globalization and Transnationalism." *Annual Review of Anthropology* 24:547–65.

Keesing, Roger. 1994. "Colonial and Counter-colonial Discourse in Melanesia." *Critique of Anthropology* 14 (1): 42–58.

Keithahn, Edward L. 1963. *Monuments in Cedar*. Seattle: Superior.

Keskitalo, Alf Isak. 1994. "Integration of Indigenous Peoples' Knowledge." In *Arctic Environment: Report on the Seminar in Integration of Indigenous Peoples' Knowledge*, ed. Bente V. Hansen, 38–54. Copenhagen: Ministry for the Environment (Iceland), Ministry for the Environment (Denmark), Home Rule of Greenland (Denmark Office).

Kirshenblatt-Gimblett, Barbara. 1990. "Objects of Ethnography." In *Exhibiting Cultures: The Poetics and Politics of Museum Display*, ed. Ivan Karp and Steven D. Lavine, 386–43. Washington DC: Smithsonian Institution Press.

Kopytoff, Igor. 1986. "The Cultural Biography of Things: Commoditization as Process." In *The Social Life of Things*, ed. Arjun Appadurai, 64–91. Cambridge: Cambridge University Press.

Krause, Aurel. 1956. *The Tlingit Indians*. 1885. 2d ed. Trans. Erna Gunther. Seattle: University of Washington Press.

Krech, Sheppard, and Barbara Hail, eds. 1991. "Art and Material Culture of the North American Subarctic and Adjacent Regions." Special issue, *Arctic Anthropology* 28 (1).

Kroeber, Alfred L. 1952. *The Nature of Culture*. Chicago: University of Chicago Press.

Kuhn, Richard G., and Frank Duerden. 1996. "A Review of Traditional Environmental Knowledge: An Interdisciplinary Canadian Perspective." *Culture* 16 (1): 71–84.

Kuper, Adam. 1994. "Culture, Identity and the Project of a Cosmopolitan Anthropology." *Man* 29 (3): 537–54.

Labrador Inuit Association. 1977. *Our Footprints Are Everywhere: Inuit Land Use and Occupancy in Labrador*. Nain: Labrador Inuit Association.

Lass, Andrew. 1989. "What Keeps the Czech Folk 'Alive'?" *Dialectical Anthropology* 14:7–19.

Latour, Bruno. 1993. *We Have Never Been Modern*. Trans. Catherine Porter. New York: Harvester Wheatsheaf.

Legros, Dominique. 1985. "Wealth, Poverty and Slavery among the 19th Century Tutchone Athapaskans." *Research in Economic Anthropology* 7:37–64.

Levin, Michael D. 1993. *Ethnicity and Aboriginality: Case Studies in Ethnonationalism*. Toronto: University of Toronto Press.

Lewis, David Rich. 1995. "Native Americans and the Environment." *American Indian Quarterly* 19 (3): 423–50.

Linke, Uli. 1990. "Anthropology, Folklore and the Government of Modern Life." *Comparative Studies in Society and History* 32:117–48.

Ljungstrom, Asa. 1993. "Narratives of Artefacts." In *Nordic Frontiers: Recent Issues in the Study of Modern Traditional Culture in the Nordic Countries,* ed. Pertti Anttonen and Reimund Kvideland, 131–46. Publication 27. Turku, Finland: Nordic Institute of Folklore.

Long, Theodore E. 1986. "Prophecy, Charisma and Politics: Reinterpreting the Weberian Thesis." In *Prophetic Religions and Politics,* ed. Jeffrey K. Haddon and Anson Shupe, 3–17. New York: Paragon House.

Longstreth, T. Morris. 1927. *The Silent Force: Scenes from the Life of the Mounted Police of Canada.* New York: Century.

Low, Denise. 1995. "Contemporary Reinvention of Chief Seattle: Variant Texts of Chief Seattle's 1854 Speech." *American Indian Quarterly* 19 (3): 407–21.

Lumley, Robert, ed. 1988. *The Museum Time Machine: Putting Cultures on Display.* London: Routledge.

Lynge, Finn. 1992. *Arctic Wars, Animal Rights, Endangered People.* Hanover NH: Dartmouth.

McClellan, Catharine. 1950. "Culture Change and Native Trade in the Southern Yukon Territory." Ph.D. diss., University of California, Berkeley.

———. 1956. "Shamanistic Syncretism in Southern Yukon." *Transactions of the New York Academic of Sciences,* ser. 2, 19 (2): 130–37.

———. 1961. "Avoidance between Siblings of the Same Sex in North America." *Southwestern Journal of Anthropology* 17 (2): 103–23.

———. 1963. "Wealth Woman and Frogs among the Tagish Indians." *Anthropos* 58:121–28.

———. 1970a. *The Girl Who Married the Bear.* Publications in Ethnology 2. Ottawa: National Museums of Canada.

———. 1970b. "Indian Stories about the First Whites in Northwestern North America." In *Ethnohistory in Southwestern Alaska and Southern Yukon: Method and Content,* ed. Margaret Lantis, 103–33. Lexington: University Press of Kentucky.

———. 1975. *My Old People Say: An Ethnographic Survey of Southern Yukon Territory.* 2 vols. Publications in Ethnology 6 (1–2). Ottawa: National Museums of Canada.

———. 1981a. "History of Research in the Subarctic Cordillera." In *Handbook of North American Indians,* vol. 6, *Subarctic,* ed. June Helm, 35–42. Washington DC: Smithsonian Institution Press.

———. 1981b. "Inland Tlingit." In *Handbook of North American Indians,* vol. *Subarctic,* ed. June Helm, 469–80. Washington DC: Smithsonian Institution Press.

———. 1981c. "Intercultural Relations and Cultural Change in the Cordillera." In

Handbook of North American Indians, vol. 6, *Subarctic,* ed. June Helm, 387–401. WashingtonDC: Smithsonian Institution Press.

———. 1981d. "Tagish." In *Handbook of North American Indians,* vol. 6, *Subarctic,* ed. June Helm, 481–92. Washington DC: Smithsonian Institution Press.

———. 1981e. "Tutchone." In *Handbook of North American Indians,* vol. 6, *Subarctic,* ed. June Helm, 493–505. Washington DC: Smithsonian Institution Press.

McClellan, Catharine, with Lucie Birckel, Robert Bringhurst, James A. Fall, Carol McCarthy, and Janice Sheppard. 1987. *Part of the Land, Part of the Water: A History of the Yukon Indians.* Vancouver: Douglas and McIntyre.

McCluskey, Sally. 1972. "Black Elk Speaks but So Does John Neihardt." *Western American Literature* 6:231–42.

McDonald, Robert. 1985. "Journals of Rev. Robert McDonald, 1862–1913." Manuscript in Yukon Archives, with index by Linda Johnson. Whitehorse, Yukon Native Language Centre.

McDonnell, Roger. 1975. "Kasini Society: Some Aspects of the Social Organization of an Athapaskan Culture between 1900–1950." Ph.D. diss., University of British Columbia.

McEachern, Allan. 1991. *Reasons for Judgment: Delgamuukw v. B. C.* Smithers, British Columbia: Supreme Court of British Columbia.

McQuesten, Leroy. n.d. "Life in the Yukon, 1871–1885." Unpublished manuscript, Whitehorse, Yukon Archives.

Marcus, George E. 1995. "Ethnography in/of the World System: The Emergence of Multi-sited Ethnography." *Annual Review of Anthropology* 24:95–117.

Merrill, William L., Edmund J. Ladd, and T. J. Ferguson. 1993. "The Return of the Ahayu:da: Lessons for Repatriation from Zuni Pueblo and the Smithsonian Institution." *Current Anthropology* 34 (5): 523–67.

Miller, Bruce G., ed. 1992. "Anthropology and History in the Courts." Theme issue, *BC Studies,* no. 95.

Miller, Christopher. 1985. *Prophetic Worlds: Indians and Whites on the Columbia Plateau.* New Brunswick: Rutgers University Press.

Miller, Daniel. 1995. *Worlds Apart: Modernity through the Prism of the Local.* London: Routledge.

Mills, Antonia. 1994. *Eagle Down Is Our Law: Wit'suwit'in Law, Feasts and Land Claims.* Vancouver: University of British Columbia Press.

Minority Rights Group, ed. 1994. *Polar Peoples: Self-Determination and Development.* London: Minority Rights Group.

Moore, Patrick. 1996. "The Story of Tes Ni'a, a Kaska Account of the Hudson's Bay Cannibals." Paper delivered at the Rupert's Land Colloquium, 31 May–4 June, Whitehorse YT.

———. 1997. "Ethnomyms and the Kaska, Sekani and Mountain Slavey Dictionary Project." Paper presented at the Alaska Anthropology Meetings, twenty-fourth annual meeting, Whitehorse, YT, 10–12 April.

Moore, Patrick, and Angela Wheelock. 1990. *Wolverine Myths and Visions: Dene Traditions from Northern Alberta*. Lincoln: University of Nebraska Press.

Morrow, Phyllis. 1995. "On Shaky Ground: Folklore, Collaboration, and Problematic Outcomes." In *When Our Words Return: Writing, Hearing and Remembering Oral Traditions of Alaska and the Yukon*, ed. Phyllis Morrow and William Schneider, 27–51. Logan: Utah State University Press.

Morrow, Phyllis, and Chase Hensel. 1992. "Hidden Dissension: Minority-Majority Relationships and the Uses of Contested Terminology." *Arctic Anthropology* 29 (1): 38–53.

Myers, Fred. 1994. "Culture-Making: Performing Aboriginality at the Asia Society Gallery." *American Ethnologist* 21 (4): 679–99.

Ned, Annie. 1984. *Old People in Those Days, They Told Their Story All the Time*. Comp. Julie Cruikshank. Whitehorse: Yukon Native Languages Project.

Nungak, Z., ed. 1983. *Northern Quebec Inuit Elders Conferences at Kangirsuk (Payne Bay) Quebec, and at Povungnituk, Quebec*. 2 vols. Inukjuak PQ: Avataq Cultural Institute.

Nuttall, Mark. 1992. *Arctic Homeland: Kinship, Community and Development in Northwest Greenland*. Toronto: University of Toronto Press.

Nyman, Elizabeth, and Jeff Leer. 1993. *"Gágiwdul.at": Brought Forth to Reconfirm. The Legacy of a Taku River Tlingit Clan*. Whitehorse: Yukon Native Language Centre; Fairbanks: Alaska Native Language Center.

Ogilvie, William. 1913. *Early Days on the Yukon*. Ottawa: Thorburn and Abbott.

Okrainetz, Glen. 1992. "Towards a Sustainable Future in Hudson Bay," *Northern Perspectives* 20 (2): 12–16.

Osgood, Cornelius. 1971. *The Han Indians: A Compilation of Ethnographic and Historical Data on the Alaska Boundary Area*. Publications in Anthropology 14. New Haven: Yale University.

Paine, Robert. 1982. *Dam a River, Damn a People? Saami (Lapp) Livelihood and the Alta/Kautokeino Hydro-electric Project and the Norwegian Parliament*. Document 45. Copenhagen: IWGIA.

Parezo, Nancy. 1987. "The Formation of Ethnographic Collections: The Smithsonian Institution in the American Southwest." In *Advances in Anthropological Method and Theory*, vol. 10, ed. Michael Schiffler, 1–47. New York: Academic.

Passerini, Louisa, ed. 1992. *Memory and Totalitarianism*. Oxford: Oxford University Press.

Pearce, Susan. 1990. *Objects of Knowledge*. New Research in Museum Studies 1. London: Athlone.

Pederson, Poul. 1995. "Nature, Religion and Cultural Identity: The Religious Environmentalist Paradigm." In *Asian Perceptions of Nature: A Critical Approach,* ed. Ole Bruun and Arne Kalland, 258–76. Richmond, Eng.: Curzon.

Pelly, David. 1986. "Where Inuit and Biologist Meet: Combining Instinct with Evidence." *Nature Canada* 15 (4): 39–42.

Peterson, Jacqueline. 1988. "Review of *Prophetic Worlds: Indians and Whites on the Columbia Plateau.*" *Ethnohistory* 3 (2): 191–96.

Pine, Frances. 1996. "Naming the House and Naming the Land: Kinship and Social Groups in Highland Poland." *Journal of the Royal Anthropological Institute* 2 (3): 443–60.

Portelli, Alessendro. 1991. *The Death of Luigi Trastulli and Other Stories: Form and Meaning in Oral History.* Albany: State University of New York Press.

Posey, Darrell. 1990. "Intellectual Property Rights and Just Compensation for Indigenous Knowledge." *Anthropology Today* 6 : 13–16.

Posey, Darrell A., and W. L. Overall, eds. 1990. *Ethnobiology: Implications and Applications.* Proceedings of the First International Congress of Ethnobiology, Brazil. 2 vols. Belém, Brazil: Museu Paraense Emilio Goeldi.

Price, Julius M. 1898. *From Euston to Klondike: A Narrative of a Journey through British Columbia and the North-West Territory in the Summer of 1898.* London: Sampson Low, Marston.

Primrose, P. C. H. 1900. "Report of Superintendent P. C. H. Primrose, Dawson District, November 10, 1899." *Annual Report of the Northwest Mounted Police,* 42, 44. Ottawa: Northwest Mounted Police.

Rice, Keren, and Laura Murray. n.d. *Talking on the Page: Editing Aboriginal Texts.* Toronto: University of Toronto Press. Forthcoming.

Richards, John. 1995. "Anthropology's Terrible Triumph." *Vancouver Sun,* 21 December, A-17.

Richards, Paul. 1993. "Cultivation: Knowledge or Performance?" In *An Anthropological Critique of Development: The Growth of Ignorance,* ed. Mark Hobart, 61–78. New York: Routledge.

Richardson, Boyce. 1993. "Harvesting Traditional Knowledge." *Nature* 22 (4): 30–37.

Ricoeur, Paul. 1979. "The Model of the Text: Meaningful Action Considered as a Text." In *Interpretive Social Science: A Reader,* ed. Paul Rabinow and William M. Sullivan, 73–101. Berkeley: University of California Press.

———. 1980. "The Value of Narrativity in the Representation of Reality." *Critical Inquiry* 7 (1): 169–90.

Ridington, Robin. 1978. *Swan People: A Study of the Dunne-za Prophet Dance.* Canadian Ethnology Service Paper 38, Mercury Series. Ottawa: National Museums of Canada.

———. 1982. "Technology, World View and Adaptive Strategy in a Northern Hunting Society." *Canadian Review of Sociology and Anthropology* 19 (4): 460–67.

———. 1987. "From Hunt Chief to Prophet: Beaver Indian Dreamers and Christianity." *Arctic Anthropology* 24 (1): 8–18.

———. 1988a. "Knowledge, Power and the Individual in Subarctic Hunting Societies." *American Anthropologist* 90 (1): 98–110.

———. 1988b. *Trail to Heaven: Knowledge and Narrative in a Northern Native Community.* Vancouver: Douglas and McIntyre.

———. 1990. *Little Bit Know Something: Stories in a Language of Anthropology.* Iowa City: University of Iowa Press.

———. 1993. "The Sacred Object as Text." *American Indian Quarterly* 17 (1): 83–99.

———. 1994. "Tools in the Mind: Northern Athapaskan Ecology, Religion and Technology." In *Circumpolar Religion and Ecology: An Anthropology of the North,* ed. Takashi Irimoto and Takaho Yamada, 273–88. Tokyo: University of Tokyo Press.

Rosaldo, Renato. 1989. *Culture and Truth.* Boston: Beacon.

Rushforth, Scott. 1992. "The Legitimation of Beliefs in a Hunter-Gatherer Society: Bearlake Athapaskan Knowledge and Authority." *American Ethnologist* 19 (3): 483–500.

———. 1994. "Political Resistance in a Contemporary Hunter-Gatherer Society: More about Bearlake Athapaskan Knowledge and Authority." *American Ethnologist* 21 (2): 335–52.

Sanjek, Roger. 1993. "Anthropology's Hidden Colonialism: Assistants and Their Ethnographers." *Anthropology Today* 9 (2): 13–18.

Saris, A. Jamie. 1995. "Telling Stories: Life Histories, Illness Narratives and Institutional Landscapes." *Culture, Medicine and Psychiatry* 19 : 37–72.

Sarris, Greg. 1993. *Keeping Slug Woman Alive.* Berkeley: University of California Press.

Sidney, Angela. 1980. *Place Names of the Tagish Region, Southern Yukon.* Whitehorse: Yukon Native Languages Project.

———. 1982. *Tagish Tlaagú/Tagish Stories.* Recorded by Julie Cruikshank. Whitehorse: Council for Yukon Indians and Government of Yukon.

———. 1983. *Haa Shagóon/Our Family History.* Comp. Julie Cruikshank. Whitehorse: Yukon Native Languages Project.

———. 1988. "The Story of Kaax'achgook. *Northern Review* 2 : 9–16.

Sidney, Angela, Kitty Smith, and Rachel Dawson. 1977. *My Stories Are My Wealth.* Recorded by Julie Cruikshank. Whitehorse: Council for Yukon Indians.

Siikala, Anna-Leena. 1992. "Understanding Narratives of the 'Other.'" In *Folklore*

Processed: In Honour of Lauri Honko on His Sixtieth Birthday, ed. Reimund Kvideland, 200–213. Studia Fennica Folkloristica 1. Helsinki: Suomalaisen Kirjallisuuden Seura.

Sissons, Jeffrey. 1993. "The Systemization of Tradition: Maori Culture as a Strategic Resource." *Oceania* 64 (2): 97–116.

Slobodin, Richard. 1970. "Kutchin Concepts of Reincarnation." *Western Canadian Journal of Anthropology* 2 (2): 67–79.

Smith, Kitty. 1982. *Nindal Kwädindür/I'm Going to Tell You a Story.* Recorded by Julie Cruikshank. Whitehorse: Council for Yukon Indians and Government of Yukon.

Spier, Leslie. 1935. *The Prophet Dance of the Northwest and Its Derivatives: The Source of the Ghost Dance.* Menasha WI: George Banta.

Stahl, Sandra Dolby. 1989. *Literary Folkloristics and the Personal Narrative.* Bloomington: Indiana University Press.

Stamps, Judith. 1995. *Unthinking Modernity: Innis, McLuhan and the Frankfurt School.* Montreal: McGill-Queen's University Press.

Stoeltje, Beverly. 1992. "Festival." In *Folklore, Cultural Performances and Popular Entertainments,* ed. Richard Bauman, 261–71. Oxford: Oxford University Press.

Stolcke, Verena. 1995. "Talking Culture: New Boundaries, New Rhetorics of Exclusion in Europe." *Current Anthropology* 36 (1): 1–13, 19–24.

Stordahl, Vigdis. 1993. "How to Be a Real Sami: Ethnic Identity in a Context of (Inter)national Integration." *Inuit Studies* 17 (1): 127–30.

Strathern, Marilyn. 1992. *After Nature: English Kinship in the Late Twentieth Century.* Cambridge: Cambridge University Press.

———. 1996. "Kinship Knowledge." Paper presented at the International Symposium on Governing Medically Assisted Human Reproduction, University of Toronto, 10–12 February.

Strathern, Marilyn, ed. 1995. *Shifting Contexts: Transformations in Anthropological Knowledge.* London: Routledge.

Suttles, Wayne. 1957. "The Plateau Prophet Dance among the Coast Salish." *Southwestern Journal of Anthropology* 13 : 352–98.

Swanton, John. 1909. *Tlingit Myths and Texts.* Bulletin 39. Washington DC: Bureau of American Ethnology.

Tanner, Adrian. 1979. *Bringing Home Animals: Religious Ideology and Mode of Production of Mistassini Cree Hunters.* St. John's: Memorial University of Newfoundland, Institute of Social and Economic Research.

Tedlock, Dennis. 1979. "The Analogical Tradition and the Emergence of a Dialogical Anthropology." *Journal of Anthropological Research* 35 : 387–400.

————. 1983. *The Spoken Word and the Work of Interpretation.* Philadelphia: University of Pennsylvania Press.

Thomas, Nicholas. 1992. "The Inversion of Tradition." *American Ethnologist* 19 (2): 213–32.

Tlen, Daniel. 1986. *Speaking Out: Consultations and Survey of Yukon Native Languages Planning, Visibility and Growth.* Whitehorse: Yukon Native Language Centre.

Tom, Gertie. 1987. *Èkeyi: Gyò Cho Chú/My Country: Big Salmon River.* Whitehorse: Yukon Native Language Centre.

Trigger, Bruce G. 1982. "Ethnohistory: Problems and Prospects." *Ethnohistory* 29 (1): 1–19.

————. 1995. "Archaeology and the Integrated Circus." *Dialectical Anthropology* 15 (4): 319–36.

Tuohy, Sue. 1991. "Cultural Metaphors and Reasoning: Folklore Scholarship and Ideology in Contemporary China." *Asian Folklore Studies* 50 (1991): 189–220.

Urquhart, M. C., ed. 1965. *Historical Statistics of Canada.* Toronto: Macmillan.

Velten, H. V. 1944. "Three Tlingit Stories." *International Journal of American Linguistics* 10 (4): 168–80.

Vergo, Peter, ed. 1989. *The New Museology.* London: Reaktion.

Vitebsky, Piers. 1995. "From Cosmology to Environmentalism: Shamanism as Local Knowledge in a Global Setting." In *Counterworks: Managing the Diversity of Knowledge,* ed. Richard Fardon, 182–203. London: Routledge.

Walker, Deward E., Jr. 1969. "New Light on the Prophet Dance." *Ethnohistory* 16: 245–55.

Wallace, Anthony. 1956. "Revitalizaton Movements." *American Anthropologist* 58 (2): 264–81.

Welsh, Peter. 1992. "Repatriation and Cultural Preservation: Potent Objects, Potent Pasts." *University of Michigan Journal of Law Reform* 25 (3–4): 837–65.

Wenzel, George. 1991. *Animal Rights, Human Rights: Ecology, Economy and Ideology in the Canadian Arctic.* London: Belhaven.

White, Hayden. 1987. *The Content of the Form: Narrative Discourse and Historical Representation.* Baltimore: Johns Hopkins University Press.

Wilson, William. 1976. *Folklore and Nationalism in Modern Finland.* Bloomington: Indiana University Press.

Wood, Z. T. 1899. "Annual Report of Superintendent Z. T. Wood, Tagish, Upper Yukon, 1898." In *Annual Report of the Northwest Mounted Police,* 42–43. Ottawa: Northwest Mounted Police.

Workman, William. 1978. *Prehistory of the Aishihik-Kluane Area, Southwest Yukon*

Territory. Archaeological Survey Paper 74, Mercury Series. Ottawa: National Museums of Canada.

World Commission on Environment and Development (Bruntland Commission). 1987. *Our Common Future*. London: Oxford University Press.

Wright, Al. 1976. *Prelude to Bonanza: The Discovery and Exploration of the Yukon*. Sidney BC: Gray's.

Yukon International Storytelling Festival and the Northern Research Institute. 1994. "'Become a World': A Tribute to Angela Sidney." Yukon International Storytelling Festival and Northern Research Institute, Yukon.

Zaslow, Morris. 1971. *The Opening of the Canadian North, 1890–1914*. Toronto: McClelland and Stewart.

Zolbrod, Paul. 1987. "When Artifacts Speak, What Can They Tell Us?" In *Recovering the Word: Essays on Native American Literature,* ed. Brian Swann and Arnold Krupat, 13–40. Berkeley: University of California Press.

Index

Aagé, 79–80
Aishihik, 9
Alaska Highway: consequences of, 23; construction of, 11
Alaska Highway Pipeline Inquiry, 11
Alaska State Museum, 110
American Museum of Natural History, 101
Ames, Michael, 115
Anderson, Johnny, 38
animal-human relations: changing relations, 52, 67; in narrative, 54–56, 76–79; social contract, 8, 57–58, 108, 122
Animal Mother: in narrative, 18
anthropology: ethnographic methods, xii, 1–2, 25, 161; as narrative, 1–3, 69, 161–62
Arctic Environmental Protection Strategy, 48, 52, 65
Arctic Monitoring and Assessment Program, 65
artistic traditions: in subarctic, 7. See also ceremonial regalia; Smith, Kitty, carvings; trade
Association of Canadian Universities for Northern Studies, 48
Avataq Cultural Institute, 48

Babcock, Barbara, 104
Baha'i, 131–34
Bakhtin, Mikhail, xii, xiii, 72, 94, 140, 154
Balikci, Asen, 120
Barbeau, Marius, 101, 105, 108, 110
Barth, Frederick, 114
Basso, Keith, 139
bear: in circumpolar narratives, 108
Bear Woman, 107–8
Bell, Roy, 143

belonging: concepts of, xiv, 3, 12–13; and kinship, 21–23; and language, 13–16; and place, 16–21
Benjamin, Walter, xiii, xvii, 115, 140, 154–55
Berger, Thomas, 51
Berton, Pierre, 74–75
Black Elk, 59
Blackjack, Roddy and Bessie, 147–49, 158
Boas, Franz, 15, 40, 101, 105
Bompas, Selina, 8
Bompas, William Carpenter, 8, 88, 175 n.40
Borneman, John, 21
Boss, Jim, 91, 163, 175 n.48
Bourdieu, Pierre, 49, 69–70, 73, 94–95
Bruun, Ole, 59
Bureau of Aboriginal Languages Services (Government of Yukon), 14, 24

Campbell, Robert, 7
Camprobber: in narrative, 148
Canadian Arctic Resources Committee, 48, 52
caribou: migration routes of, 53–54; in narrative, 54–56
Carmack, George, 74–75, 79–80
Carmack, Kate (Shaaw Tláa), 74–75, 79–80
carvings. See under Smith, Kitty
ceremonial regalia, Tlingit, 99, 145–47
Charlie, Dawson, 74–75, 78, 80
Checkpoint Charlie Museum, 50
Chief Seattle, 59
Chilkoot Pass, 10
Christianity, 119, 121, 129–31. See also missionaries

circumpolar issues: environmental concerns, 49–68; political alliances, 138, 140–41, 143, 155–58, 183 n.3

clan: Dak̲l'weidí, 38, 93; Deisheetaan, 25, 38; G̲aanax̲.ádi, 178 n.30; G̲aanax̲teidí, 178 n.30; Kiks.ádi, 27, 36, 38; Łukaax̲.ádi, 146, 158; Yanyeidí, 149–50

classifications and consequences: in academic research, 13–14, 49; in bureaucratic practice, 58, 64–66; in colonial encounters, 74, 81, 95–96; in historical writing, xiv, 3–5; in law, 86–87; in museums, xvi, 111–12

Clifford, James, 98–99, 113, 139

Cohen, Percy, 118–19

Collins, F. H., 152

Commissioner of Yukon, 16, 168 n.15

communication: storytelling strategies, xv, 12–13, 40–44, 66–68, 145–53

Conservation of Arctic Flora and Fauna (CAFF), 65

Constantine, Charles, 92

copper-clawed owl: in narrative, 18, 106

Council for Yukon First Nations (formerly Council for Yukon Indians), 24, 48

Crow: in narrative, 20, 100, 109–10, 181 n.24

Crow (Kajìt; moiety), 14. See also kinship

culture: as a concept, 1–3; cultural translation, 43–44, 98–99, 114, 139, 143–44, 162, 164–65. See also communication

Daanawaak, 145–46

Dalton Post (Shäwshe), 113

Darnell, Regna, 101, 139

Dauenhauer, Nora and Richard, xiii–xiv, 27, 36, 108, 110, 146

Dawson, Rachel, 127

Dawson City, 10, 83

de Certeau, Michel, 1

de Laguna, Frederica, 105, 108, 110

Delgamuukw v. B.C., 63–64

Dene Cultural Institute, 48

Dennis, Bert, 38

dialogue: in ethnography, 25, 40, 139; in oral tradition, 71–72, 153–55

Dukt'ootl', 110, 113, 114, 178 n.30

Dúshka, 105, 109

environmental issues, xv; animal rights movement, 60–61; and local knowledge,

51–60, 66–68; in Siberia, 61–62; stereotypes in literature, 50, 58–62

epidemics, 73, 79, 89, 105, 127–28

festivals: elders' festival, 15–16, 57–58. See also Yukon International Storytelling Festival

Fienup-Riordan, Ann, 60

fish: in narrative, 57–58

Fogelson, Ray, 162

Fort Selkirk, 7

Fox: in narrative, 18

Fox, Christian, 82, 90

Friedman, Jonathan, 157

frog: in narrative, 76–78

frontier imagery, 73, 81, 92–93, 163–64

Furniss, Elizabeth, 163–64

Garfield, Viola, 108, 110

generational differences, 14, 23

Giddens, Anthony, 68

glaciers: in narrative, 18–19, 106, 177 n.20

gold rush: centennial celebrations of, 92, 97; discovery of gold, 75, 80; Klondike, xv–xvi, 4, 9–10, 47, 72–97

government: and northward expansion, xv–xvi, 9–12, 23, 51–53, 57, 71–74, 92–97

Greer, Sheila, 103

Grove, Alan, 96

Hammond, Austin, 145–47, 157–58

Handler, Richard, 112

Hawksley, John, 151–52

Henderson, Patsy, 38, 78

Henderson, Robert, 75

Henry, Percy, 16

Hensel, Chase, 58, 97

history: oral and written, xv–xvi, 4–12, 71–97, 116–20. See also oral tradition

Honigmann, John, 120

Hooper Bay Traditional Dance Group, 143

Hudson Bay Program, 65–66

Hume, May Smith, 107–11

Hutshi, 9

Hymes, Dell, 40–41, 139

indigenous rights, 62–67. See also environmental issues, animal rights movement; land claims

Innis, Harold, xiii, xvii, 71, 81, 94, 95, 140, 155

International Union for the Conservation of Nature, 48, 52
International Working Group for Indigenous Affairs, 65
International Year for the World's Indigenous Peoples, 65
Inuit, 64–65
Inuit Circumpolar Conference, 48, 65
Inuit Cultural Institute, 48

Jack, Joe, 128
Jim, Daisy (Daisy Mason), 80, 174n.19
Jim, Mrs. Tagish (Gokhakat), 90
Joe, John, 18, 129
Johnson, A. P., 27
Johnson, Mark, xii
journey: as narrative theme, 36, 80, 107–8, 122–23

Kaak'achgóok, xv, 27; story of, as told by Angela Sidney, 28–35
Kaats', 107–8, 110, 113, 114
Kalland, Arne, 48, 59
Kan, Sergei, 119
Kapferer, Bruce, 58
Keish (Skookum Jim), 47, 74–81, 92–93
Keithahn, Edward, 108, 110
killer whale: in narrative, 110–11
kinship: behavioral guidelines, 75–76, 89–92, 105–7; and belonging, 14, 21–23; in narrative, 36–39, 110–11, 145–53, 157–58. See also clan
Klondike gold rush. See under gold rush
Klondike Nugget, 81, 83–84, 86
knowledge: indigenous, concept of, 47–50, 52–53, 56–57; local, 40, 45–68, 98–99, 128, 135–36, 141; and power, 58, 68–70, 71–72, 92–97. See also classifications and consequences; environmental issues; oral tradition; traditional ecological knowledge
k'och'en ("cloud people"): in narrative, 9, 123–27
Kodeneha, Maggie, 38–39
Kroeber, Alfred, 101
Kwanlin Dan First Nation, 143, 153

Laberge, Lake, 82–83
Labrador Inuit Association, 48
land: mapping of, 13–14; and mobility, 16–17; in narrative, 16–21, 145–53, 157–58

land claims: in Alaska, 147; in British Columbia, 63–64; in Yukon, 16–17, 20–21, 23–34, 141, 153, 155–59, 163
languages, indigenous: and generational differences, 14; instruction of, in schools, 14; multilingualism, 13, 16; place-names as linguistic evidence, 13, 168n.13; transcription of, xxiii–xxv; and translation issues, xiii–xiv, 46, 84–85
Latour, Bruno, 68–69
law, codified, 71, 81–89, 94–95
Leer, Jeff, 149
Legros, Dominique, 120
life stories, xi–xiii. See also Ned, Annie; Sidney, Angela; Smith, Kitty
Lisle, F. H., 84
London, Jack, 73
Lowell glacier (Nàlùdi). See glaciers

MacBride Museum, 100, 107
Mackenzie Valley Pipeline Inquiry, 51, 135–36, 157
Maori, 66
Marsh Lake incident: 74, 81–83, 89–97; and appeals, 88–89; and trial, 83–88
material culture: Northwest Coast, 99, 102; and oral tradition, 98–104, 111–15, 145–47, 157–58; Subarctic, 102–3, 112
May, Karl, 58
McClellan, Catharine, 27, 78, 105, 110, 119, 120, 129, 132–33
McClintock River, 82
McDonald, Robert, 8, 121, 180n.16
McDonnell, Roger, 120
McGuire, Thomas, 83–87
McIntosh, William, 82, 96
Meehan, Billy, 82–83, 87, 90
missionaries, 5, 7–8, 121, 130. See also Bompas, William Carpenter; McDonald, Robert
moiety: Crow (Kajìt) and Wolf (Ägunda), 14. See also kinship
Morrow, Phyllis, 58, 97
Mountain Man: in narrative, 147–48
museums, xvi, 98–104, 111–12, 115
Myers, Fred, 139

Naa Kahidi, 145
Naatsilanéi, 110, 113, 114
Nàlùdi (Lowell glacier). See glaciers
Nantuck brothers. See Marsh Lake incident

narrative: as concept, 1–3; coherence of, xii–
  xiii, xiv–xvii, 3–4, 40–44, 47, 107–15,
  157–58, 164–65; as explanation, 75–81,
  118, 119–20, 133–37, 181 n.22. *See also*
  oral tradition; storytelling
Ned, Annie, 45, 69, 70, 103, 129–30, 164;
  and life history, xii, 45–47, 135, 164; use
  of stories, 20, 53–57
Ned, Johnny, 129–30, 135
Nielsen, Erik, 51
Northern Native Broadcasting Yukon, 24
Northern Storytelling Festival, 142–43. *See
  also* Yukon International Storytelling
  Festival
Northwest Mounted Police, 93, 81–89, 113
Nunavik project, 65
Nyman, Elizabeth, 149–51, 158

Ogilvie, William, 74
oral tradition: as history, xv, 36, 63–64, 92–
  94, 116–18; and material culture, 98–
  104, 111–15, 145–47, 157–58; as social
  process, 26, 40–44, 47, 136–37, 153–
  59; transcription of, xiii–xiv, 15–16. *See
  also* history, oral and written; narrative;
  storytelling

Pattullo, Duff, 95
performance. *See under* storytelling
place-names: and land claim negotiations,
  20–21; as linguistic evidence, 13,
  168 n.13; in narrative, 17–20
Portland Museum of Art, Rasmussen Collection, 98–99
prophecy: oral traditions about, 116–18,
  122, 123–24; scholarly literature about,
  117–20, 134–35
Prophet Dance, 119, 179 n.4, 180 n.5

resource management. *See* environmental
  issues
Ricoeur, Paul, 36
Ridington, Robin, 27–28, 120
Rosaldo, Renato, 135
Rudd, Edwin, 82, 97
Rushforth, Scott, 135–36

Sapir, Edward, xii, 72, 101
Saris, A. J., 94
Saro-Wiwa, Ken, 154
Sarris, Greg, xiii, xvii, 114, 139, 165
Scarff, Jessie, 151–53, 158

Service, Robert, 73
Shaaw Tláa (Kate Carmack), 74–75, 79–80
shamans: Małal, 127–28, 131, 135; Major,
  131–32, 135; Nasq'a, 129; as prophets,
  121, 123–24, 180 n.18; use of Christian
  symbols, 131–33; use of songs, 182 n.36
Sidney, Angela, xiii, xv, 39, 90–92; and life
  history, xii, 75–76, 127–28, 131–33, 164;
  use of stories, 18, 25–44, 76–78
Sidney, Peter, 37–38, 42
Skookum Jim (Keish), 47, 74–81, 92–93
Slobodin, Richard, 120
Smith, Billy, 106
Smith, Kitty, 16, 20; carvings, xvi, 104–7,
  108–9, 112–15; and life history, xii, 75,
  80, 89–90, 91, 99–101, 104–15, 164; use
  of stories, 18–19, 123–27
solstice: in narrative, 32–33, 36
song: in narrative, 35, 37, 42, 55, 148–49
Spier, Leslie, 119
Stolke, Verena, 162
storytelling, xi–xii, 1–4; and audience, 28,
  39–40, 42–43, 142, 144–45, 156–58,
  164; in carvings, 107–11; and performance, 25–44, 145–58. *See also* narrative;
  oral tradition
Strathern, Marilyn, 69
Supreme Court of British Columbia, 63–64
Supreme Court of the Northwest Territories, 88–89, 96
swan power, 127
Swanton, John, 27, 105, 108, 110

Tagish police post, 82–83
Taku River, 149–50
Tatl'èrma, 89, 105
Tedlock, Dennis, 139
Teslin Lake, 15
textual analysis: limitations of, 40–41
Tl'adaake Tene, 90, 92
Tl'anaxéedékw ("Wealth Woman"), 76, 78
trade: aboriginal, 5–6, 9; artistic traditions
  and, 7; European fur trade, 5–8; Hudson's
  Bay Company, 5, 7
traditional ecological knowledge (TEK), xv,
  47–58, 61, 64–66. *See also* knowledge, local
Tukaq Theater, 143

Umbrella Final Agreement, 159
UNESCO, 48, 52
United Nations Conference on the Environ-
  ment (Earth Summit), 48, 65

United Nations Man-in-the-Biosphere program, 48

Vitebsky, Piers, 61–62, 65

Wade, F. C., 84
Weber, Max, 117, 118, 119
Wenzel, George, 60–61
Wolf (Ägunda), 14. *See also* kinship
World Bank, 48
World Commission on Environment and Development (Bruntland Commission), 48
World Conservation Strategy, 48, 65
World War II, 11, 37
World Wildlife Fund, 48, 53, 56

Yukon Arts Centre, 144
Yukon College, 39
Yukon First Nations Land Claims Settlement Act (Bill C-33), xvii, 141
Yukon First Nations Self-Government Act (Bill C-34), 141
Yukon Historical and Museums Association, xvi, 24, 45, 138–59
Yukon International Storytelling Festival, xvi, 24, 138–59
Yukon Native Language Centre, xiv, 14, 24, 117–18, 167n.6
Yukon Territory: establishment of, 10, 83, 96